Computerised
Book-Keeping

Visit our How To website at www.howto.co.uk

At www.howto.co.uk you can engage in conversation with our authors – all of whom have 'been there and done that' in their specialist fields. You can get access to special offers and additional content but most importantly you will be able to engage with, and become a part of, a wide and growing community of people just like yourself.

At www.howto.co.uk you'll be able to talk and share tips with people who have similar interests and are facing similar challenges in their lives. People who, just like you, have the desire to change their lives for the better – be it through moving to a new country, starting a new business, growing their own vegetables, or writing a novel.

At www.howto.co.uk you'll find the support and encouragement you need to help make your aspirations a reality.

How To Books strives to present authentic, inspiring, practical information in their books. Now, when you buy a title from How To Books, you get even more than just words on a page.

An accredited textbook of
The Institute of Certified Bookkeepers

Computerised
Book-Keeping

Dr Peter Marshall

howtobooks

99832

Published by How To Books Ltd,
Spring Hill House, Spring Hill Road,
Begbroke, Oxford OX5 1RX. United Kingdom.
Tel: (01865) 375794. Fax: (01865) 379162.
info@howtobooks.co.uk
www.howtobooks.co.uk

British Library Cataloguing in Publication Data
A catalogue record for this book is available from the British Library

ISBN: 978-1-84528-397-1

Produced for How To Books by Deer Park Productions, Tavistock, Devon
Typeset by PDQ Typesetting, Newcastle-under-Lyme, Staffordshire
Cover design by Baseline Arts Ltd, Oxford
Printed and bound in Great Britain by Bell & Bain Ltd, Glasgow

NOTE: The material contained in this book is set out in good faith for
general guidance and no liability can be accepted for loss or expense
incurred as a result of relying in particular circumstances on statements
made in the book. The laws and regulations are complex and liable to
change, and readers should check the current position with the relevant
authorities before making personal arrangements.

Contents

Contents

Preface

Book-keeping has moved on in many ways since the manual book-keeping version of this book was first published in 1992, but one way in particular has had a huge impact and students and practitioners will have to develop skills in this area if they are to find work. Employers now require book-keeping and accounting staff to have skills in computerised accounting.

The subject has moved on, but not moved away from the traditional knowledge. The principles and theory of book-keeping are just the same now as they have been since the 14th century, and maybe even earlier than that. However, computerisation can now increase the productivity with which the data is recorded and carry out many of the calculations automatically. This is why employers require their accounting staff to have these skills.

In today's commercial world, firms have to compete hard for business and this requires them to keep costs to a minimum, as all costs are reflected in the prices they have to charge for their products. The wages of accounting staff are examples of such costs, and this area is one in which very significant savings can be made. If firms don't make those savings, their prices will not compete with those that do and they will not survive.

It's no good trying to go straight to computerised book-keeping, though, and missing out the learning of manual book-keeping. Once a few problems occur in the accounts, a person who has only learned how to input data will be stumped. Employers will still require their staff to fully understand the principles and theory of double-entry book-keeping.

The manual book-keeping version of this book (*Mastering Book-Keeping*) has been very successful over the years, as its eight editions and accreditation by the Institute of Certified Book-keepers demonstrates. Its success has been due to the fact that attention was given not just to recording the facts and techniques of the subject accurately and comprehensively, but to studying the problems that feature in the teaching and learning situations and presenting the material in a way that would best overcome them. Classes were observed, teachers and students interviewed and questionnaires administered. The same approach was used in the production of this book.

The connection between computerised and manual book-keeping is always evident in the text. If you have read *Mastering Book-Keeping* already, you will feel comfortable with this new textbook.

This book is aimed at students of the subject, but, like the manual book-keeping version, it will serve as a useful handbook long after qualification. The material and structure take account of the requirements of all the major examination boards, and specimen papers are included.

The Sage family of packages has, for a long time, been regarded as the industry standard, and this is why this software has been chosen here as a medium through which to introduce book-keepers and business people to computerised book-keeping.

Most software packages use similar formats, so if a student masters Sage they will quickly and easily be able to transfer those skills to the other software packages.

Sage products are always evolving, but the routines and formats remain the same, so regardless of what version of the software you have at any time, the skills you will learn here will be appropriate.

Peter Marshall

ICB examination papers and model answers are reproduced by kind permission of The Institute of Certified Bookkeepers, IAB examination papers, marking scheme and model answers are reproduced by kind permission of The International Association of Bookkeepers, and OCR exam papers are reproduced by kind permission of Oxford, Cambridge and RSA Examinations.

1 A period of transition

With the increasing globalisation of trade and industry at all levels, it is becoming increasingly necessary to achieve some degree of harmony in accounting practices between countries. The standards that applied in the UK since 1970, i.e. Statements of Standard Accounting Practice (SSAPs) and Financial Reporting Standards (FRSs), are being gradually phased out and replaced by International Accounting Standards (IASs) and International Financial Reporting Standards (IFRSs). All companies listed on EU Stock Exchanges already use the international standards and in time they will be used by all UK businesses.

Here are some examples of the changes in terminology with which you will have to become familiar. In the international standard terminology, instead of turnover the term *revenue* is used, instead of stock the term *inventory* is used, and debtors and creditors are called *accounts receivable* and *payable*. Provisions tend to be referred to as *allowances,* the profit and loss account is known as the *income statement* and any profit that is brought down to the balance sheet is termed *retained profits*. Debentures are known as *loan notes,* fixed assets are called *non-current assets* and long-term liabilities are called *non-current liabilities*.

2 The role and significance of the professional association

One of the distinguishing characteristics of all professions is the existence of professional associations. Such bodies maintain and improve the reputation of the profession by the regulation of conduct, the improvement of skills and the validation of qualifications.

The Institute of Certified Bookkeepers is based at 1 Northumberland House, Trafalgar Square, London WC2N 5BW, under the Royal Patronage of His Royal Highness Prince Michael of Kent GCVO. The other professional association for book-keepers is The International Association of Book-keepers (AIB), whose registered office is at Burford House, 44 London Road, Sevenoaks, Kent TN13 1AS.

Book-keeping became a regulated profession under the Money Laundering Regulations of 2007. As a result of this, book-keepers now have special legal duties imposed upon them, and failure to comply with them has serious legal consequences. All practising book-keepers must be registered with a supervisory body. Both professional bodies mentioned here are treasury-appointed supervisory bodies under the Money Laundering Act and, as such, will monitor, guide and supervise members to ensure compliance.

In addition, membership provides proof of proficiency, which is recognised worldwide. It offers assistance with career development, not only through the provision of training and qualifications, but also through notification of job vacancies, updates on legislation and advice, and guidance on private practice. Members also get the opportunity to meet and associate with others in the same profession in local groups and forums.

Note: A discerning reader will spot that the term book-keeper is spelt in two different ways on this page. This is not a mistake. There are actually three correct spellings of this term: bookkeeper, book-keeper and book keeper. The two institutes use different spellings.

Figure 1. The homepage of the ICB website: www.bookkeepers.org.uk.
Reproduced with kind permission.

Figure 2. Website page of The IAB. www.iab.org.uk. Reproduced with kind permission.

3 Data security

When a business keeps a substantial number of personal details in computerised accounting records, it may be obligated to register with the Information Commissioner. The person who decides how data will be used and for what purpose is referred to in the Act as the data controller, while a person on whom data is kept is referred to as a data subject. It is essentially so that data subjects are aware of what is held and how it is used.

It is not necessary to inform the Information Commissioner if:

- the data controller is only using the data for sending and receiving invoices and statements;
- the data subjects are companies and no individuals can be identified in them;
- the data is only used to process payroll and prepare statutory returns.

However, if a data controller is going to make accounting data available to management or any other department for non-accounting purposes, e.g. marketing, statistical, planning or control purposes, it must register. It must disclose the kind of data held, the purpose for which it will be used and how subjects can access their own data.

Legal obligations in respect of personal data

Businesses registered under the Data Protection Act 1998 must comply with certain standards of practice contained in Schedule 1 of the Act. These require that the personal data shall:

- be obtained only for specified and lawful purposes and must not be used in any manner incompatible with such purposes;
- be relevant and adequate but not excessive for the purpose for which it has been collected;
- be accurate and kept up to date;
- not be kept for any longer than necessary for the purpose for which it was collected;
- only be processed in accordance with the subject's rights under the Act;
- be protected by appropriate organisational and technical measures against unauthorised and unlawful use, or accidental loss or damage;
- not be taken outside of the country to any country where there is not adequate legal protection of the rights and freedom of data subjects in respect of the processing of their personal data.

In many businesses today accounting information *will* be used for non-accounting purposes so it is very likely that anyone who controls such data will need to register and comply with the Act. To access the full text of the Act, click on www.opsi.gov.uk/ads/adsl998/19980029.htrn. The Information Commissioner's general website is www.ico.gov.uk.

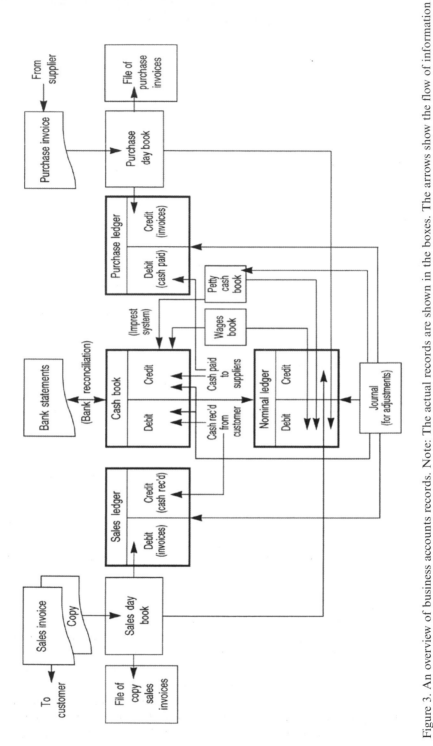

Figure 3. An overview of business accounts records. Note: The actual records are shown in the boxes. The arrows show the flow of information between the various records. The boxes shown in bold are divisions of the ledger. There is an additional month-end information flow between ledger divisions when cross-referencing is made in folio columns.

6

4   The flow of documents and processes

This chapter outlines the paper trail between buyer and seller in a typical business transaction and the processes within each firm that each document triggers.

Estimate or quotation

Sometimes it is not possible to give a precise quotation and an estimate is regarded as the best that can be done. The quotation must be for an exact figure while an estimate is only a rough figure. However, the final costs of work or supplies are expected to be within 10% of the estimated figure and courts are likely to be sympathetic to the purchasing party in actions where this figure has been exceeded.

Request for quotations

Often when a business wishes to purchase goods and services from another, requests for quotations will be sent out to a number of potential suppliers. Any company interested in competing to supply goods to the business will begin to calculate the lowest prices at which it is prepared to supply the goods or services. It will then prepare a quotation or estimate (according to whichever was requested) and send it to the potential customer.

When the customer receives the estimates or quotations they will compare them all on the basis of prices and perceived quality of the goods or services being offered, taking into account such things as delivery dates and past experience of dealing with that particular supplier.

Purchase order

When a final selection is made, the buyer will normally issue a purchase order. This will state the quantity, type of goods, prices and the special conditions of the contract, such as the terms of business, the timescale in which payment is agreed to be made, e.g. strictly 30 days. Delivery instructions and any other special conditions which may apply will be included, e.g. there may be a penalty clause for late completion of work, entitling the buyer of services to compensation of a specific sum, or a specific percentage of the total.

Delivery note

If the supplier accepts this purchase order then a delivery note will normally be made out and sent with the goods. This will normally be in at least triplicate form and will specify the goods. Some multipart, carbonised sales forms contain three copies of the delivery note and two copies of the sales invoice. The delivery notes, being the bottom two copies, may have the cash columns blocked out. In certain aspects these invoices and delivery notes will be the same, including the boxes for name and address, order number and details of goods, but the cash details will normally be omitted on the delivery notes.

The delivery note will be passed to the stores, where it will trigger the packing and shipment of the goods to the customer. At the same time the stock records will be adjusted to show the goods have been booked out from stock and have become the responsibility of the delivery driver and remain so until he or she returns a signed delivery note confirming they have been received by the customer in good order.

Where the order is for services
If the purchase order is for services rather than goods, e.g. building work, then a job order sheet may be produced by the supplying firm and passed to the works department for the manager to allocate the job to a worker or workers.

Customer signs to confirm delivery
When the goods arrive, a copy of the delivery note is signed by the customer after he or she has checked the goods are those that were ordered and have been received in good condition. There will usually be a second copy for the customer to file. These retained copies are source documents for updating the stock records, which at the end of the year, after verification against a physical stock check, will be used in the balance sheet as one component of the current assets section (Closing Stock).

Production of an invoice
The signed delivery note will be passed to the sales office of the supplier, where it will trigger the preparation of an invoice. This may already have been prepared as part of a quadruplicate or quintruplicate set and sent to the customer with the delivery note, or it may be sent by post once a signed delivery note is received to confirm the goods it is charging for have been received by the customer.

In a manual system one copy of the invoice will go to the accounts department, where its details will be entered into the sales day book. In a computerised system the sales day book may be updated automatically with the invoice details when the invoice is produced on the system.

Purchase returns note
Sometimes goods are returned by agreement with the supplier, because they are faulty or not what was ordered. In such a case a purchase returns note will be created by the buyer, which is essentially the opposite of a delivery note, describing the goods being returned and the reason.

Production of a credit note
The receipt of a purchase returns note will normally, after checking it is justified, trigger the production of a credit note at the supplier's end (essentially the opposite of an invoice). When the customer receives this, it will be entered in the purchase returns day book and this, in turn, will be

posted to the debit side of the relevant bought ledger account to reduce the indebtedness of the company to that particular supplier.

Production of a statement

At the end of the month (or sooner if it is the firm's policy) the sales day book details will be posted to the ledger divisions – the sales account in the nominal ledger and the personal account details in the sales ledger. The ledger divisions will be balanced and the resulting balances will be reproduced in statements and sent to customers, informing them of the amount they owe, whether it is overdue and when it should be paid by. The statements will also include any interest or penalties that have been agreed for late payment and details of any early settlement discount the customer can claim.

Often the statements will be age-analysed, i.e. stating which parts of the total amount have been outstanding for one month, which parts of it have been outstanding for two months, and so on. If the debt is overdue for payment, a strong demand will normally be annotated, such as *This account is overdue for payment. Please settle by return.* Such demands may become increasingly strong the older a debt becomes.

Statements will not normally give details of the goods or services supplied. Their purpose is merely to deal with the financial indebtedness of the customer, but some statements may show such details.

Often a remittance advice slip will be included with the statements (attached or as a separate slip). It will give the necessary details for the cashier to tie up the payment with the relevant account. This is partly for the convenience of the customer to save them preparing a covering letter to accompany the cheque.

Production of a cheque

The receipt of the statement by the customer is usually what triggers the production of the cheque payable to the supplier. Any remittance slip that came with the statement will be filled in and sent with it to the supplier.

The details from the cheque stub will be entered into the cashbook to credit the bank with the funds it is transferring to the supplier. If any early settlement discount has been received it will be posted to the discount received account. The other side of each part of this transaction will be posted to the debit side of the supplier's personal account in the bought ledger, to record that the business has been settled by bank funds, less any discount the suppliers have allowed.

Figure 4 provides a schematic illustration of the flow of documents in a single business transaction and the processes triggered by each one.

Symmetry of the processes of purchases and sales

This same flow of documents takes place in respect of goods supplied by the firm as for goods supplied to the firm. The roles are just reversed.

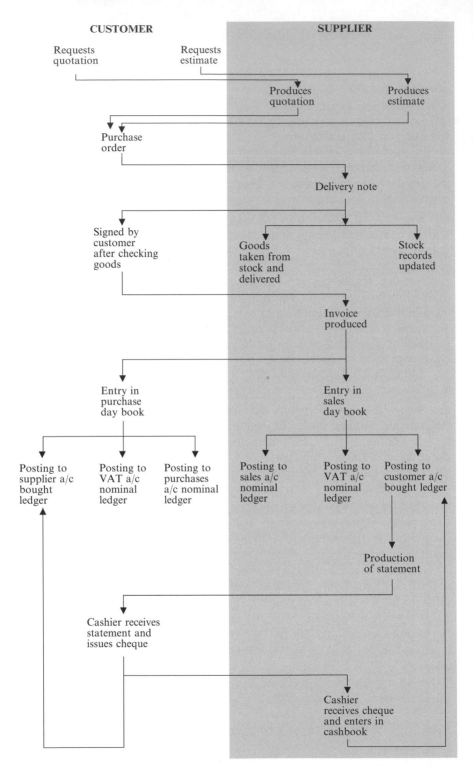

Figure 4. An illustration of the flow of documents and the processes which each triggers in a transaction between two businesses.

Details you will need:

- start date of the first financial year;
- the VAT scheme your company uses;
- who will use the system?

Allocate a password to all users. Select a password that is easy for you to remember but which is unlikely to be known or guessed by an unauthorised person. The password can be a combination of letters and numbers.

- List of customers' names and addresses, telephone numbers, bank details, e.g. sort codes and account numbers.
- Detailed list of the firm's products.
- List of opening ledger balances.

Step by step

1. Turn on the computer.
2. Double click on the Sage Accounts icon on the desktop.
3. If there is no such icon on the desktop, double-click on the Start button in the bottom left-hand corner of the screen.
4. Click on All Programs.
5. Click on Sage Accounts in the list to open the Sage Accounts folder. *The system desktop will appear.*

There are three ways of viewing the system. These are:

- the Customer Dashboard;
- the Customer Process map;
- the Customer List view.

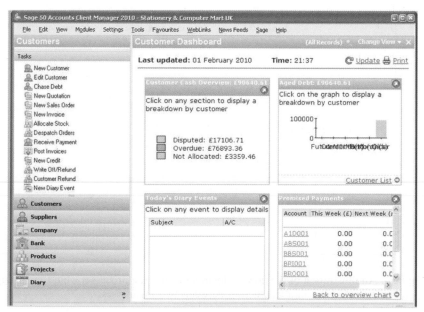

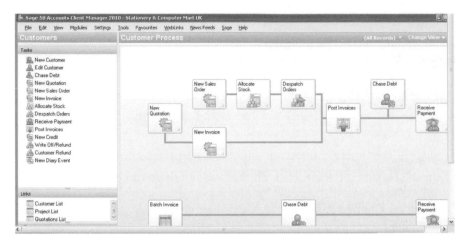

It is worth exploring these three windows before going any further. Each has a bar or column down the left-hand side known as the navigation bar. The navigation bar contains three sections:

- the tasks pane;
- the links list;
- the modules bar.

There are two toolbars on each of these windows:

- a browser toolbar;
- a modules toolbar.

We'll start with the buttons at the bottom of the navigation bar. These buttons take you to the different parts of the accounts and different areas of activity, e.g. sales, purchase or banking. The links list, in the middle pane on the left, contains links to other related pages. The tasks list at the top of the left pane is a list of things that you might want to do in any of these areas of the accounts.

Entering the default values

You have to set up the system first, before you can use it to do the accounts. There are a number of defaults and other settings to be inputted. Here's how to do it.

Step by step

1. In the Dashboard view, click on the Setting tab on the browser toolbar. *A drop-down menu will appear.*
2. Click on Change Password.
   A Change Password dialogue box will appear.

3. Enter the password you wish to use in the dialogue box.
4. Confirm the entry of the password.
   This is to comply with the Data Protection Act, which provides that any system containing confidential information on individuals must be protected against unauthorised access. Use of the password satisfies this requirement.
5. Click on OK.

Company preferences

If you run the Easy Start-up Wizard you will have been asked for your company preferences. If you did not run this wizard, enter your company preferences now. To do this:

Step by step

1. Click the back arrow to go back to the Settings tab on the browser toolbar and this time, on the drop-down menu click on the second option – Company Preferences. *A dialogue box will appear.*

2. Enter the name of the firm on line 1.
3. Enter the full address and also the e-mail and web addresses.
4. Click on the VAT tab near the top of the page.
    Another dialogue box will appear.
5. Enter the VAT reference number.
6. Click on OK to finish.

Fixed asset and product defaults

You now need to set up your categories of fixed assets and products.

Step by step

1. Click on the Settings tab on the browser toolbar again and this time click on the first option – Configuration.
    A Configuration Editor window will appear.

2. Click on the Products tab in the second-top row.
    A list of blank categories will appear, ready to be filled in with categories of your choice.
3. Click on the first blank line to highlight it.
4. Click on the Edit button.
    An Edit Product Category dialogue box will appear.

5. Enter the name of the first fixed-asset category you wish to add to the list.
6. Click on the OK button.
7. Click on Apply.
8. Repeat the process for all the fixed-asset categories there are in the company.

VAT codes

All the current UK and EU VAT codes are already pre-programmed into Sage 50 and the standard rate, which is given the code T1, is preset as the default code.

The other codes are:

- T0. Zero rated.
- T2. Exempt.
- T4. Sales to customers in other European countries.
- T7. Zero-rated purchases from suppliers in other European countries.
- T8. Standard-rated purchases from suppliers in other European countries.
- T9. Transactions to which VAT does not apply. For example, banking, journal entries and error corrections.

Up-to-date information on rate changes and new rates can be found on the HMRC website or by contacting HMRC direct (see p119 for website URL).

To change any of the tax rates or enter additional ones proceed as follows.

Step by step

1. In the Configuration Editor window click on the Tax Codes tab.
   A list of codes and their rates will appear.

2. Click on the code that needs to be changed to highlight it, or click on the next blank space if a new code is to be added to the list.
3. Click on the Edit button.
   An Edit Tax Code box will appear.
4. Enter the new percentage rate.
5. Tick the EC Code box if the tax concerned is a rate relating to transactions with other European countries.
6. Enter the description of the tax concerned, for example zero rated.
7. Click on OK.
8. Click on Apply.

Financial year parameters

If you have not set up the parameters of the financial year at the installation stage, do it now. Here's what to do:

Step by step

1. Click back with the back arrow to return to the Settings tab on the modules toolbar and click. This time select Financial Year from the drop-down menu.

It is sometimes quicker to highlight the option by pressing the F key on your keypad, rather than moving your mouse to it, especially if your hands are already on the keypad. If your hand is already on the mouse, however, that might be the easiest way to highlight the option. The same goes for all other options on the drop down menu. You can open them by clicking on the underlined letter in the name.

A Financial Year dialogue box will appear.

2. Input the start date of your current financial year.
3. Click on Change.
4. Click Yes.
5. Click Yes again.
   A Change Financial Year dialogue box will appear.

6. Select the year from the drop-down menu by clicking on the arrow to the right of the Month field.
7. Click on OK.

Setting up account statuses

Account Status notes are generated when an invoice is raised in the name of a person or firm with a history that affects their credit-worthiness. It may, for example, be that their account is 'on stop' for any of the following reasons:

- non-payment;
- bad debt;
- they have exceeded their credit limit.

There are ten different, commonly used account statuses pre-programmed into the Sage 50 software. If you need to add an additional one:

Step by step
1. Click on Configuration Editor.
2. Click on the tab marked Account Status.
   A menu of account statuses will appear.

3. Scroll down to the first blank space and click to highlight it.
4. Type in the account status label you want to add.
5. Click on the Edit button.
   An Edit Account Status box will appear.

6. Enter the status name.
7. Tick the appropriate box if you want the system to place such accounts on hold.
8. Click on OK.
9. Click on Apply.

Setting the currencies

If your company uses several currencies, you will need to set up the current exchange rates for them. To do this:

Step by step

1. Click on the Settings tab on the module toolbar.
2. On the drop-down menu, click on the Currencies option.
   A list of currencies will appear.

3. Click on the first foreign currency you are likely to use in your business transactions.
4. If it does not appear in the list, scroll to the first blank line.
5. Click on Edit.

An Edit Currency box will appear.

6. Type in the name of the currency.
7. Type in the currency code.
8. Type in the currency symbol, e.g. $ for dollar, € for euro.
9. Type in the current exchange rate between that and the currency of the country in which your business is domiciled.
10. Type in the major and minor units into which the currency is divided, e.g. dollars and cents.
11. Click on the OK button.
12. Click on Close.
13. Exchange rates should be checked before entering any transactions, because they change frequently. To check the current exchange rate, click on a reputable currency exchange website, e.g. http//:www.XE.com.

Setting up customer and supplier defaults

The process is more or less the same for both customer and supplier account defaults.

Setting up customer defaults

To save time looking up a customer's credit limit or the discounts to apply, these details need to be input as default values at the start of the year, or as soon as you start using the Sage 50 system.

To enter customer default values:

Step by step

1. Return to the Settings tab on the Modules toolbar and click.
   A drop-down menu that you have seen several times already will appear.
2. Click on the Customer Defaults option.
   The Customer Defaults window will appear.

Customer Defaults		
Record	Statements	Ageing	Discount

Defaults
Country	United Kingdom	GB
Currency	1 Pound Sterling
Std Tax Code	T1 17.50	Def. N/C 4000
Department	1

Discounts
| Discount % | 0.00 | Type | Invoice Value |
| | | Price List | |

Account status
| Default | 0 Open |
| Terms Agreed | ☐ |

OK   Cancel

3. Click on the Record tab.
4. Type in the country in which the customers are based.
5. Type in the currency in which you will trade with these customers.
6. Type in the standard VAT code that will apply. The standard tax code T1 is the code for the standard rate, currently $17\frac{1}{2}\%$.
7. Type in the default nominal ledger account number to use if no individual account number is input.
   Sage 50 allocates numbers between 4000 and 4999 for customer nominal ledger account codes.
8. Type in the default customer department details if this detail is considered useful.
9. Type in the default percentage, if any, of trade discount to allow to customers.
10. Input the name of the price list that will normally apply.
11. Set up the default terms of credit for customers to be used if no special terms are to be applied.
12. Click on the Statements tab and enter the details.

13. Click on the Ageing tab at the top of the window and enter the details. These are the units in which age of debts is to be measured, e.g. weeks or months. (The ageing details are important to ensure the debtor and creditor ratios of the firm are kept in balance. If the company's customers are paying their bills more slowly than its suppliers are being paid, the company may well become insolvent.)
14. Click on the Discount tab.
15. Enter details of any regular discount you intend to give the customer.
16. Click on OK to save the details.

Entering supplier defaults
Step by step
1. Return to the Settings tab on the modules toolbar and click.
   A drop-down menu that you have seen several times already will appear.
2. Click on Supplier Defaults.
   The Supplier Defaults window will appear.

3. Click on the Record tab.
4. Enter the country in which the suppliers are based.
5. Enter the currency in which transactions with these suppliers will be conducted.
6. Enter the tax code that applies.
7. Type in the nominal ledger account number to use if no individual account number is input.
   Sage 50 allocates the numbers between 5000 and 5999 for supplier nominal ledger account numbers.
8. Type in the department within the supplier firm, if appropriate.
9. Click in the Terms Agreed box, if relevant.
10. Click on the Ageing tab and enter the details. These are the units in which age of debts is to be measured, e.g. weeks or months.

11. Click on OK to save the details.

Product defaults

Product Defaults need to be set up to avoid these details having to be entered each time a transaction is recorded. To do this:

Step by step
1. On the Settings tab, select Product Defaults.
   The Product Defaults window will appear.

2. Each product should be given a nominal ledger account code.
3. Type in this code for each product.
4. Select from the drop-down menu the VAT code that applies to this product.
5. Enter the units in which the product is sold, e.g. 1, 10, 12, 20, 100, etc.
6. Enter the category into which the product is placed, if appropriate.
7. Select from the drop-down menu the department to which the product relates.
8. Select from the drop-down menu the EC VAT description that applies, if appropriate.
9. Select the level of accuracy required in terms of decimal places for quantity.
10. Click OK to save the details.

Control accounts

In Sage 50, control accounts have preset nominal ledger account numbers, but these can be changed if desired. To do this:

Step by step
1. On the Settings tab, select Control Accounts.
   The Control Accounts window will appear.

2. Click on any nominal ledger you wish to change.
3. Click on the arrow that appears at the right of the code to see the options for change.
4. Select the appropriate code.
5. Click on OK to save the details.
6. Click on Close.

Finance rates

Your company may charge interest on late payment of invoices. If this is the case, the interest rate that applies needs to be set up so that the system can automatically calculate the interest charges as the debts age. To do this:

Step by step

1. On the Settings tab, select Configuration.
   The Configuration Editor window will appear.

2. Click on the Terms tab on the second row.
    The Customer Finance Rates box will appear within that window.
3. Click on Add.
    The Customer Finance Rates dialogue box will appear.
4. Enter the date from which the interest charge is to be applied using the calendar icon at the right of the date box.
5. Type in the bank base rate as a percentage.
6. Type in any additional charge to be added to the interest rate, e.g. in many tenancy agreements the interest on arrears is charged at 4% above the Bank of England base rate. In such a case, the figures to be entered here, if they were being entered at the time of writing this book, would be 0.5% for the base rate percentage and 4% for the additional percentage.
7. Click on OK to save the details.
8. Click on Close to finish.

To get a full appreciation of just how much time and effort a computerised accounting system can save, let's remind ourselves how many parts make up a complete business transaction and how many stages there are in the flow of documentation that record it, each time-consuming on its own and each requiring special skills to record. Figure 4 on page 10 illustrates this.

Each of these stages has to be properly recorded and analysed so that:

- profit or loss can be calculated;
- taxes can be properly calculated;
- payments can be successfully obtained for goods and services supplied;
- creditors can be paid for goods purchased;
- credit accounts can be properly managed;
- profitability can be assessed on production and service provisions and costs controlled;
- properly informed forecasts and decisions can be made.

Using a computerised system, such as Sage 50, automates most of this. Once you have entered your set-up details, which you only have to do once, all you have to input are the prime entries. The ledger-posting, debt-ageing and statement production are done automatically.

Recording daily details: books of prime entry

Double-entry accounts are kept in the ledger, but daily details of transactions are not normally entered directly into it. It would become too cluttered and difficult to use. For convenience we enter all the day-to-day details of transactions into other books, traditionally known as *daybooks* or *books of prime entry*. Sage 50 does not use these terms. It refers to them, instead, as windows for different kinds of transactions. Here is a list of the different daybooks in a manual system side-by-side with their counterpart names in a Sage 50 computerised system:

Traditional manual accounting	Sage 50 computerised accounting
Purchase daybook	Batch supplier invoice window
Purchase returns daybook	Batch supplier credits window
Sales daybook	Batch customer invoice window
Sales returns daybook	Batch customer credits window
Journal	Nominal ledger journals window
Journal	Accruals window
Journal	Prepayments window
Cash book	Bank payments window
Cash book	Supplier payments window
Cash book	Bank cash window
Cash book	Batch purchase payments window
Cash book	Bank receipts window
Cash book	Cash receipts window
Cash book	Bank transfer window

Let's begin with recording sales.

Source documents for the book-keeper

The sources of information we need to enter into the daybooks to record sales and sales returns are invoices and credit notes.

An invoice is a bill. It is a document that informs a customer that a firm has supplied goods or performed a service and is now asking for payment. The invoice will contain the name and address of the customer, the name, address and contact details of the supplier (usually in the form of the heading), the goods supplied or service performed, the price, any discounts agreed, the VAT payable by the customer and the terms of trade, e.g. immediate payment, payment within 7 days, payment within 30 days, deduct x% for payment within 7 days, interest will be charged on late payment, etc.

A credit note is the opposite of an invoice. So equal and opposite are they that they usually have the same reference number typed on them so that the latter can easily be identified as a document that negates an invoice of the same reference number.

A credit note is issued when an invoice is to be cancelled, perhaps because the order has been cancelled, or because the goods or services have been invoiced twice in error, in which case the credit note will cancel one of them out. Another situation that can give rise to a credit note is where the value of goods or services has been successfully challenged and a reduction of price agreed. In such a case, the value of the credit note may be anything from a small reduction to a 100% reduction.

When a firm receives invoices or credit notes for goods it has purchased, they are known as purchase invoices and credit notes inwards, respectively. When it sends them out, they are called sales invoices and credit notes outwards. Whether the documents refer to sales or purchases, their format is basically the same. After all, what is a purchase invoice to one party in the transaction is a sales invoice to the other, and so it goes for credit notes too.

The production of invoices is usually triggered by receipt of signed delivery notes for *goods sold* and by time sheets or some kind of job completion docket for services rendered. Where manual systems are in use, except in very small firms, where such details may be known by heart, product or service descriptions, codes and prices are sourced from sales, or service catalogues. Trade terms are dictated by company policy and any special terms that are allowed to particular customers may be listed in a customer's *special terms* file. In a Sage 50 accounting system many of the details are entered and stored in the computer, so there is no need to look them up when creating invoices. The software does all that for you, entering product descriptions, prices and trade terms automatically, thus saving a great deal of time and effort.

In essence, the two kinds of primary record are the same, other than the fact that rather than pages in a bound book these exist as pages on a computer screen.

Sales invoices can be automatically created from Sage 50. If this facility is used, the stage of gathering together the sales invoice copies to use as source documents is bypassed, because the information will have been stored when the invoices were created and the system knows where to find it and how to use it when writing up the sales daybook. More will be said about this later in Chapter 30. For now, we will deal with recording invoices that have been produced manually in order to follow the same format as *Mastering Book-Keeping* (manual version).

If invoices have been created outside Sage 50, you will have to gather the copies to input as if you were using a manual system. This type of sales data input is known as *batch invoice processing*.

Setting up the customer accounts

You only have to set up an account once for each customer. After that you only have to enter the account number when making an entry and all the other details will be automatically filled in. The benefit of inputting all the other information on making the initial customer record will become clear when you start dealing with things like credit control.

You get there by clicking on the Customers button on the navigation bar, which is visible at the bottom left-hand corner of any of the desktop views. The modules toolbar in the Customers window provides all the principal tools you will need (14 options).

To create a new customer record, click on the New icon on the modules toolbar. *A Customer Record Wizard will appear and guide you through the twelve windows of the process.*

However, you can also use the Record icon on the modules toolbar. This is quicker.

Step by step
1. Click on the Record icon on the modules toolbar.
   A Customer Record window will appear.

2. Click on the Details tab.
3. Enter the customer's account number (select from the drop-down menu).

4. Enter the company name.
5. Enter the opening balance (select from the drop-down menu).
6. Enter the customer's address.
7. Select the country from the drop-down menu.
8. Enter the name of the contact within the company.
9. Enter the customer's telephone numbers and fax number.
10. Enter the customer's website address.
11. Enter the customer's e-mail address.
12. Tick the appropriate boxes if letters and/or statements are sent to the customer by e-mail.
13. Click on the Credit Control tab if particular credit terms have been agreed with the customer.
14. Click on Save.
15. Repeat the process for each new customer record you need to create.
16. Click on Close when finished.

Viewing customer records

You can view the transaction history for a customer quickly and easily.

Open the Customer Record window for the customer whose transactions you wish to view (see page 27).

The type of transaction is indicated by use of the following codes:

- SI Sales invoice;
- SR Sales receipt;
- SC Sales credit note;
- SD Sales discount;
- SA a sales receipt, on account.

Step by step
1. Click on the Activity tab. If you are interested in a particular transaction, select the date parameter required to reveal it.
2. Scroll to the transaction you wish to view in detail. You can limit the search by clicking on the finder arrow at the right of the Show field.
3. Double-click on the transaction to reveal the whole record for that order.
4. Click on OK.
5. Click Close when finished.

If it is all sales orders you are interested in, click on the Orders tab at the top of the Customer Record.

Price lists

Your company may wish to operate different price lists for different categories of customer, e.g. trade, wholesale and retail. To create a price list:

Step by step
1. On the module toolbar in the Customers window click on the Price List icon.
   A Price Lists box will appear.

2. Click on New.
    A New Customer Price List window will appear.

3. Type in the name or code of a price list, e.g. list A.
4. Type in the description of the price list, e.g. trade price list January 2010.
5. Click on Save.
6. Select the Customers tab and click on Add.
    A list of customers and price lists that apply will appear.

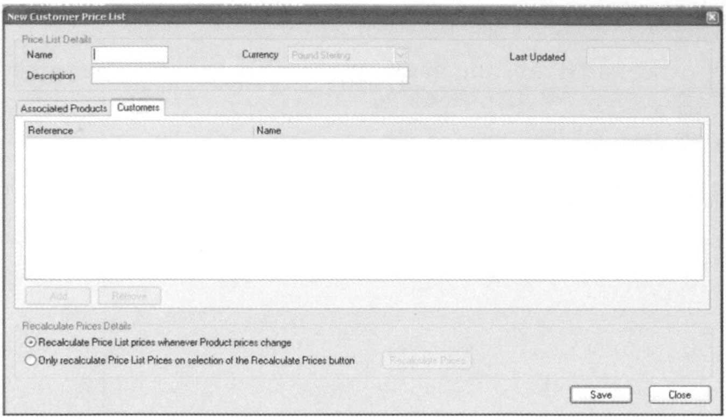

7. Scroll to the customer to whom you wish the new price list to apply.
   If this customer is currently on a different list, you will be asked if the customer is to be transferred to the new list.
8. Click on Yes.
9. Click Yes to all if all customers are to be similarly transferred.
10. Click on OK.
11. Click on Save.
12. Click on Close.
13. Click on Close again.

Invoices produced manually

Invoices produced manually (see Figure 5) are known in computerised book-keeping as *Batch invoices*. To record them in the computerised accounts:

Invoice

D. Davidson (Builder)   Delivered to:
1 Main Road   Broad Street
Anytown   Anytown
Lancs   Lancs

P356   20/12/200X

20	bags of cement	10.00	200.00
15	5 litre tins of white emulsion	1.00	15.00
32	bags of sand	5.00	160.00
40	metres of 100mm x 50mm pinewood	1.00	40.00

                                                     415.00
                 VAT @ 17½%   72.63
                                                     487.63

E&OE

Figure 5. Example of an invoice.

Step by step

1. Click on the Invoice icon on the modules toolbar in the Customers window.
   A Batch Customer Invoices window will appear.

2. In the first column (account number) click on the downward arrow to reveal the list of customer account numbers. Alternatively, type in the appropriate account number.
3. Change the invoice date if appropriate in the second column.
4. In the A/C column enter the invoice number.
5. Type a reference, if relevant, in the third column.
6. Change the nominal ledger code (N/C) if required.
7. Enter or change the department code if required.
8. Enter the net invoice value. If you only have the gross value, enter that in the net box and click on Calc. Net or the F9 shortcut key on the computer keyboard and the system will calculate the net value and fill in the appropriate net and gross boxes.
9. Click on save to make the dual posting to the ledger.
10. Click on Close.

Credit notes produced manually

Credit notes produced manually are known in computerised book-keeping as *batch customer credits*. To record them in the computerised accounts:

Credit Note

D. Davidson (Builder)   Delivered to:
1 Main Road   Broad Street
Anytown   Anytown
Lancs   Lancs

P3756   20/01/200X

60   Door hinges   0.50   30.00
                                                     ‾‾‾‾‾
                                                     30.00

                  VAT @ 17½%   5.25
                                                     ‾‾‾‾‾
                                                     35.25
                                                     ‾‾‾‾‾
E&OE

Figure 6. Example of a credit note.
E&OE stands for errors and omissions excepted.

Step by step

1. Click on the Credit icon on the modules toolbar in the Customers window. *A Batch Customer Credits window will appear.*

2. In the first column (account number) click on the downward arrow to reveal the list of customer account numbers. Alternatively, type in manually the appropriate account number.
3. Change the credit note date if appropriate in the second column.
4. In the A/C column enter the invoice number.
5. Type a reference, if relevant, in the fourth column.
6. Change the nominal ledger code if required.

7. Enter or change the department code if required.
8. Enter the net credit note value.
9. If you only have the gross value, enter that in the net box and click on Calc. Net or the F9 shortcut key on the computer keyboard and the system will calculate the net value and fill in the appropriate net and gross boxes.
10. Click on Save to make the dual posting to the ledger.
11. Click on Close.

Chasing overdue payments is extremely important. The older a debt is, the less likely it will be settled.

Secondly, the sales/debtors ratio needs to be kept in balance with the purchases/creditors ratio, otherwise cash-flow problems will start to occur.

Thirdly, it enables the business to calculate interest charges where the transaction allows for these to be applied.

The method of doing this involves age analysis of debts. The Sage 50 system can do this automatically.

Step by step

1.   On the modules toolbar in the Customers window click on the Aged tab.
     The Aged Balances Date Defaults box will appear.

2.   Enter the current date (the date of the report being generated).
3.   Enter the date to which the aged balances are required to be shown.
4.   Click on OK.
     The Aged Balances window will appear.

A/C	YTD	Credit Limit	Balance	Future	Current	1 Month(s)	2 Month(s)	3 Month(s)	Older
A1D001	5220.54	1000.00							
ABS001	3070.45	4000.00	2533.31						2533.31
BBS001	5974.24	2000.00	4309.77						4309.77
BRI001	1029.00	0.00							
BRO001	14742.39	4000.00							
BUS001	4959.81	4000.00	2066.62						2066.62
CASH001	30561.30	0.00							
CGS001	3922.44	3000.00	2028.03						2028.03
COM001	4452.08	4000.00	2807.04						2807.04
DST001	3947.99	2000.00							
FGL001	10867.60	1000.00	11260.26						11260.26
GRA001	4846.01	4000.00	4149.09						4149.09
HAU001	2295.85	4000.00	1975.16						1975.16
JSS001	3001.20	1000.00	972.07						972.07
KIN001	16062.58	6000.00	7398.35						7398.35
MAC001	10592.14	4000.00	6927.16						6927.16

Future	Current	1 Month(s)	2 Month(s)	3 Month(s)	Older	Balance	Debtors
0.00	0.00	0.00	0.00	0.00	90640.61	90640.61	90640.61

5.   If you wish to view the data in graph format, click the Graph tab.
6.   If you wish to see a breakdown of the figures, click on the Detailed button at the bottom left.
7.   When you have finished viewing, click on Close.

If you wish to change the units in which the ages of the debt is shown:

Step by step

1. Go to the Customer Defaults window.

2. Click the Ageing tab.

3. Select the desired ageing units, e.g. Calendar months.
4. Click on OK.

If you wish to change the payment terms or any other terms of trade for any customer or customers:

Step by step

1. Click the Customers button on the navigation toolbar.

2. Scroll to the account concerned (or hold down the Control key and highlight more than one account, if required).
3. Click the Record tab.
4. Click on the Credit Control tab at the top of the customer's record.
   The Credit Control box will then appear containing all the information you entered when the account was set up. You can now add or change details e.g. you may wish to change the credit limit amount, the terms of trade, the credit position, place the account on hold or release it from hold.

5. Click on Save.
6. Click on Close.
7. Click on Close again.

Dealing with disputed invoices

If a customer disputes their bill, you may choose to place their account on hold until the dispute is resolved. To do so:

Step by step

1. On the modules toolbar in the Customers window click on the Dispute icon.
   The Disputed Items window will appear.

2. Click on the finder arrow in the account number box at the top left and scroll to the account concerned. Click on it to highlight it.
The customer's account history will appear in the Disputed Items window.

No	Type	Date	Ref	Details	T/C	Amount	Disput	Dispute Reason
1010	SI	24/04/2008	58	A4 Carbon Copy Book - Tripli...	T1	33.40		
1011	SI	24/04/2008	58	Shorthand Notebook - 80 Sh...	T1	41.90		
1012	SI	24/04/2008	58	AT Mini Tower Case	T1	13.97		
1013	SI	24/04/2008	58	ATX Desktop Case	T1	27.94		
1014	SI	24/04/2008	58	CDR08432 Read/Write CD D..	T1	286.83		
1015	SI	24/04/2008	58	10gb Hard Drive	T1	46.56		
1016	SI	24/04/2008	58	DIMM 32mb 100Mhz	T1	167.63		
1017	SI	24/04/2008	58	15" Monitor	T1	167.63		
1018	SI	24/04/2008	58	17" Monitor	T1	130.38		
1019	SI	24/04/2008	58	MTH2000 Motherboard	T1	223.50		
1020	SI	24/04/2008	58	PCR600 Processor	T1	149.00		
1021	SI	24/04/2008	58	PCR650 Processor	T1	121.06		
1022	SI	24/04/2008	58	PCR900 Processor	T1	716.42		
1023	SI	24/04/2008	58	LP100 Laser Printer	T1	223.50		
1024	SI	24/04/2008	58	LP100 Laser Printer Toner	T1	35.82		
1025	SI	24/04/2008	58	32mb PCI Video Card	T1	147.77		

A/C ABS001 Name ABS Garages Ltd

Save Discard Dispute Close

3. Click on the transaction you wish to flag as being disputed.
4. Click on Dispute.
   A Details dialogue box will appear.

Details

Select a reason to explain why this item is being disputed.

Reason code 4 - Faulty goods

OK Cancel

5. Use the finder arrow to select the relevant reason for the dispute – the reasons will have been programmed in at the configuration stage.
6. Click OK.
7. The transaction will now be flagged with a letter 'D'.
8. Click on Save.
9. Click on Close.
10. Click on Close again.

To remove the 'D'. flag once the dispute is resolved, open the Disputed Items window and click on the Dispute button.

Generating sales reports

A wide variety of report types have been programmed into Sage 50. To generate a report:

Step by step

1. In the Customers window click on the Reports icon on the modules toolbar.
   The Report Browser window will appear.

2. Click on the folder containing the general category of the type of report you want to generate.
   A subfolder listing the types of reports available will appear.
3. Click on a specific report type within that folder.
4. Click on the Preview option.
5. If satisfied, click on Generate Report.
   The report will then be printed.
6. Click on the Close button.

When you are viewing a customer's record, if you need to contact the customer for credit control or any other purpose you can simply click on the Phone button on the Customers toolbar, and this will automatically call the customer from the system. This will only work if the computer modem uses your normal telephone line.

Sage 50 is pre-programmed with a wide variety of standard letters to suit most needs. You can also add your own if there isn't one that suits you. To send out a standard letter:

Step by step
1. Open the Customers window and select the customer to whom you wish to send a standard letter, or click on Clear to remove the highlighter from the screen if you want the letter to go to all customers.
2. Click on the Letters button on the modules toolbar.
   A list of standard letters will appear.

3. Click on the appropriate standard letter.
4. Click on the Preview option.

| Date: | 01/02/2010 | | | Stationery & Computer Mart UK | | | | | Page: | 1 |
| Time: | 22:46:18 | | | Aged Debtors Analysis (Contacts) - By Balance (Descending) | | | | | | |

Report Date: 01/02/2010   Customer From: ABS001
Include future transactions: No   Customer To: ABS001
Exclude later payments: No

++ NOTE: All report values are shown in Base Currency, unless otherwise indicated ++

A/C	Name	Credit Limit	Turnover	Balance	Future	Current	Period 1	Period 2	Period 3	Older
ABS001	ABS Garages Ltd Mike Hall 0191 254 5909	£ 4,000.00	3,070.45	2,533.31	0.00	0.00	0.00	0.00	0.00	2,533.31
	Totals:		3,070.45	2,533.31	0.00	0.00	0.00	0.00	0.00	2,533.31

End of Report

5. When satisfied, click on Generate Report.
   The letter, ready to send, will appear (see opposite).
6. If you are satisfied with the letter, click on OK to print.
7. Click the X at the top right-hand corner of the Letters box to close.

Gift Aid Declaration

Stationery & Computer Mart UK

Details of Donor:

Account Ref: AID001

Contact Name.   Jim Thomas

Address: 67a Station Road

                                           Blackpool
                                           Lancashire
                                           BP12 7HT

I want the charity to treat*the enclosed donation of £ .... as a Gift Aid donation

*the donation(s) of £ ....which I made on ....../....../...... as (a) Gift Aid donation (s)

*all donations that I make from the date of this declaration until I notify you otherwise as Gift Aid donations

*all donations I have made for the six years prior to this year, (but no earlier than 6/4/2000) and all donations

*all donations that I make from the date of this declaration until I notify you otherwise as Gift Aid donations

*all donations I have made for the six years prior to this year, (but no earlier than 6/4/2000) and all donations
I make from the date of this declaration until I notify you otherwise, as Gift Aid donations.

*delete as appropriate

You must pay an amount of Income Tax and/or Capital Gains Tax at least equal to the tax that the charity reclaims on your donations in the appropriate tax year (currently 28p for each £1 you give).

Signature:...   Date :...............................

Notes :
1. You can cancel this Declaration at any time by notifying the charity.
2. If in the future your circumstances change and you no longer pay tax on your income and capital gains equal to the tax that the charity reclaims, you can cancel your declaration.
3. If you pay tax at the higher rate you can claim further tax relief in your Self Assessment tax return.
4. If you are unsure whether your donations qualify for Gift Aid tax relief, ask the charity.. Or, refer to help sheet IR65 on the HMRC web site (http://www.hmrc.gov.uk/home.htm).
5. Please notify the charity if you change your name or address.

Generating customer statements

Statements are sent periodically to customers to inform them of the amount of their indebtedness to the company (see page 9 for full treatment of statements). To generate customer statements:

The first four steps are the same as for generating standard letters except that you are using the customer's statements instead of customer letters list.

Step by step

1. Open the Customers window and select the customer to whom you wish to send a statement, or click on Clear to remove the highlighter from the screen if you want statements to go to all customers.

2. Click the Statements button on the modules toolbar.
   A list of statement formats will appear.

3. Click on the appropriate format.

4. Click on Generate Report.
   The selection criteria box will appear.

5. Enter the customer reference range.

6. Enter the date parameters.

7. Click on OK to preview and use zoom if you need to.

8. Click on Print.

9. Close each window you opened when finished.

In a conventional, manual book-keeping system the details of the purchase invoices and credit notes inwards would be written up in the purchase and purchase returns daybooks in the same format as sales and sales returns would be written up in the sales and sales returns daybooks. In the Sage 50 computerised system the purchase daybook is replaced by a series of batch suppliers invoice windows, one for each line of the conventional purchase daybook.

Each line of the traditional purchase daybook is replaced with a batch suppliers invoice record. The page contains most of the information categories that a traditional purchase daybook page does and the former allow for additional references that will be useful if the data is also going to be used for cost centre analysis. Do not be concerned if you don't understand this concept at this stage. It is a management accounting concept.

These windows are not, in themselves, part of the double-entry accounts; they are rather sources from which the software will compile the accounts.

Time-saving automated processes

The same time- and effort-saving advantages are gained here as they are in relation to recording sales and sales returns details in the Sage 50 system, as the program does much of the work for you from information it has in its memory. For example, you only need to type in the customer's account number and the system will look up all the other details and fill in the spaces. Click on the calendar at the right of the date box and it will offer you a calendar of dates to choose from. VAT is calculated automatically and the invoice columns are summed.

Here's how to record batch purchase invoices (invoices that were produced manually) using Sage 50.

To do things with the bought (purchases) ledger you need to be in the Suppliers window. You get there by clicking on the Suppliers button on the navigation bar. The modules toolbar in the Suppliers window provides all the principal tools you will need (14 options).

To create a new supplier, click on the New icon on the modules toolbar. *The New Suppliers record wizard will appear and guide you through the 12 windows of the process.*

However, a quicker way is to use the Record icon on the modules toolbar.

Step by step
1.   Click on the Record icon on the Modules toolbar.
     The Suppliers Record window will appear.
2.   Click on the Details tab.
3.   Enter the supplier's details, i.e.:
     • account number;
     • name of the supplier company;
     • opening balance by selecting from the drop-down menu;
     • supplier's address;
     • country from the drop-down menu;
     • name of the contact within the company;

- supplier's telephone numbers and fax number;
- supplier's website address;
- supplier's e-mail address.
4. Tick the appropriate boxes if letters, remittances and orders are sent to the supplier by e-mail
5. Click on the Credit Control tab if particular credit terms have been agreed with the supplier.
6. Click on the Save button.
7. Repeat the process for the next new supplier record to be created, and so on.
8. Click on the Close button when finished.

Viewing supplier records

Step by step
1. From the Suppliers window, select the supplier's record you want to view and click on the Activity tab.
   The Activity window will appear.
2. If you are interested in a particular transaction, use the finder arrow at the right of the Show field to select the date parameter required.
3. Scroll to the transaction you wish to view in detail.
4. Double-click on the transaction to reveal the whole record for that order.
5. Click on OK.
6. Click on Close when finished.

If it is merely all purchase orders that you are interested in, you can just click on the Orders tab at the top of the Suppliers record.

How to write up the purchase records

What you need:

- a computer on which Sage 50 has been installed and configured into which the relevant details of all the suppliers to the firm to date have been entered and stored;
- the purchase invoices (batch invoices) that have not yet been entered.

Step by step
1. Click on Suppliers on the navigation bar.
   The Suppliers window will appear.
2. Click on the Invoice icon on the toolbar.
   A batch suppliers invoices window will appear.
3. Input the name of the supplier in the A/C box at the top left of the window or use the finder arrow to find the name.
   The supplier's stored details will be automatically entered into the information categories.
4. Input the date, nominal ledger account code, any reference that is relevant, the VAT code that applies and the invoice details. The nominal ledger account code is the ledger address to which the nominal aspect of the dual posting will be made.

5. If you only have the gross total, enter it in the Net box and click on the Calc button or press the F9 shortcut key on your computer keyboard and the system will calculate the correct value, overwrite it into the Net box and correctly fill in the VAT and Gross Total boxes for you.
6. Click on Save to make the dual postings (postings to the ledger will be explained in Chapter 15).
7. Repeat the process for all other invoices in the batch.
8. Click on Close to finish.

Example: A. Frazer, a retail stationer, makes the following purchases during April 2010:

Apr	1	Morgan and Baldwyn	20	Pen and pencil sets @ £4
	3	Morgan and Baldwyn	40	Calculators @ £5
	15	S. Jones	20	Assorted books @ £3.50
	21	A. Singh Wholesale	40	Assorted books @ £4
			80	Diaries @ £0.50
	30	Morgan and Baldwyn	25	De-luxe writing cases @ £6

The example below shows how he would record the transactions in Sage 50.

Batch Supplier Invoices

A/C Morgan and Baldwyn   Tax Rate   17.50
N/C De-Luxe Writing Case   Total   646.25

A/C	Date	Ref	Ex.Ref	N/C	Dept	Project Ref	Cust Code	Details	Net	T/C	VAT
101	01/04/2010			5004	2			20	80.00	T1	14.00
101	03/04/2010			5007	2			40	200.00	T1	35.00
102	15/04/2010			5010	2			20	70.00	T1	12.25
1094	21/04/2010			5013	2			40	160.00	T1	28.00
1094	21/04/2010			5020	2			80	40.00	T1	7.00
101	30/04/2010			5021	2			25	150.00	T1	0.00

| | | | | | | | | | 550.00 | | 96.25 |

Save   Discard   Calc. Net   Memorise   Recall   Close

Recording supplier credit notes (purchase returns)

Sometimes goods a company has purchased have to be returned to the supplier. It may be because they are faulty or arrived damaged, maybe they are not the goods that were ordered, maybe the order was cancelled before the goods were delivered, or maybe they were not ordered at all and the firm erroneously received goods that were ordered by someone else. In conventional manual accounting these returns are entered in the purchase returns daybook. The Sage 50 system equivalent of this is a Batch Supplier Credits window.

S. JONES (WHOLESALE STATIONERY SUPPLIES) LTD
210 Barton High Street, Barton, Barshire

Credit Note No: SJ /02206   15/3/201X

To authorised return of faulty
desk diaries   200.00

VAT @ 17½%   35.00
                                                                          235.00

Name of customer
D. Davidson
1 Main Street
Anytown
Lancs.

Figure 7. Example of a credit note inwards.

Look at the credit note shown above. Our company purchased a quantity of desk diaries from S. Jones (Wholesale Stationery Supplies) Ltd, and unfortunately found that some of them were faulty. We told them about the problem and they agreed that we could return them. S. Jones then issued us with a credit note to the value of the faulty goods, plus VAT, a total of £235.00. The credit note is dated 15 March. The record of this credit note in our Sage 50 system would be as shown below.

Batch suppliers credits outwards

To record supplier credit notes proceed as follows.

Step by step

1. On the modules toolbar in the Suppliers window click on the Batch Supplier Credits icon.

   A Batch Supplier Credits window will appear. The supplier's stored details will be automatically entered into the information categories.

2. Input the date, nominal ledger account code, any reference that is relevant, the VAT code that applies and the invoice details. The nominal ledger account code is the ledger address to which the nominal aspect of the dual posting will be made.

3. If you only have the gross total, enter it in the Net box and click on the Calc button, or press the F9 shortcut key on your computer keyboard and the system will calculate the correct value, overwrite it into the Net box and correctly fill in the VAT and Gross Total boxes for you.

4. Click on Save to make the dual postings (postings to the ledger will be explained in Chapter 15).

5. Repeat the process for all other credit notes in the batch.

6. Click on Close to finish.

Ageing balances

Ageing a debt owed by a customer or owed to a supplier refers to categorising it according to the time it has been outstanding.

Analysing debts into aged balances enables a firm to see how long it is taking to pay out its average £1 and how long it is taking to collect its average £1 in. If these are not kept in balance so that the money comes in at least as quickly as it goes out, a firm will eventually become insolvent, even if it is making significant profits.

It is common to give customers a 30 days' credit period and expect the same from suppliers, but many firms now expect payment immediately or within 7 days.

Another reason why age analysis of debts is important is that the longer a debt remains outstanding the more likely it is to become a bad debt and either have to be collected by legal action or written off as uncollectable.

Sage 50 does the age analysis for you. Here is how to set the process in motion:

Step by step
1. In the Suppliers window, scroll to the supplier whose account you wish to age analyse and click on it, unless you wish to age all of your suppliers' accounts, in which case miss out this stage and proceed straight to the next one.
2. Click on the Aged icon on the Suppliers toolbar.
   An Aged Balances Date Defaults box will appear.
3. Input the current date and the date to which you wish the process to go back.
4. Click on OK.
   An Aged Balances window will appear, showing the aged balance as at the date you inputted into the defaults box.
5. To view the transactions that make up the aged balances, scroll to each and click on Details at the bottom left corner of the window.
6. Close all windows when finished.

Communicating with suppliers
When you are viewing a supplier's record, if you need to contact the supplier for any reason you can simply click the Phone on the Suppliers toolbar, and this will automatically call the supplier from the system. This will only work if the computer modem uses your normal telephone line.

Sage 50 is pre-programmed with a wide variety of standard letters to suit most needs. You can also add your own if there isn't one that suits you. To send out a standard letter:

Step by step
1. Open the Suppliers window and select the supplier to whom you wish to send a standard letter, or click on Clear to remove the highlighter from the screen if you want the letter to go to all suppliers.
2. Click on Letters on the modules toolbar.
   A list of standard letters will appear.
3. Click on the appropriate standard letter.
4. Click on the Preview option.
5. When you've found the appropriate standard letter, click on Generate Report.
   The letter, ready to send, will appear.
6. If you are satisfied with the letter, click on OK to print.
7. Click the X at the top right-hand corner of the Letters box to close.

Producing supplier reports

A wide variety of report types have been programmed into Sage 50. To generate a report:

Step by step

1. In the Suppliers window click on the Reports icon on the modules toolbar. *The supplier reports window will appear.*
2. Click on the folder containing the general category of the type of report you want to generate.
3. A subfolder will appear listing the types of reports that are available.
4. Click on a specific report type within that folder.
5. Click on the Preview option.
6. If satisfied, click on the Generate Report button.
7. With some choices a criteria box will appear into which you have to enter supplier and date parameters.

The report will then be printed

8. Click on Close.

Bank payments

In a conventional accounting system the bank cashbook includes records for both bank and cash transactions, with the petty cash book being reserved for only small payments and operated on an imprest system. The Sage 50 system does not distinguish between cash and petty cash. All cash transactions are treated as petty cash and there is a separate account for it.

The single document in which all banking transactions are recorded in a conventional manual system is replaced in the Sage 50 system by separate accounts for bank and cash, and each has a number of individual input windows.

There are windows already set up in the system for three types of bank account – a current account, a deposit account and a building society account. There is only one cash account preset in the system but you can add others if you need. A company credit card is already preset on the system and you can add others if you need to.

A separate window for each type of transaction

Unlike in a manual system, where all types of banking transaction are recorded on the same page, in Sage 50 each type of transaction has its own window.

In a conventional manual accounting system all cash and cheques that the firm receives are entered on the left-hand (debit) side of the bank cashbook and all cheques it writes and cash it pays out are entered on the right-hand (credit) side. In Sage 50, however, there is no left or right sides for entries. Instead, each transaction is entered into a window specifically designed for that type of transaction.

- The Bank Payments window for recording miscellaneous, one-off payments.
- The Suppliers Invoice Payments window for recording payments to individual suppliers.
- The Batch Purchase Payments window for recording payments to all suppliers.
- The Bank Receipts window for recording non-invoice receipts.
- The Customer Receipts window for recording all monies received from particular customers.
- The Bank Transfer window for recording bank transfers.
- The Recurring Entries window for setting up recurring entries.

To view the bank accounts:

Step by step
1.   Click on the Bank button on the navigation bar.
     The Bank Accounts window will appear.

2. Scroll to the account you wish to do something with and click.
   The chosen bank account record window will appear.

3. Click on the appropriate tab according to whatever detail you wish to view.
4. Click on Close when finished.

Setting up additional bank accounts

To set up your bank account details:

Step by step

1. Click the Bank button on the navigation bar to open the Bank Accounts window, unless you are already there.
2. Scroll to the account you wish to edit.
   The Bank Record window for that account will appear.
3. Click on the Record icon on the toolbar.
4. Change the current balance as appropriate and enter or amend any other details as required.
5. Click on the Bank Details tab.
   A further set of defaults will appear.

6. Enter or amend any other details as required.
7. Click on Save.
8. Click on Close.

Recording miscellaneous non-invoice payments

Step by step

1. In the Bank Accounts window click on the Payments icon on the toolbar.
   The Bank Payments window will appear.

2. Use the finder arrow in the first column to locate the appropriate account.
3. Check the date is correct.
4. Enter the cheque number or other suitable reference.
5. Enter the nominal ledger code for the payment.
6. Enter the details of the payment to be posted in the Details column.
7. Enter any early settlement discount claimed, if relevant (see page 92 for explanation).
8. Change the VAT code if the payment is not for a standard rated chargeable purchase.
9. Click on Save.
   The details will be posted to update the ledger divisions.
10. Repeat steps 2 to 7 for all other such receipts to be recorded.
11. Click on Save to update the nominal ledger and bank account.
12. Click Close to finish and return to the Bank Accounts window.

To make payments to a specific supplier, remain in the Bank Accounts window and select the account from which you wish to pay the supplier.

Step by step
1. Click on Suppliers on the toolbar.
   The Supplier Payment window for that account will appear.

2. In the payee field, use the finder arrow to find and select the supplier's account number.
3. Change the date on the top line if necessary using the calendar button. Enter the cheque number in the appropriate field.
4. Enter the amount in the Payment column against the relevant invoice number or simply click on Pay in Full if appropriate.
5. Enter any early settlement discount claimed, if relevant (see page 92 for explanation).
6. Do likewise for customer payments.
7. Repeat steps 5 and 6 for any other invoices being paid with this cheque.
8. Click on Save.
9. Click on Close to finish to return to the Bank Accounts window.

To record payments to several suppliers:

Step by step
1. In the Bank Accounts window, select the relevant bank account.
2. Click on Batch.
   The Batch Purchase Payments window will appear.
3. Then do one of the following:
   - to record settlement of all the accounts listed just click on Pay All;
   - to record settlement of individual accounts in the list, select the transaction concerned and click on Pay In Full;
   - to record part payment to any account, enter the amount paid in the Payment column against the invoice concerned.
4. When all payments have been recorded, click on Save.
5. Click on Close to finish and return to the Bank Accounts window.

Recording payments that are not in settlement of debts

To record the banking of payments received that are not in settlement of invoices:

Step by step

1. In the Bank Accounts window click on the Receipts icon on the toolbar. *The Bank Receipts window will appear.*

2. Select the appropriate bank account using the finder arrow at the right of the Bank field.
3. Enter or change the date as appropriate.
4. Enter the cheque number or another suitable reference in the Reference field.
5. Enter the nominal ledger account number to where the dual posting is to be made.
6. Enter the department if this detail is needed.
7. Enter the reason for the posting in the description field.
8. Enter the net value of the transaction.
9. Enter the VAT, if applicable.
10. Repeat steps 4 to 9 for any other receipts that are to be recorded.
11. Click Save to post the entries to the ledger.
12. Close all windows when finished.

Recording money received from customers

When receipts are from customers in settlement of invoices, the system speeds things up for you. You don't have to enter the nominal ledger codes for the dual posting. The system deals with that automatically for you. To record receipts from customers:

Step by step

1. In the Bank Accounts window, scroll to the bank account into which the payment/s is/are being deposited and click on the Customer icon on the toolbar.

The Customer Receipts window will appear.

Customer Receipt - Company Credit Card										
Bank Details			**Customer Details**			**Receipt Details**				
Account Ref	1240		Account			Date	02/02/2010			
Name	Company Credit Card		Name			Amount	0.00			
Balance	9358.97					Reference				

Show All   From 02/02/2010   To 02/02/2010

No.	Type	A/c	Date	Ref	Ex.Ref	Details	T/C	Amount £	Disputed?	Receipt £	Discount £

Analysis Total   0.00

Save   Discard   Pay in Full   Wizard   Automatic   Dept.   Close

2. Type in the sales ledger account number of the customer from whom a payment has been received and banked.
    A list of invoices and part invoices outstanding will appear.
3. Enter the current date using the calendar button at the right of the Date field.
4. Enter an appropriate reference.
5. To record settlement of an invoice in the list, select the transaction concerned and click on Pay in Full.
6. To record part payment of any invoice, enter the amount paid in the Receipt column and the value of any discount given in the Discount column against the invoice concerned.
7. Repeat steps 1 to 5 for any other receipts that are to be recorded.
8. Click on Save to post the entries to the ledger.
9. Close all windows when finished.

Bank transfers

If you need to make a bank transfer from one of your bank accounts to another this is how to do it:

Step by step

1. In the Bank Accounts window, scroll to the bank account from which money has to be moved.
2. Click on the Transfer icon on the toolbar.
    The Bank Transfer window will appear.

3. Enter, in the Account To field, the nominal ledger account number of the bank account to which you are recording money as having been transferred.
4. Enter any reference deemed appropriate.
5. Enter the department number, if relevant.
6. Enter the amount of the transfer.
7. Enter the correct date.
8. Click on Save.
9. Click on Close.
10. Click on Close again.

To set up recurring entries

For identical value payments that have to be made regularly, typically each month, Sage 50 automates part of the process. It stores the details and on the payment day asks you on starting up if you want to post the recurring payments that have fallen due. To set up a recurring bank entry:

Step by step

1. In the Bank Accounts window, click on the Recurring icon on the toolbar. *The Recurring Entries window will appear.*

2. Click on Add.
   The Add/Edit Recurring Entries window will appear.
3. Use the finder arrow at the right of the Transaction Type field to select a type from the list.
4. Use the finder arrow at the right of the Bank Account field to select the bank account from which the recurring payment is to be made.
5. Do likewise to select the nominal ledger account number to which the other side of the dual posting is to be made.
6. Type in a relevant reference.
7. Describe the transaction in the Details field.
8. Enter the payment frequency start date and total number of payments in the relevant fields in the Frequency section of the window.
9. Enter the net amount, using the VAT code and any VAT that has to be added to the payment. The net and VAT amounts are entered via the keyboard icons at the right of the relevant fields and the VAT code is entered by means of the finder arrow on the field.
10. Click on OK when satisfied. This will return you to the Recurring Entries window.
11. Repeat the process for all other recurring entries to be set up.
12. Click on Process and then on Process All.
13. Click on Close when finished.

Writing cheques in the system

In a conventional manual system the cashier is the one who writes cheques on the firm's bank account, whether or not they have the authority to sign them on the firm's behalf. Sage 50 provides the facility for cheques to be printed direct from the system and as the book-keeping entries are made automatically it cuts out the need to write up cheque stubs and post to the cash book from them. To print cheques in Sage 50:

Step by step
1. In the Bank Accounts window, scroll to the bank account on which a cheque is to be drawn.

2. Click on the Cheques icon on the toolbar.
   The Print Cheques window will appear.

3. If a starting cheque number has not been entered in the relevant field (i.e. if there are no cheques in the list), enter one now.
4. Highlight those transactions for which cheques are to be printed.
5. Click on Print Cheques.
   The Cheque Layouts window will appear.

6.   Select a suitable layout from the list.
7.   Click on the Run button.
     A Confirm dialogue box will appear.

8.   If the cheque printed correctly, Click on the Yes button.
9.   Click on Close when finished.

Printing bank statements

You can print out your reconciled bank statement at any time using the Sage 50 system:

Step by step

1.   In the Bank Accounts window, select the account for which you wish to print a statement.
2.   Click on the Statement icon on the toolbar.

The Print Output box will appear with the Preview radio button already ticked.

3. Click on Run.
   A Criteria box will appear.

4. Enter the date range for which you want transactions included using the finder arrows on the two parameter boxes to bring down the calendar on which to check off the To and From dates.
   A preview of the statement will appear.

```
Date:    02/02/2010                                                    Page:   1
Time:    22:11:48                    Bank Statement

1200
Bank Current Account                          Stationery & Computer Mart UK
Currency:    Pound Sterling                   Sage House
                                              Benton Park Road
Bank Balance: £        -20091.04              Newcastle Upon Tyne
                                              NE7 7 LZ


Date From:    01/01/1980
Date To:      02/02/2010

No      Date      Ref       Details            Payments  £   Receipts  £   Balance   £
                            B/Fwd Balance                                   -6,511.96
```

5. Click on Print Options on the toolbar of the Preview window if you are satisfied with the preview.
    A Print dialogue box will appear.
6. Click on the OK button to print the statement.
7. When finished, close the Preview window by clicking the X at the top right-hand corner.

Bank reconciliation

Every cashier tries to keep the cashbook as accurate and up to date as possible. Receipts and payments are inputted each day, then, at regular intervals, the firm receives bank statements from the bank – weekly, monthly or quarterly. Unfortunately, the balance shown on the cashbook hardly ever agrees with the one shown on the bank statement. There can be various reasons for this.

Unpresented cheques

When you get the bank statement and compare the balance with that shown in your records, you may see that some cheques you drew have not yet been presented to the bank for payment. They simply don't appear on the bank statement at all, as yet. The cashier enters cheque transactions within a day or two of handling the cheques but it could be days or even weeks before the payee presents them to the bank for payment.

Bank lodgments

Payments into the bank may have been recorded promptly in the accounts, but if they haven't yet been recorded by the bank, or if the statement was sent out between the time the cashier lodged the bankings in the night safe and the time he/she actually paid them in over the counter, they will not show up on the statement.

Automatic payments
Payments by direct debit or standing order may have been omitted by the cashier, but they will still appear on the bank statement.

Bank charges and interest
A cashier may know nothing about these until the bank statement arrives, containing the details.

Returned cheques
A customer's cheque may have been returned unpaid – in other words, 'bounced'. The cashbook will show the money having been received, but the bank won't have received funds for the cheque, so the statement will show a contra entry.

Errors
The cashier could simply have made an error. Bank errors can happen, but they are rare.

The bank reconciliation
If a discrepancy arose from just one source it would be easy enough to deal with, but usually there are several discrepancies, some distorting the credit side and some distorting the debit side.

To remove this confusion and explain the discrepancies, the cashier carries out a bank reconciliation. The cashier, after all, is responsible for the firm's money, so if the bank disagrees with the cash balance in the firm's records, the cashier must clearly show the reasons why.

This process can take time and cause headaches in the manual system. While the computerised system is not quite clever enough to sort out all the problems in reconciling bank statements and bank account balances that don't match, nevertheless it takes on some of the burden and makes the process easier for the cashier. Here's how you do it using Sage 50:

What you need to hand:

* cheque stubs;
* paying-in slips;
* bank statement.

Compare the opening balances of the bank account on Sage 50 and that for the same date on the statement received from the bank. If they match, proceed to step 2. If they don't, you'll have to investigate the reason why. There is no point at all in using the automatic reconciliation function if the opening balances don't match. A reconciliation of the previous month's banking figures will be needed.

If the opening figures match, then follow this procedure:

Step by step
1.   Return to the Bank Accounts window.

2. Scroll to the account to be reconciled.
3. Click on the Reconcile icon on the toolbar.
   A Statement Summary window will appear.

4. Enter the statement reference, the date of the bank statement and the closing balance in the relevant fields.
5. Enter the amounts and dates of any interest earned and account charges incurred in the relevant fields. This detail can be taken from the bank statement.
6. Click on OK.
   The Bank Reconciliation window will appear.

It has two panes. The top pane presents all the transactions recorded in the bank account in the Sage 50 system and the bottom pane is for you to move those that are also represented in the bank statement to. To do this:

7. In the upper pane, double click on each transaction in turn that is also represented in the bank statement or highlight it and click on the match transactions button to the right of the panes to move the entry to the lower pane. Tick each item on the bank statement as you go.
8. When the balances on the bank statement and the bank reconciliation match, click on Save.
9. Click on Close to return to the Bank Accounts window.

If when you have worked through all the transactions in the upper pane, and if the balance of the bank account on Sage 50 and the balance as per the bank statement still do not match, proceed as follows:

Go through the bank statement line by line and look for transactions that are not represented in the Sage 50 accounts. Such items are likely to be interest earned or bank charges incurred but not spotted on the bank statement earlier, or they might be returned cheques or direct debits. Cross the ticks you made on the bank statement, so that you can easily spot any unmatched items.

If you erroneously process any transaction as matched, then just double click on it in the lower pane or highlight it and click on the Unmatch button to reverse the process.

When you find any such items that are not represented in the accounts, enter them by means of adjustment as follows:

Step by step

1. In the Bank Reconciliation window, click on the Adjust button.
   An Adjustment dialogue box will appear.

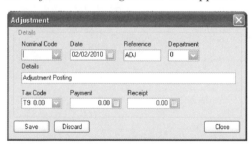

2. Enter the relevant details, including the nominal ledger code to which dual posting of the transaction is to be posted, the department (if this detail is required), a description of the transaction, the VAT code that applies to this kind of transaction and the value. Make sure you enter the latter in the right column, according to whether it is an outgoing (Payment field) or an income (Receipt field).
3. Repeat the process for all adjustments you have to make.
4. Click on Save.
5. Click on Close to return to the Bank Reconciliation window.

The only afterthoughts you can't enter in the Adjustment box are omitted customer receipts and supplier payments. To put right such omissions as these, you have to save the reconciliation, go back to the Customers and/or Suppliers windows and input them in the normal way. Then you can reopen the reconciliation by clicking on the Reconcile icon on the toolbar of the Bank Accounts window, then selecting the Use Saved option when asked whether you wish to use this or discard it.

When the process is complete, click on Reconcile at the bottom left of the window. The reconciliation will be saved in the archive and you can view it at any time by clicking on View History button in the Bank Reconciliation window.

The reconciliation statement produced by Sage 50 does not conform to any of the traditional formats as represented in *Mastering Book-Keeping*.

Generating a bank report

A wide variety of report types have been programmed into Sage 50. To generate a bank report:

Step by step
1. Click on the Reports icon on the modules toolbar.
    A Report Browser window will appear.

2. Double click on the folder containing the general category of the type of report you want to generate.
    A subfolder will appear listing the types of reports that are available.
3. Click on a specific report type within that folder.
4. Click on the Preview option.
5. If satisfied, click on Generate Report.

A Criteria box will appear:
- *transaction dates (to and from);*
- *transaction numbers (to and from).*

6. Enter the details and click on OK.
7. Click on Print to print the report.
8. Close all windows when finished.

Checking liquidity

You can check the cash-flow situation by clicking on the Cash Flow icon on the toolbar of the Bank Accounts window.

A three-paned Cash Flow window will appear showing:

- *all outstanding receipts and payments;*
- *balances on all bank accounts side by side with the overdraft limits on those accounts;*
- *a summary of the current aggregated bank balances, the receipts and payments due within the selected period, e.g. one week, or one month, etc., and the forecasted aggregated bank balances at the end of this period.*

In a conventional manual accounting system a specifically formatted book is used for recording petty cash transactions. It is like the conventional cashbook but with analysis columns added. This is so that the many small purchases can be aggregated with other purchases of the same type and only column totals posted to the ledger.

However, in Sage 50, since the postings are done automatically and there are not the limitations of space in the books that there is in the case of a manual book-keeping system, there is no justification for using specifically formatted input sheets for petty cash. Sage 50, therefore, simply uses the same windows as for banking transactions.

The petty cash account is identical in format to the banking account. Furthermore, Sage 50 does not have separate cash and petty cash accounts and nor does the banking account have a separate section for larger cash transactions, as is the case with the conventional cashbook in a manual system.

However, there is nothing to stop you setting up a separate account for larger cash transactions if you wish. You can set up any number of bank and cash accounts. Here, it will be assumed that you do not need a separate account for large cash transactions and so only a petty cash account will be used.

The petty cash float
The petty cashier looks after a small float such as £50 or £100 in notes and coins. It is used to pay for miscellaneous small office expenses such as staff travel expenses, window cleaning or small office items needed quickly. The petty cashier keeps account of all such transactions.

Using the imprest system
From time to time the cashier will reimburse the petty cashier for the amount he/she has spent on the firm's behalf and the float is replenished to the original amount. This is called an imprest system, and the original amount of the float (e.g. £50) is called the imprest amount.

Keeping the petty cash secure
The petty cashier is personally responsible for the petty cash, so he/she should:
● keep it locked away;
● limit the number of people who have access, preferably to one person;
● reconcile cash to records regularly (petty cash vouchers + receipts + cash = imprest value).

Recording petty cash transactions
To enter up the petty cash records you will need to have to hand all the cash purchase invoices for the period.

Value Added Tax (VAT)
VAT may not be shown as a separate item on cash purchase invoices for small amounts and where a conventional manual system is in use the petty cashier

would have to calculate the VAT content, if any, on each invoice. In Sage 50, however, the petty cashier does not have to do this. They can simply place the gross total in the Net box and then click on Calc Net and the system will overwrite the Net box with the correct net value and fill in the VAT box with the correct VAT figure. If the payment is for a purchase that is not chargeable for VAT at the standard rate the tax code must be changed in the T/C column against this item.

Starting a new petty cash system

When starting a new petty cash system a sum of money will be entrusted as a float to the petty cashier, let's say £50. Normally a cheque is drawn on the current account and given to the petty cashier to cash. It can just as well be done by bank transfer though, avoiding the need for a cheque. Even if a cheque is used, it is still simpler to treat it as a bank transfer in the accounts. To enter the bank transfer:

Step by step

1. In the Bank Accounts window, click on the Transfer icon on the toolbar or click on Record Transfer in the tasks pane on the top left-hand side. *The Bank Transfer window will appear.*

2. Enter the account from which the money is being transferred and the account that it is being transferred to, using the finder arrows on each relevant field.
3. Enter the cheque number in the reference field (or if it is a direct bank transfer use some other suitable reference).
4. Type in a description of the transaction, e.g. imprest.
5. Enter a department name if deemed appropriate.
6. Enter the amount of the transfer.
7. Overtype the date of the transfer if it is not the current date.
8. Click on Save.
9. Click on Close when finished.

If you are changing from a manual system to a Sage 50 system and you already have an imprest system in place, you will need to set up an opening balance on the petty cash account. This is how to do it:

Step by step

1. In the Bank Accounts window, select Account Type.
2. Scroll to Petty Cash and click on the Record icon on the toolbar.
    The Bank Record-Petty Cash window will appear.

3. Click on the icon at the right of the Current Balance field.
    The Opening Balance Setup window will appear.

4. Enter a suitable reference, the date and the opening balances of receipts and payments.
5. Click on Save.
    The Opening Balance Setup window will disappear and leave only the Bank Record-Petty Cash window.

6. Enter the imprest amount in the Minimum Limit field.
7. Click on the Bank Details tab and enter the bank details if you have not already done so at setup stage.

9. Click on the Contact tab and complete the details if you have not already done so.
10. Click on Save.
11. Click on Close when finished.

Recording payments out of petty cash

The payments from the petty cash tin can be written up as a batch whereafter a request can be made for a cheque to replenish the imprest amount. Here's how to enter up a batch of petty cash dockets:

Step by step

1. In the Bank Accounts window, scroll to the petty cash account and click on the Payments icon on the toolbar.

   A Bank Payments window will appear.

2. In the first column, use the finder arrow to locate the account number of the petty cash account.
3. Enter in the second column the date of the first transaction to be entered.
4. Type in the reference number allocated to the first receipt slip.
5. Enter the nominal ledger code to which the payment is to be posted.
6. Enter a department number if departmental cost centring is required.
7. Enter brief details of the transaction, e.g. window cleaning.
8. Type in the amount of the payment.
9. Change the value of the TC if the transaction concerned is not chargeable for VAT at the standard rate.
10. Click on Save to post the details to the nominal ledger and the petty cash account.
11. Repeat the process for all petty cash invoices.

    The gross total of the batch of transactions is shown in the total box at the top right of the window and the Net and VAT totals are shown in the two total boxes at the bottom right.
12. Click on Close to return to the Bank Accounts window.
13. Click on Close again to finish.

13 Journalising

In a manual system, opening balances, bad debts and depreciation are dealt with by means of a prime entry in the Journal, but Sage 50 has quicker and simpler methods for these, which are explained in Chapters 21, 32 and 39 respectively. Nevertheless, the journal remains an appropriate vehicle for dealing with the same types of transactions as it does in a manual system.

To make journal entries:

Step by step

1. Click on Company on the navigation bar.
   The Nominal Ledger window will appear.

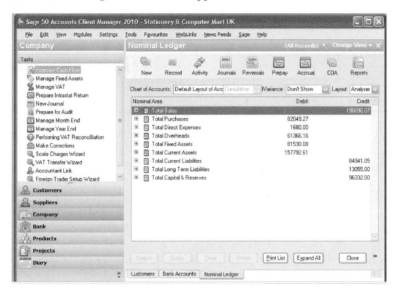

2. Click on the Journals icon on the toolbar.
   The Nominal Ledger Journals window will appear.

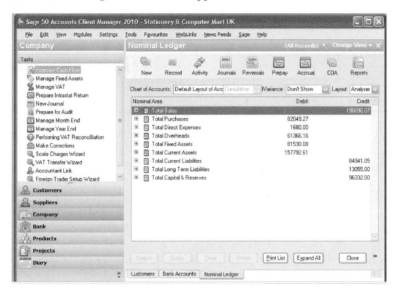

3. Enter a suitable reference, e.g. Depreciation 2009.
4. Click the calendar button at the right of the date field to select the current date.
5. Enter the nominal ledger code of the first of the assets you are going to depreciate.
   The name of the asset will be filled in automatically.
6. Write a brief explanation in the Details field, e.g. Depreciation on motor van.
7. Change the VAT code if the transactions are not chargeable for VAT at the standard rate, as this is the default rate and if you do not change it this will be the rate that is posted.
8. The VAT will not be calculated for you. If VAT is a part of the complex transaction you must calculate it yourself and enter it as a debit or credit payment, e.g. in the hypothetical case of journalising the purchase of a printer and posting the dual entry to capital introduced, the journal entries would be as follows.

	Debit	Credit
Capital introduced	117.70	
Printer		100.00
VAT		17.50
	117.50	117.50

9. Enter the amounts concerned, both debit and credit.
   There may be different numbers of debit and credit parts to the transaction, but both sides of the transactions must add up to the same amount, so that a zero balance shows in the balance field at the top right.

   If the two sides of the transaction you are journalising don't balance, the system will not let you save the entries. This prevents an error which would lead to the trial balance failing to balance in a manual system and so saves a lot of time and trouble.

   Sometimes it is a good idea to make combination double entries. An example of this is the case of sales of various fixed assets and a single bank payment.

   If an error is made, reverse it by clicking on the Reverse Journals icon on the toolbar in the Nominal Ledger window.
10. Take a backup copy and print out a copy in case anything goes wrong during the reversal process. To do this, click on File on the browser toolbar and select the Backup option from the drop-down menu.
    A message box will appear asking you if you want to check your data.

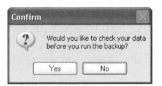

11. Click on Yes.
    A Backup window will appear. It has three tabs:

Backup

| Backup Company | Advanced Options | Previous Backups |

Company Details

You are about to create a backup of:

Company Name: Stationery Computer Mart UK

Found In: X:\DOCUMENTS AND SETTINGS\ALL USERS\APPLICATION
            DATA\SAGE\ACCOUNTS\2010\COMPANY.000\

Where do you want the company backed up to?

We have suggested a filename and location to save this backup to. If you are happy
with this suggestion click OK. If not enter a filename and use Browse to select the
location for your backup.

Backing Up to removable media? Insert the device before clicking OK.

Backing Up to CD? Refer to the Help now.

Filename : SageAccts Stationery & Computer Mart UK 2010-02-12 17-34-18.001

Location :

[Browse...]

[OK] [Cancel] [Help]

- *Backup Company*;
- *Advanced Options*;
- *Previous Backups*.

12. Select the first tab if you wish to back up everything.
    Select the second if you only want to save part of your files, e.g. the data or
    the templates.
    Select the third to call up previous backups.
13. When you have selected from the tabs, change the filename to something
    suitable. Change the location if you wish.
14. Click on OK and the backup will begin.

An information box will appear when the process has completed successfully.

If a journal entry is one you will make regularly, set the system to memorise it as a skeleton journal entry by clicking on the Memorise button at the bottom of the Nominal Ledger Journals window. When you need to make the journal entry again, you can quickly recreate it.

14   Accruals and prepayments

Accruals and prepayments are adjustments we need to make to the accounts at the end of the year (or other management accounting period).

- Accruals are sometimes called accrued expenses, expense creditors or expenses owing. They are a liability for expenses for goods or services already consumed, but not yet billed (invoiced).
- Prepayments are an asset of goods or services already paid for, but not yet completely used. Prepayments are, therefore, in a sense the opposite of accruals.

Example of accrued expenses

Suppose we are drawing up accounts for the year ended 31 March. We know there will be an electricity bill for the three months ended 30 April, a month after the end of our financial year. By 31 March, even though we haven't had the bill, we would already have used two months' worth of it, but as things stand the cost of this won't appear in our accounts because it is too soon to have received a source document (i.e. the invoice) from which to enter it. Still, electricity clearly was an expense during the period, so we have to 'accrue' a sensible proportion. For example:

Electricity account period	1 February to 30 April
Estimated charge	£630.00 (three-month period)
Period falling within our accounts	1 February to 31 March (two-month period)
Charge accrued for period:	$\dfrac{£630.00}{3 \text{ months}} \times 2 \text{ months} = £420.00$

Wages and rent

Other items that often have to be accrued are wages and rent. The firm receives the benefit of work and of premises before it pays out wages and rent (assuming rents are payable in arrears; if rent is payable in advance we would need to treat it as a prepayment).

Example of prepayment

A prepayment arises, for example, where an insurance premium or professional subscription is paid annually in advance but only one or two months' benefit has been used by the end of the year. We must adjust the figures so that we don't charge the whole amount against profits for the year. Clearly, much of the benefit remains as an asset for use in the next year. Here's an example, again assuming that our accounting period ends on 31 March:

Professional subscription for calendar year:	£100.00
Period falling within our accounts:	1 January to 31 March
Period falling into next accounting period:	1 April to 31 December (nine months)
Prepaid for next year:	$\dfrac{£100.00}{12} \times 9 = £75.00$

ACCRUALS	PREPAYMENTS
The balance c/d will be a debit one, but the ultimate effect on the expense account (the balance b/d) will be a credit entry.	The balance c/d will be a credit one, but the ultimate effect on the expense account (the balance b/d) will be a debit entry.

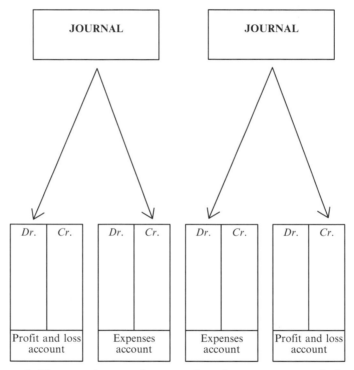

Figure 8. The opposite ways that accruals and prepayments are dealt with in the accounts.

The amount of the accrual is treated as a carried-down balance (c/d) on the debit side of the expense account concerned (e.g. wages, heat and light, etc.), which will have the effect of increasing the balance b/d on the credit side. The amount of a prepayment is treated in the opposite way, as a carried-down balance on the credit side of the relevant expense account, which will have the effect of increasing the balance b/d on the debit side.

Accounting for accruals in Sage 50
To deal with accruals in Sage 50 is a much simpler process. Here's how you do it:

Step by step
1. In the Nominal Ledger window, click on the Accrual icon on the toolbar. *The Accruals window will appear.*

N/C										
ACR										

Current Item: 4
No Of Items: 3

N/C	Details	Dept	Accrual N/C	Value	Months	Monthly Amount	sted
7502	Telephone Accrual	0	2109	200.00	4	50.00	4
7502	Telephone Accrual	0	2109	225.00	4	56.25	4
7502	Telephone Accrual	0	2109	300.00	4	75.00	3
				0.00	0	0.00	0

Save   Wizard   Print List   Close

2. Click on the finder arrow in the N/C field to locate the relevant nominal ledger account to which an accrual is to be posted, e.g. Rent account, and click on it to select it.
3. Enter the description of the accrual in the details column, e.g. Rent accrued.
4. Enter the department number to which it applies if cost-centre analysis is needed. Enter the estimated total expense over the accrual period.
5. Enter the number of months over which the accrual is to be posted (maximum 12).
   The monthly amount is automatically calculated and entered. The last column shows you a running total of how many accruals have already been posted for this entry.
6. Click on Save.
7. Click on Close to return to the Nominal Ledger window.

There is a wizard to guide you if you get stuck.

Accounting for prepayments in Sage 50

Likewise for prepayments, recording them in the Sage 50 system is simple and uncomplicated. When the prepayments process is run on Sage 50 the payment concerned will be shown in the accounts as spread over the number of months to which it relates, e.g. a pre-paid insurance premium may be spread over the ensuing 12 months.

When the month-end procedure is run, the part of the payment that relates to that month will be all that is posted to the nominal ledger expense account, because that will be the only part of the pre-paid service that has been used. The rest will remain an asset to be used in subsequent months.

This is how you deal with prepayments:

Step by step

1. In the Nominal Ledger window, click on the Prepay icon on the toolbar. *The Prepayments window will appear.*

N/C	Details	Dept	Prepayment N/C	Value	Months	Monthly Amount	sted
7100	Rent Prepayment	0	1103	1800.00	4	450.00	4
7100	Rent Prepayment	0	1103	2000.00	4	500.00	4
7100	Rent Prepayment	0	1103	2500.00	4	625.00	3
				0.00	0	0.00	0

(Prepayments window — N/C and PRP fields at top; Current Item 4, No Of Items 3; Save, Wizard, Print List and Close buttons)

2. Click on the finder arrow in the N/C field to locate the relevant nominal ledger account, which has been prepaid, and click on it to select it.
3. Enter the description of the prepayment in the Details column.
4. Enter the department number to which it applies if cost-centre analysis is needed. Enter the value of the prepayment in full.
5. Enter the number of months over which it must be spread (maximum 12). *The monthly amount is automatically calculated and entered. The last column shows a running total of how many prepayments have already been posted for this entry.*
6. Click on Save.
7. Click on Close to return to the Nominal Ledger window.

There is a wizard to guide you if you get stuck.

The company's official record

The ledger is the official record of a company's accounts. We sometimes speak of the general ledger, the bought ledger, sales ledger and cashbook separately, as if they were separate 'ledgers', but to an accountant the ledger is a single unit, even if it is made up of physically separate books. The ledger is really a 'system' rather than a book. Whatever form it takes – books or computer disks, etc. – 'the ledger' means the master record of all the company's financial affairs.

The divisions of the ledger

The nominal ledger is a division so named to distinguish it from the personal division of the ledger. In the nominal ledger the impersonal aspects of transactions are posted, e.g. purchases, sales figures, wages, stationery and asset purchases. The personal ledger is the division where the personal side of each transaction is posted, i.e. the credit to suppliers' accounts when the company has purchased something, and the debit to customers' accounts when the company has sold something.

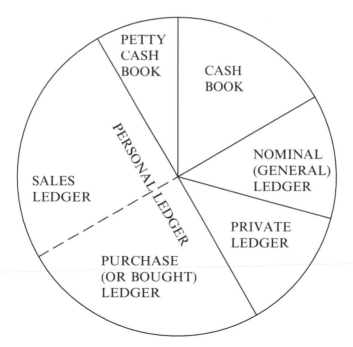

Figure 9. The divisions of the ledger.

Different accounts within the ledger

Each division of the ledger contains a number of different accounts, one for each item of expense, revenue, asset or liability as they will appear in the final accounts. For example, there will be an account for purchases, an account for sales, an account for wages, and a separate account for each asset such as Motor car 1 account, Motor car 2 account or Printing machine account, and so on.

In accounting nothing should ever be posted into the ledger except from the books of prime entry. In Sage 50 you can't fail on this one, as the only pages you are offered are those of *books of prime entry*. The paper pages of the traditional books of prime entry are replaced with windows that appear on the computer screen. It is only into these that raw accounting data can be entered.

Automatic ledger posting in Sage 50

In fact, you don't even have to do the ledger posting parts of the process. The system does that for you. You just do the prime entries. If you compare the size of the ledger chapter here with the ledger chapter in the manual book-keeping version of this book, you will see what a huge amount of time and effort computerised accounting saves. Ledger posting and balancing is a major part of manual book-keeping and all this is done automatically in Sage 50. You don't even have to enter the folio columns.

A sales ledger page in manual book-keeping (see page 56 in *Mastering Book-Keeping*) is replaced below with a customer record window in activity view with the debit, credit and balance figures in the upper pane.

15 The nominal ledger (cont)

The purchase ledger page in Figure 35 of *Mastering Book-Keeping* is replaced below with a supplier record window in activity view to demonstrate the different way that the material is dealt with in computerised accounting.

Important points to understand

Of all the things students find difficult to grasp in book-keeping, two in particular stand out.

The first is knowing whether to debit or credit an account – which is the debit aspect and which the credit aspect of the transaction?

The second is knowing which nominal ledger accounts to post the impersonal side of transactions to, i.e. knowing how to classify expenses and revenues into the right account names in the first place.

In the main, these things are taken care of in Sage 50 as the posting is done automatically. However, you still need to understand what it means to debit or credit an account if you are to really know the meaning of the records you are making and you will not be able to make journal entries correctly in Sage 50 if you do not understand these terms.

Understanding debits and credits

The word debit comes from the Latin verb *debere*, meaning 'to owe'; debit is Latin for 'he or she owes'. In business, a person owes to the proprietor that which was loaned or given to him by the proprietor.

The word credit comes from the Latin verb *credere*, meaning 'to trust' or 'to believe'. Our creditors believe in our integrity, and trust us to pay them for goods and services they supply; so they are willing to deliver them without asking for immediate payment.

Perhaps this will help a little in understanding personal ledger accounts; but what about the impersonal accounts of the nominal ledger? Whenever an account has a debit balance it means that it 'owes' the proprietor the value of it (and vice versa for credit balances), as if that account were a person.

As for how to name the overhead expense accounts, with the exception of limited companies (whose final accounts formats are governed by law, see page 37 in *Mastering Book-Keeping*) there is no hard-and-fast rule. Each company and each accountancy practice will have defined its own range. The range of asset and liability account names is a little easier to suggest, since the anticipated balance sheet effectively governs the range of accounts which will be set up. There is a good degree of consistency between companies in this respect and the range that tends to be used can be memorised in terms of four levels of classification. Sage 50 gives you a wide range of pre-named ledger accounts, and you can add more of your own if you need to.

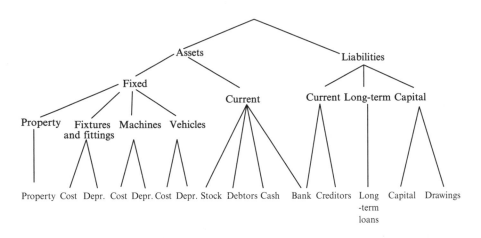

Figure 10. The architecture of the ledger.

Viewing the nominal ledger accounts

While you don't have to post the ledgers yourself in Sage 50, you still need to view them from time to time, so you will need to know how to do this. It's not the same as in a manual system, where you physically open the pages to the account you wish to view.

To view the nominal ledger:

Step by step
1. Click on the Company button on the navigation bar.
    The Nominal Ledger window will appear showing a list of accounts.

2. You can alter the layout to analysis or graph form if you wish, by clicking on the finder arrow at the right of the Layout field.
3. Click on Close when finished.

Viewing nominal ledger transactions

You can view the transactions in a variety of formats.

Graphs are useful to compare actual figures against budgeted figures or comparables from previous years. To view the data in this way:

Step by step

1. In the Nominal Ledger window, select the account you wish to view.
2. Click on the Record icon on the toolbar.
3. Click on the Graphs tab at the top of the window.
4. Click on the sixth icon from the left. This offers you a variety of graph types to choose from.
5. To select a different graph format, click the Graph icon on the toolbar.
   The range of graph types will appear.

6. Click on the format you prefer.
7. If you wish to save the document, click on the Disk icon on the toolbar and type in a file name for it.
8. Click on the Printer button if you wish to download the graph to send to a colleague or display it on a notice board.
9. You can also use the graph in a report by clicking on the Camera button to copy it and then post it into the report documents.
10. Click on Close to return to the Nominal Ledger window.

To view the activity on a particular ledger account in tabular form:

Step by step
1. In the Nominal Ledger window, select the account you wish to view. You can select more than one if required.
2. Click on the Activity tab.
    The activity window will appear.

3. Click on the Show button to select the date range.
4. Scroll to the transaction in which you are interested in the upper pane.
   All the items relating to that transaction will appear in the lower pane.
5. Click on Close when finished to return to the Nominal Ledger window.

Transaction codes used in the ledger in Sage 50

Code	Transaction type
BP	Bank payment
BR	Bank receipt
CP	Cash Payment
CR	Cash Receipt
JC	Journal Credit
JD	Journal Debit
SA	Sales Receipt, on Account
SC	Sales Credit
SD	Discount Allowed on Sales Receipt
SI	Sales Invoice
SR	Sales Receipt
PA	Purchase Payment on Account
PC	Purchase Credit
PD	Discount Received on Purchase Payment
PI	Purchase Invoice
PP	Purchase Payment
VP	Visa Credit Card Payment
VR	Visa Credit Card Receipt

Using the Search filter

An alternative way to view something in a ledger account is to use the Search filter.

There is a Search button at the bottom of all the module windows except for the Bank windows. If you want to search for something in all the modules, use the Search button in the Financials module as this module searches all the other modules.

To carry out such a search:

Step by step

1. In the Financials module window, click on Search button.
   A Search box will appear.

2. Click on the finder arrow in the Join column and select the only option offered, which is 'Where'.
3. Click on the Field column and select the variable for which you are searching.
4. Click in the Condition column and use the finder arrow to select the condition that applies, i.e. either 'is equal to' or 'is not equal to'.
5. Type in the Value column the value for which you are searching.
6. Click on Apply.

Adding nominal ledger accounts

If you need to add a ledger account not already included in the list this is how you do it:

Step by step

1. In the Nominal Ledger window, click on the Record icon.
    The Nominal Record window will appear.

Month	Actuals	To end Dec 2007
B/F	0.00	0.00
Jan	0.00	0.00
Feb	0.00	0.00
Mar	0.00	0.00
Apr	0.00	0.00
May	0.00	0.00
Jun	0.00	0.00
Jul	0.00	0.00
Aug	0.00	0.00
Sep	0.00	0.00
Oct	0.00	0.00
Nov	0.00	0.00
Dec	0.00	0.00
Future	0.00	0.00
Total	0.00	0.00

2. Enter a nominal ledger account number for the new nominal ledger account you wish to set up.
3. Press the tab key.
4. Type in the name of the new account.
5. Type in the budget or comparable values for the account.
6. Click on Save.
7. Click on Close to finish or repeat from Step 2 to set up another new account.

Deleting an unwanted nominal ledger account

To delete an unwanted account in the nominal ledger:

Step by step

1. On the Nominal Ledger window, click on the Record icon.
2. Select the account you wish to delete.
3. Click on Delete at the bottom of the window. *The system will not let you delete an account if there is a balance remaining on it.*
4. Click on Close to return to the Nominal Ledger window.

RED HOUSE CEMENT WORKS
Mulvy Island Road
Anytown, Anyshire.

Invoice No: 002345

	£ p
100 Bags of cement @ £10	1,000.00
Less 35% trade discount	350.00
	650.00
Plus VAT	113.75
Total	763.75

Terms strictly 30 days net

Figure 11. Example of the way trade discount may be shown on
a wholesaler's invoice to a retailer.

S. JONES (WHOLESALE STATIONERY SUPPLIES) LTD
210 Barton High Street, Barton, Barshire

Invoice No: 00322   10/2/201X

10 reams of printer paper @ £7	70.00
Plus VAT 17½%	12.25
	82.25

2½% early settlement discount
Deduct £2.06 if paid within
14 days.

Customer
Razi & Thaung
15 Bolton Road
Finchester

Figure 12. Example of the way early settlement discount may be shown on
an invoice.

Trade discounts

A trade discount is one given by wholesalers to retailers, so that the retailers can make a profit on the price at which they sell goods to the public. In the Red House Cement Works example, the trade discount is 35% of the recommended retail price. However, trade discounts have no place as such in a company's accounts. They are deducted before any entry is made in any of the books. As far as the wholesaler is concerned, his price to the retailer is simply £6.50, so £6.50 is the amount the wholesaler and retailer enter in their records.

Early settlement discounts

Early settlement discounts are inducements offered to persuade customers to settle their debts to the company early. Typically, a discount of 2½% might be offered for payment within 14 days. But the details can vary. Example:

	£
Building materials supplied:	200.00
Less 2% discount for settlement within 7 days:	4.00
	196.00

Companies offer such discounts for two reasons:

* to speed up cash flow;
* to reduce the chance of debts becoming bad debts (the longer a debt remains outstanding, the more likely it is to become a bad debt).

If you enter your records daily, you will not know whether or not an early settlement discount will be taken. You will only know once the actual payment arrives, so you have to enter the figure without any deduction of discount into your records. When the debt is paid, if a discount has been properly deducted the credit entry to that customer's account will be 2½% less than the account shows. You then need to enter the discount as a credit to his account and a debit to 'discount allowed account' in the nominal ledger. This will make up the shortfall. It has the same effect as cash on the customer's personal account – and so it should. The offer shown on the invoice is like a 'money-off voucher', and we would expect to treat that the same as cash.

Discounts and VAT

An early settlement discount is based on the invoice total (including VAT). Whether it is claimed or not will not alter the net sale value or the VAT amount that will be entered in the records.

Making the prime entries of discounts claimed

You make your prime entry of an early settlement discount claimed by a customer in the Customer Payment window. If it is your company that is claiming such a discount from a supplier then the prime entry is made in the Supplier Payment window. Both payment windows are accessed from the Bank Account window.

Before entering such discounts claimed or received, the book-keeper must check that they have been properly claimed by reference to the time limit for early settlement discount.

The dual ledger postings for each item in the discount column will be made automatically, thus saving time and cost.

Manual book-keeping

Control accounts perform a number of useful functions in manual book-keeping. They:

- subdivide the work in a large company so that the individual clerks can be responsible for a single division of the ledger, using the control total to balance it;
- are a means of compartmentalising the accounts so that error-checking can be carried out more easily;
- are a means of reducing the potential for fraud;
- serve as a useful summary for each ledger division.

Sage 50

In Sage 50 computerised book-keeping, the first three of these functions are redundant.

There is no need to subdivide the ledger work as a moderate-sized computerised system can handle huge amounts of data on its own.

There is no need to compartmentalise the accounts for error-checking purposes. That strategy is only relevant because it helps to minimise the effects of human perceptual limitations when a person is looking for an error, like marking the floor into squares to search each one meticulously when you have dropped something tiny. The computer does not have these perceptual limitations.

Nor does the control accounting in a computerised system lend itself to fraud protection, like the control accounting in a manual system does, because being an automatic function of the system it will not mean that different people post the two sides of the dual posting. That is where the protection comes from in a manual system. If different people post the two sides of the dual posting, an unauthorised transfer would be quickly noticed.

Nevertheless, the control accounts used in Sage 50 serve as useful summaries of ledger balances for management purposes, and control totals are readily available not just for ledger divisions but for all ledger accounts.

Control Accounts

Control Account	N/C
Debtors Control	1100
Creditors Control	2100
Default Bank	1200
VAT on Sales	2200
VAT on Purchases	2201
Sales Discount	4009
Purchase Discount	5009
Retained Earnings	3200
Default Sales	4000
Accruals	2109
Prepayments	1103
Bad Debts	8100
Mispostings	9999
Suspense	9998

The book-keeper does not have to do anything to create control accounts in Sage 50. These are automatically produced as a consequence of inputting the primary data, e.g. purchases, sales, banking, etc.

Trial balance as at 31 March 201X

Ledger balances

Sales		100,000
Fixtures and fittings	15,000	
Freehold premises	40,000	
Motor van	8,000	
Debtors	10,000	
Stock (opening)	10,000	
Cash at bank	10,000	
Cash in hand	50	
Capital		63,050
Bad debts	2,000	
Bad debts provision		2,000
Drawings	6,450	
Depreciation	2,350	
Provision for depreciation on motor van		1,600
Provision for depreciation on fixtures and fittings		750
Purchases	60,000	
Motor expenses	750	
Heat and light	800	
Wages	10,000	
Postage and stationery	550	
Repairs and renewals	250	
Creditors		12,000
Interest and banking charges	200	
Carriage	3,000	
Closing stock	9,000	9,000
	188,400 =	188,400
	(debit balances) =	*(credit balances)*

Figure 13. A typical trial balance, listing all the debit and credit balances in the ledger.

A listing of ledger balances

The trial balance is unlike anything we have seen so far, but it is quite simple to understand. It is just a listing of all the ledger balances at a particular moment in time. The balances are listed in two columns – one for the debit balances and one for the credit balances. In a manual system it is a means of checking the accuracy, because if all the ledger divisions have been correctly posted the two columns will balance. Remember, for every transaction there have been two postings, a debit and a credit, so the sum of all the debits should equal the sum of all the credits. See the example opposite.

This error-checking function of the trial balance is redundant in Sage 50, however, because the system controls the double entry automatically and the possibility of an error of posting unequal values to the two sides in any dual posting is not going to happen.

However, the trial balance still serves as a useful summary of all ledger balances at a glance.

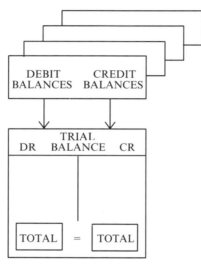

This is how to produce a trial balance in Sage 50:

Step by step

1. In the Financials window Click on the Trial icon on the toolbar.
   The Print Output window will appear.

2. Select Preview.
3. Click on Run.
   A Criteria box will appear.

4. Using the finder arrows at the right of each field, enter the date parameters and the number of transactions to include, if relevant. If all transactions are to be included, as will be usual, leave this value at zero.
5. Click on OK.
   The Trial Balance preview window will appear.

6. If you require a printout, click on Print.
7. Click on OK.
8. Click on Close when finished.

19   Revenue accounts

Revenue accounts are a pair of ledger accounts called the trading account and the profit and loss account. They are much like any other ledger account except that they are not ongoing (except for limited companies, dealt with later). Also, they are needed by more people outside the company, for example:

- HM Revenue and Customs to assess tax liability;
- shareholders to see how the business is doing;
- prospective purchasers to value the business;
- prospective lenders to assess the risk of lending to the business, and its ability to pay interest.

But we adapt these accounts to a more easy-to-read version. The two sides of the accounts are represented in progressive stages of addition and subtraction. So the revenue accounts forwarded to interested parties don't look like ledger accounts at all.

The trading account

This shows the gross profit, and how it is worked out:

$$\text{Sales} - \text{Cost of goods sold} = \text{Gross profit}$$

To work out the cost of goods sold (i.e. cost of sales), the equation is:

$$\text{Purchases} + \text{Opening stock} + \text{Direct costs} - \text{Closing stock} = \text{Cost of sales}$$

Direct costs include carriage inwards, packaging, warehousing costs and salespeople's commission.

When the balances are transferred from the nominal ledger to the trading account, sales returns are deducted from the sales and only the balance posted to the trading account. After all, they are merely 'unsales', so to speak. The same goes for purchase returns.

Stock

Stock is dealt with three times in the revenue accounts and balance sheet – once as opening stock and twice as closing stock. Suppose we started the year with £1,000 worth of stock, we purchased a further £10,000 of stock during the year, but had none left at the end of it. Altogether, it means we sold assets of £11,000 during the year. Purchases and opening stock must be the same kind of asset, since they were both finished goods on the shelf; otherwise we could not have sold them both and had nothing left to sell. Clearly, stock and purchases need to be treated in the same way in the final accounts.

This year's opening stock was, in fact, last year's closing stock. Throughout this year it was an asset, appearing on the debit side of the ledger. So this year's closing stock must also be carried forward to next year as an asset; it, too, must stay on the ledger, just like all other assets at the end of the year. The only balances that must be transferred out permanently to the revenue accounts are those for expenses and revenues (which, of course, are not assets).

Physical stock-take

Closing stock will not even be in the ledger until we have done a stock-take (a physical counting and valuation of the stock in hand). We must then post to the debit side of the stock account in the nominal ledger the actual asset value of stock remaining and being carried forward into next year.

Why we need a counter-entry for stock

The counter-entry is posted to the credit of the trading account. Why? Let us go back to our basic example. Opening stock was posted as a debit in the trading account because it was assumed it had all been sold, along with the purchases for that year. But what if we had bought £12,000 worth but still had £2,000 worth left? An entry to the opposite side would have to be made for this. Closing stock is a credit posting in the trading account.

Another way of looking at this is if we had purchased £12,000 worth of stock but only sold £10,000, it would be as if we had purchased only £10,000 worth for sale during the year. The other £2,000 worth would be for sale in the next year. So it is right that closing stock is deducted from purchases.

Direct expenses in the trading part of the revenue account

The last item that is transferred into the trading account section is direct expenses. These include expenses without the occurrence of which the sales or services would not have been made. Examples are salespeople's commissions, carriage inwards and outwards, warehousing costs and packaging, as opposed to rent, heat and light charges and office wages, which would have to be paid whether sales were made or not.

Contribution to overheads

Gross profit is not the same thing as net profit. Gross profit is first and foremost a contribution to overheads. It is only when overheads are paid for that any net profit may or may not be available for shareholders.

The profit and loss account

The profit and loss account sets out the calculation of net profit like this:

$$\text{Gross profit} + \text{Other income} - \text{Expenses} = \text{Net profit}$$

There are two sides to every posting. As each posting is made to the revenue account, an opposite posting is made to the original ledger account from where its balance came. These postings close down the revenue and expense accounts ready for a fresh start in the next accounting period.

TRADING ACCOUNT

Sales			100,000
Purchases		58,000	
Opening stock	12,000		
Closing stock	10,000	2,000	60,000
Gross profit			40,000

BALANCE SHEET (EXTRACT FROM)

Current assets	
Stock	10,000
Debtors	8,000
Cash at bank	2,000
Cash in hand	50
	20,050

Figure 14. Stock appears three times in the final accounts. Closing stock appears twice (although it is conventional to only use the adjective 'closing' in the trading account to distinguish it from 'opening stock').

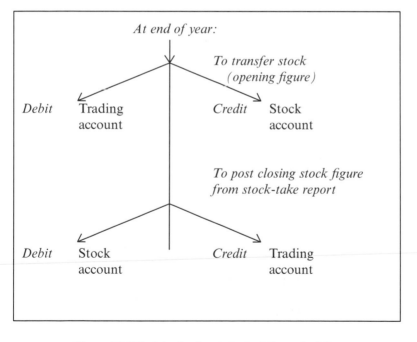

Figure 15. What to do about stock at the end of the year.

Generating revenue accounts in Sage 50

In manual book-keeping, drawing up a trading, profit and loss account can be a time-consuming process, but in Sage 50 it's just a matter of a few clicks.

The standard format of the revenue accounts in Sage 50 does not refer to the trading account by title; it just places all the elements of both the trading account and the profit and loss account under the heading of Profit and Loss Account, but the division between the part which has always traditionally been entitled the Trading Account and that which has traditionally been referred to as the Profit and Loss Account is there and clear to see. You can always enter the trading account title on the printout if desired. Here's how to compile the revenue account:

Step by step
1.   In the Financial Window click on the P&L Account icon on the toolbar. *A Print Output box will appear.*

2.   Check Preview is selected.
3.   Click on Run.
     A Criteria box will appear.

4.   Select the accounting period required on the date parameter boxes, using the finder arrows.
5.   If you do not wish the dates themselves to be included in the parameters or you wish some other conditions to be applied, select the appropriate conditions using the finder arrow on the first box, otherwise leave this one alone.
6.   Select a print layout, again using the finder arrows.
7.   If you do not wish all the transactions to be included in the preview of this profit and loss account, select the number of transactions you do wish to be

included in the preview, otherwise leave it on the default value of 0, which Sage 50 interprets as all transactions.

8. Click on OK.

The Profit and Loss Account preview will appear.

9. If a printout is required, click on Print and then on OK.
10. Click on Close when finished to return to the Financials window.

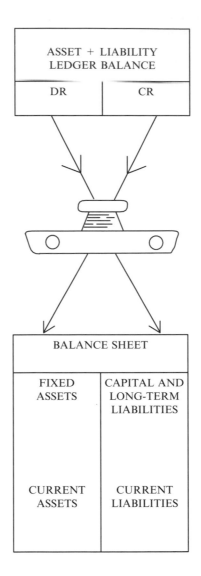

Figure 16. The balance sheet as a snapshot of the financial affairs.

A financial snapshot

Unlike the trading, profit and loss account, the balance sheet is not an 'account' as such. Rather, it is a useful snapshot of the firm's financial situation at a fixed point in time. It sets out clearly all the firm's assets and liabilities, and shows how the resulting net assets are matched by the capital account.

The balance sheet always goes hand-in-hand with the revenue accounts. We need it to show:

- where the net profit has gone (or how the net loss has been paid for);
- how any net profit has been added to the capital account;
- how much has been taken out as 'drawings' and whether any of it has been used to buy new assets (stating what those assets are);
- source data for ratio analysis.

Management data
Accounting ratios can be worked out to help decision-making. For example, the ratio of current assets to current liabilities shows how easily a firm can pay its debts as they become due (a ratio of 2:1 is often seen as acceptable in this respect).

Five main components of the balance sheet
The balance sheet tells us about five main categories:

1. Fixed assets. These are assets the business intends to keep for a long time (at least for the year in question). They include premises, fixtures and fittings, machinery and motor vehicles. Fixed assets are not for using up in day-to-day production or trading (although a small part of their value is used up in wear and tear, and that is treated as an expense – 'depreciation'). Property should be valued at net realisable value or cost, whichever is the lower.
2. Current assets. These are assets used up in day-to-day trading or production. They include stock, debtors, cash at bank and cash in hand.
3. Current liabilities. These are amounts the business owes to creditors, and which usually have to be paid within the next accounting year. They include trade creditors and bank overdraft.
4. Long-term liabilities. A business may also have financial obligations that do not have to be settled within the next accounting year. These include long-term loans, for example to buy plant, equipment, vehicles or property.
5. Capital. This means the property of the owner of the business. He or she has invested his personal property in the business – cash, any other assets, and profits ploughed back. The business holds the value of all this for him/her in safekeeping; it must deliver it up to him/her on cessation of the business, or earlier if he/she requires. Capital is, in a way, a liability to the business, but it's a rather different one from the other liabilities, which is why we don't include it with them.

Postings to capital account
There are four types of posting that are made to capital account in the ledger: opening capital, extra capital injections, drawings and the addition of profit.

Terminology

'Capital' should not be confused with 'working capital', which is a very different thing (Current assets − Current liabilities). Do not confuse capital with capital expenditure either. That just means expenditure on fixed assets rather than on expenses.

The assets and liabilities must balance against capital in the balance sheet, to embody the fundamental double-entry equation:

$$Assets - Liabilities = Capital$$

Generating a balance sheet

This is what you do to generate a balance sheet in Sage 50:

Step by step

1. In the Financial window click on the Balance icon on the toolbar.
    A Print Output box will appear.

2. Check Preview is selected.
3. Click on Run.
    A Criteria box will appear.

4. Select the accounting period required on the date parameter boxes, using the finder arrows.
5. If you do not wish the dates themselves to be included in the parameters or you wish some other conditions to be applied, select the appropriate conditions using the finder arrow on the first box, otherwise leave this one alone.
6. Select a print layout, again using the finder arrows.
7. If you do not wish all the transactions to be included in preview of this

balance sheet select the number of transactions you do wish to be included in the preview, otherwise leave it on the default value of 0, which Sage 50 interprets as all transactions.

8. Click on OK.

   The Balance Sheet preview will appear.

9. If a printout is required, click on print and then on OK.
10. Click on Close when finished to return to the Financials window.

21 Asset depreciation

When assets drop in value

So far we have recorded figures, analysed them, summed and balanced them and learned the standard ways of doing so. Now, with depreciation, calculations involving percentages need to be made.

Depreciation is the drop in value of an asset due to age, wear and tear. This drop in value is a drain on a firm's resources, so it must be recorded in the accounts as an expense. Also, the value of the asset in the books needs to be written down, to reflect its value more realistically. A company car, for example, loses value over time. So do plant, equipment and other assets. All have to be written down each year.

There are many methods of depreciating assets and a full treatment of these can be found in my other book *Mastering Book-Keeping* 9th edition. The most commonly used methods, however, are the straight-line method and the diminishing balance method. Other than totally writing off an asset, these are the only two methods that are used in Sage 50 and therefore are the only two that will be dealt with here.

The straight-line method

The straight-line method involves deducting a fixed percentage of the asset's initial book value, minus the estimated residual value, each year. The estimated residual value means the value at the end of its useful life within the business (which may be scrap value). The percentage deducted each year is usually 20% or 33$^{1}/_{3}$% and reflects the estimated annual fall in the asset's value. Suppose a company buys a motor van for £12,100. It expects it to get very heavy use during the first three years, after which it would only be worth £100 for scrap. Each year we would write it down by one-third of its initial value minus the estimated residual value, i.e. £4,000 per year. On the other hand, suppose we buy a company car for £12,300; we expect it to get only average use and to be regularly serviced. We expect to sell it after five years for £4,800. In that case we would write down the difference of £7,500 by one fifth (20%) each year, i.e. £1,500 per year.

This method is useful where value falls more or less uniformly over the years of the asset's lifetime.

Diminishing balance method

The diminishing balance method also applies a fixed percentage, but it applies it to the diminishing value of the asset each year, not to the initial value. It is used for assets which have a long life within a company and where the biggest drop in value comes in the early years, getting less as time goes on.

Suppose a lathe in an engineering workshop cost £40,000 to buy. In the first year it will fall in value much more than it ever will in later years. The guarantee may expire at the end of the first year. The bright smooth paint on the surface will be scratched and scarred; the difference between its appearance when new and its appearance a year later will be quite obvious. But the next year the change will seem less; who will notice a few more scratches on an already scarred surface? Nor will there be a great drop due to the guarantee expiring, for it will not have started out with one at the beginning of the second year. And so it will go on; the value of the asset will depreciate by smaller and smaller amounts throughout its life. Most people would agree that a three-year-old machine has less value than an otherwise identical two-year-old one, but who could say that a 16-year-old machine really has any less value than a 15-year-old one? Since the value of these assets erodes in smaller and smaller amounts as the years go by, we use the diminishing balance method of calculation.

Worked example of depreciation using the straight-line method

Suppose a lorry costing £100,000 has an estimated lifespan within a company of five years and an estimated residual value at the end of that period of £3,000.

Using the straight-line method and a rate of 20%, the effect would be as shown below.

	£	£
Cost		100,000
Less estimated residual value		3,000
Amount to be depreciated over five years		
(provision for depreciation)		
Yr 1 97,000 × 0.2 =	19,400	
Yr 2 97,000 × 0.2 =	19,400	
Yr 3 97,000 × 0.2 =	19,400	
Yr 4 97,000 × 0.2 =	19,400	
Yr 5 97,000 × 0.2 =	19,400	
	97,000	97,000

Note A Statement of Standard Accounting Practice (SSAP) was issued in December 1977 and revised in 1981 for the treatment of depreciation in accounts (SSAP12). The student can refer to this for further information.

Accounting for depreciation using Sage 50

Using Sage 50, all that is required to account for depreciation is a few appropriate clicks.

Fixed asset register

A fixed asset register is a prerequisite for calculating depreciation using Sage 50.

What you need for each fixed asset to be recorded:

- date of purchase;
- cost price;
- method of depreciation to apply;
- annual rate of depreciation to apply;
- nominal code for depreciation in the profit and loss account;
- nominal code for depreciation in the balance sheet.

Making the Fixed Asset Registry Entry
Step by step
1. Click on Modules on the browser toolbar.
2. Select Fixed Assets Register from the drop-down menu and click.
   The Fixed Assets window will appear.

3. Click on the Record icon on the toolbar.
   A Fixed Asset Record window will appear.

4. Assign a unique code for the asset and enter it (leaving no spaces between the characters).

5. Enter the description.
6. Enter the serial number.
7. Enter the location or employee who has charge of the asset.
8. Enter the date of purchase.
9. Select the supplier using the finder arrow on the right of the Supplier field.

Details of finance outstanding on the asset

Sage 50 does not allow you to record details of finance used to purchase an asset, a detail that may be helpful at the time of disposing of an asset. However, there is nothing to stop you including a short note on this in the description if required.

Setting up the monthly depreciation posting schedule

What you have done up to now is merely made a record of the fixed asset. That is not part of the accounts. You now have to set up a monthly posting schedule to automatically post an amount of depreciation each month which will show on the monthly profit and loss account. Here's how to do it:

Step by step
1. Click on the Posting tab in the Fixed Asset Record window.
2. Select the department number using the finder arrow at the right of the Department field, if it is deemed important to include this detail.
3. Enter the nominal ledger code for the asset category concerned in the profit and loss account using the finder arrows. There are only four from which to choose:
   - Plant and machinery depreciation   0021
   - Office equipment depreciation   0031
   - Furniture and fittings   0041
   - Vehicle depreciation   0051
4. Enter the code for the asset category in the balance sheet using the finder arrow. Again there are only four from which to choose but they are a different four.
   - Plant and machinery depreciation   8001
   - Office equipment depreciation   8002
   - Furniture and fixtures depreciation   8003
   - Motor vehicles depreciation   8004
5. Select the method of depreciation to employ, using the finder arrow.
6. Select the annual percentage rate to be applied using the finder arrow. This cannot be changed once you've set it, except to 'write off'.
7. Enter the net cost price.
8. Enter the current book value.
9. Click on Save.

Assuming you choose the straight-line method, at the end of each month thereafter, an amount equal to a twelfth of the annual depreciation that has been set up will be posted to the debit of a depreciation expense account, which will end up in the profit and loss account. An equal amount will be posted to a depreciation fund for the particular asset category, the balance of which will be deducted from the asset category figure 'at cost' in the balance sheet, to show the value of such an asset after depreciation.

If you instead select the diminishing balance method, a progressively smaller amount will be deducted from its value each month and posted as an expense to the profit and loss account.

Viewing the financial facts of an asset

The financial facts of an asset, including its cost price, depreciation and net book value, can be viewed by a single click on Valuation in the Fixed Assets window.

Disposal of fixed assets

When an asset is to be disposed of the process is really simple in Sage 50. You just click on the Disposal icon on the toolbar in the Fixed Assets window and follow the instructions of the disposal wizard.

The categories into which expenses, revenues, assets and liabilities are analysed in the final accounts are collectively known as the chart of accounts. A standard chart of accounts that will suit most needs is preset in Sage 50. If it does not fully meet your requirements, you can add new categories or edit existing ones.

To view what layouts are available proceed as follows:

Step by step

1. Click on the COA icon on the toolbar in the Nominal Ledger window.
   The Chart of Accounts window will appear.

2. To view the details of any chart of accounts listed, simply scroll to it and double click.
   The Edit Chart of Accounts window will appear.

3. Close windows when finished.

Starting a New Chart of Accounts

If you wish to start a new chart of accounts proceed as follows:

Step by step

1. Click on the Add button in the Chart of Accounts window.
   A New Chart of Accounts name box will appear.

2. Enter the name of the new chart of accounts you wish to create and click on Add.
   The Edit Chart of Accounts window will reappear.

3. You can now overwrite material and add new material as required.
4. When satisfied with your new chart of accounts, click on Save.
5. To select a chart of accounts other than the default one, simply scroll to it on the list.
6. Close all windows when finished.

To generate a nominal ledger report:

Step by step

1. In the Nominal Ledger window click on the Reports icon on the modules toolbar.
    The Report Browser window will appear.

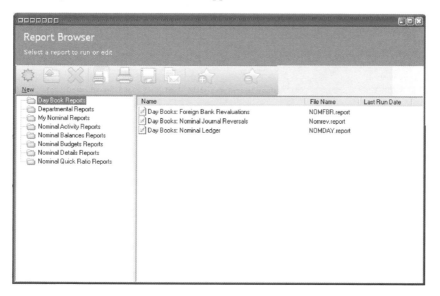

2. Click on the folder containing the general category of report you want to generate.
    A subfolder will appear listing the types of reports that are available.
3. Click on a specific report type within that folder.
    A Criteria box will appear asking for details such as the date parameters.

4. When you have filled in the details, click on the OK button.
    The Report Preview will appear.

5. Click on Print if a printout is required.
   A Print Fund Nominal Activity window will appear.

6. Adjust page and copy parameters if necessary and click on OK to print.
7. Click on Close when finished.

A tax on purchases

Value added tax (VAT) is very different from income tax and corporation tax. The last two are claimed at the point of receiving income. VAT is claimed at the point of spending that income. Also, a business is a source of taxation for income tax and corporation tax, but for VAT it is simply a kind of collector. A taxable firm has to collect VAT on the sale price of all its goods and services from its customers and pay it over to HM Revenue and Customs (HMRC) as output tax. Of course, the firm is also a customer of other firms, because it needs to buy goods and services itself. But the VAT it pays on these purchases (input tax) can be set against the VAT it has collected from its customers; it only has to pay the balance (difference) to HMRC. (If the balance is a negative one, then HMRC refund the balance to the firm.) So in the end, it is only private individuals who actually pay VAT, plus firms too small to have to register for VAT (though they can still register if they wish).

Fashion house sells suit, for which it had paid factory £55 + VAT, to wholesaler for £100 + 17.5% VAT (collects £17.50 VAT to pay to HMRC but reclaims the £9.62 VAT it had itself paid to the fashion house). Therefore fashion house remitted a net £7.87 to HMRC.	Wholesaler sells to retailer for £140 + 17.5% VAT (collects £24.50 VAT but reclaims the £17.50 it had itself paid to the wholesaler). Therefore the wholesaler remitted £7 to HMRC.	Retailer sells suit to customer for £196 + 17.5% VAT. (Collects £34.30 VAT but reclaims the £24.50 it had itself paid to the wholesaler.) Therefore the wholesaler remitted £9.80 to HMRC.

So in the chain from fashion house to consumer the VAT content has grown at an increasing rate and the total amount of VAT that has gone to the HMRC is £24.67 (£7.87 + £7 + £9.80 = £24.67).

Figure 17. VAT is collected at various stages in the chain of transactions from manufacturer to end-user.

Which businesses need to register for VAT?

The answer is any business whose turnover in the past year was at least £67,000, unless it reasonably expects that by the end of the next month the annual turnover to date will fall below that threshold figure. If a company's sales in the next month alone are likely to be at least £67,000 it must register for VAT. If its annual turnover subsequently falls below £62,000 it can deregister if it wishes.

Registration is also compulsory without any threshold level if a business:

- sells excise goods such as tobacco or alcohol;
- makes any sales of assets on which a VAT refund has been claimed by a predecessor in the chain. These are known as Relevant Goods in VAT terminology.

Which businesses have to keep VAT accounts?

All registered businesses must keep full VAT accounts. Firms that are not registered do not need to account for VAT and will ignore the fact that part of the invoice totals they enter in their purchase and petty cash records represent VAT. They cannot reclaim VAT they have paid to suppliers nor charge VAT on their invoices to customers. VAT does not appear anywhere in their accounts.

VAT periods

VAT periods are normally quarterly, but a business can elect to account to HMRC on a monthly basis instead. If the business supplies mainly or exclusively exempt and/or zero-rated goods and services it will usually receive a VAT refund. In such cases it is better if the business elects to account on a monthly basis so that the refunds arrive sooner and start earning interest in the bank sooner. The managers will have to decide whether the refunds are of a significant size to warrant the extra work involved in tripling the number of VAT returns that have to be completed and filed (monthly instead of quarterly).

VAT rates

There are a number of VAT statuses falling into two main categories:

- exempt;
- taxable.

In the second category there can be an infinite number of different tax rates applying to different kinds of goods or services. The rate can be 0%, or any number of positive rates. 'Zero-rated' does not mean 'exempt'. They are two different things.

From 1991 until the time of writing the standard rate of VAT has been 17½%, except for the period between 1 December 2008 and 31 December 2009 when it was reduced to 15% as a measure designed to help stimulate the economy. There is also currently a reduced rate of 5%, which applies to domestic fuel and some energy-saving materials. Food and children's clothing are currently zero-rated. VAT rates in existence at the time of writing are:

- Standard rate   Most goods and services
- Reduced rate   Domestic fuel and some energy-saving materials
- Zero rate   Food and children's clothing

Exempt goods and services include such things as postal and banking services and any goods supplied by an exempt business.

Keeping up to date

VAT rates change from time to time and up-to-date information can be obtained from notices published on HMRC's website, www.hmrc.gov.uk. Notice No.700 is the general VAT guide and there is a comprehensive range of booklets to cover a multitude of subjects.

Other terms you need to know

- Inputs.
- Input tax.
- Outputs.
- Output tax.
- VAT on acquisitions from other EU states.

Inputs are the taxable goods and services the business has purchased. Outputs are the taxable goods and services it has supplied to its customers and for which it must remit to HMRC. Input tax is the VAT it has been charged by its suppliers and which it can deduct from the figure it has to remit to HMRC. VAT is not charged by suppliers from other EU states, but such a figure has to be remitted to HMRC directly by the purchaser rather than indirectly via the supplier. There is a special box on the VAT return for this figure.

Invoicing and VAT

VAT has to be calculated on the net invoice value after deduction of any trade discount. Do not confuse this with early settlement discount (see page 92). That is a different issue and does not affect the VAT calculation on the invoice.

When making out the invoice:

- all the goods and/or services being charged for should be added up;
- trade discount, if any, should be deducted;
- VAT is calculated on the remainder.

Requirement to keep VAT records

Registered businesses have to keep records of VAT paid and received at the various rates, including zero, and also a record of all exempt supplies they make. Different kinds of businesses record VAT differently.

Partly exempt businesses

Where a firm sells exempt, zero- and positive-rated goods the accounting gets a bit complex. It becomes necessary to apportion their turnover. There are special schemes for retailers to make it easier to make the apportionments. However, as there are a number of such schemes they are outside the scope of this book. Here we can only focus on the mainstream VAT requirements and methods of accounting.

VAT relief on bad debts

If a debt owing to the business is more than six months old, the output tax paid on the invoice can be reclaimed from HMRC. If it is in the end paid, the output tax reclaimed must be repaid to HMRC.

VAT that cannot be reclaimed

- *VAT on cars used by the business.* Businesses cannot usually reclaim VAT on cars purchased for use in the business.
- *Goods taken from the business for private use.* If the owner of a business takes goods from the business for his or her own private use, their drawings account must be debited with the full amount which the business paid for the goods, including the VAT , while, on the other hand, the purchases account must be credited with the net amount and the VAT account credited with the VAT content.

VAT and the final accounts

The collection of VAT is not part of the essence of business transactions; it is just a duty that is imposed on businesses by HMRC that has to be carried out alongside them. Consequently it does not figure in the profits or losses of the firm and so will not appear anywhere in the profit and loss account. It will show in the balance sheet, however, as the business, if it is registered for VAT, will almost certainly hold funds that are owed to VAT or have money owed to it in the form of a repayment of VAT at the date of the balance sheet. The latter will, therefore, be likely to contain a figure for VAT in either its current assets or its current liabilities.

At the end of the VAT period a business has to complete and send in a VAT return to HMRC. Accuracy in accounting and prompt filing of returns is required by HMRC. Penalties apply for late filing.

Completing the VAT Return

At the end of each of the three months, prior to the end of the current VAT period:

- the total net sales will have been posted to the credit side of the sales account in the nominal ledger and the total VAT to the credit side of the VAT account in the same ledger;
- the total net sales returns will have been posted to the debit side of the sales account in the nominal ledger and the total VAT to the debit side of the VAT account in the same ledger;
- the total net purchases will have been posted to the debit side of the purchases account in the nominal ledger and the total VAT to the debit side of the VAT account in the same ledger;
- the total net purchase returns will have been posted to the credit side of the purchases account in the nominal ledger and the total VAT to the credit side of the VAT account in the same ledger.

If VAT was overpaid or underpaid at the end of the last VAT period, it will show in the ledger as a balance b/d at the start of the period with which you are now dealing.

If any debts have been written off during the period, they will have been debited to the sales account and the VAT content which applied debited to the VAT account, both in the nominal ledger.

Different formats for manual and computerised systems

There are certain differences in the format used when filing a return online to those that apply for paper returns. For example, if there is nothing to enter in a box in an online form you enter 0.00, while in a paper form you are required to write NONE. A negative value (a figure to be subtracted) must be written with a minus sign before it while a negative value on a paper form must be represented by bracketing the figure. No minus signs must appear on a paper VAT return.

However, Sage 50 will take care of all this for you. The program will automatically calculate the VAT and complete a VAT return which is acceptable to HMRC as long as you enter the date parameters of the period for which it is to account.

Sage 50 has the standard VAT rate set up as the default rate (coded T1), and Codes T0 and T9 have been preset as the zero rate and VAT-exempt codes.

There are three accounts in the nominal ledger that deal with VAT. They are the sales tax control account (code 2200), the purchase tax control account (code 2201) and the VAT liability account (code 2202).

When the VAT return is due to be sent in, you enter the date range of the VAT period and the output tax total will be subtracted from the input tax total and you will be informed of what the balance is and whether it is payable by you to HMRC or by them to you.

You then need to carry out a reconciliation process between the two control accounts mentioned and your VAT return and then transfer the funds to the VAT liability account.

When you make a bank payment to HMRC for this, the counter-posting goes to the VAT liability account, leaving a zero balance.

Submitting a VAT Return online

If you want to submit the VAT Return online you will have to set up an HMRC Gateway account (see page 127).

Before running the VAT Return process, carry out a verification check. This highlights possible errors in the accounts, such as potential audit queries like duplications and VAT queries such as high VAT values. It is not a foolproof check, in that it cannot cover every possible error, but it is much better than no check at all.

To carry out the verification proceed as follows:

Step by step

1. In the Financials window click on the Verification icon on the modules toolbar.
    A Verify System window will appear.
2. Check the appropriate radio button on the window to confirm the kind of check you want to carry out.
3. Click on OK.
    An Accounts Verification Settings window will appear.

4. Tick the boxes as appropriate to instruct the system as to the kinds of checks you want to carry out. Your selections may include, for example, looking for:
    *   duplications;
    *   invoices not updated within 14 days;
    *   payments on account;
    *   transactions with possibly wrong VAT rates entered;
    *   sales or purchases from other EC states with no VAT number entered.
5. Click on OK.
    A Date Range box will appear.

6. Enter the date parameters details and click on OK to run the check.
7. When you have run the verification click on the x in the top right-hand corner to close the Verification window.

Completing your VAT Return

This is how to complete your VAT Return:

Step by step

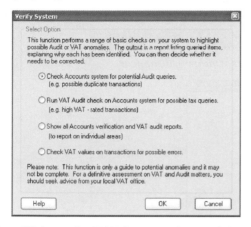

1. Click on the VAT icon on the modules toolbar in the Financials window. *The Value Added Tax Return window will appear.*

2. Enter the date parameters (inclusive dates) in the top right corner boxes.
3. Click on the Calculate button.
   A message will appear informing you of any unreconciled transactions or transactions outside the date parameters and asking you to confirm whether you want to include them.

4. Click on Yes or No as appropriate. If you don't include them, they will remain showing as unreconciled on the audit trail and you will be alerted to them again when you do your next VAT return.
5. Click on any of the VAT subtotals if you wish to explore details.
A VAT Breakdown window calculation will appear

VAT Breakdown - VAT due on Sales

VAT due in this period on sales   1   0.00

T/C	Sales Invoices	Sales Credits	Receipts	Journal Credits
T0	0.00	0.00	0.00	0.00
T1	0.00	0.00	0.00	0.00
T2	0.00	0.00	0.00	0.00
T3	0.00	0.00	0.00	0.00
T5	0.00	0.00	0.00	0.00
T6	0.00	0.00	0.00	0.00
T15	0.00	0.00	0.00	0.00
T20	0.00	0.00	0.00	0.00
	0.00	0.00	0.00	0.00

Subtotal   0.00
Adjustment   0.00
Total   0.00

Close

6. Double click on a tax code in this window if a transactional breakdown is required.
A VAT Breakdown – Transactions window will appear.
7. Close each window that has been opened and return to the VAT Return.
8. Click on the Reconcile button.
A Confirm box will appear, asking if you want to flag the transactions for VAT.

9. Click on Yes.
10. Click on Print to print out your VAT Return if required.

VAT Return Report

VAT Return Type	Output
☑ VAT return	○ Printer
☐ Summary	⊙ Preview
☐ Detailed	○ File

Run   Cancel

11. Click on Close when finished.

The confirmation that the transactions have been reconciled for VAT can be found in the audit trail, as all reconciled transactions will have an R in the VAT column.

The VAT liability account

The next thing to be done is to transfer the VAT liability to the VAT liability nominal account. The VAT Transfer Wizard will guide you through the process.

Step by step

1. Click on Modules.
2. Select Wizards.
3. Click on VAT Transfer Wizard.

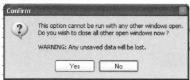

A Confirm box will appear informing you that to run this function you must close all other windows and warning you that you will lose unsaved data in doing so.

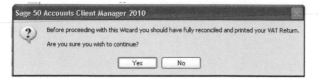

4. Click on Yes.
   A window asking you to confirm that you wish to continue will appear.

5. Click on Yes.
   A welcome to the VAT Liability Transfer Wizard window will appear.

6. Click on Next.

   A window asking you to confirm the VAT liability nominal ledger account code will appear.

7. Click on Next.

   A window asking you to confirm the date and amounts to be posted will appear.

8. Click on Next.
    A window asking you to confirm the posting details will appear.

9. Click on Finish.

e-VAT submissions

From April 2010 all businesses, barring a few exceptions, have had to submit their VAT Returns and pay VAT accounts online.

This is how to enable e-VAT submissions in Sage 50:

Step by step

1. Set up an HMRC Gateway account by visiting the HMRC website (www.hmrc.gov.uk) and follow the instructions.
2. In the Settings window in Sage 50, click on Company Preferences.
    A Company Preferences window will appear.

3.   Click on the VAT tab.
4.   Tick the Enable e-VAT submissions box.
5.   Enter your user ID.
6.   Enter your password and confirm it by entering it again in the box below.
7.   Enter your name, telephone number and e-mail address.
8.   Click on OK to finish.

Once the account has been set up, you can make online VAT submissions. To do this proceed as follows:

Step by step
1.   On the browser toolbar click on Modules.
2.   Click on the Financials option on the drop-down menu.
     The Financials window will appear.
3.   Click on Company in the navigation bar.
4.   In the tasks pane click on Manage VAT.
     The Value Added Tax Return window will appear.
5.   Click on the required VAT Return to highlight it.
     The VAT Return will appear.

Value Added Tax Return		
Stationery & Computer Mart UK	For the period	01/02/2010
Sage House	to	28/02/2010
Benton Park Road		
Newcastle Upon Tyne		
VAT due in this period on sales	**1**	0.00
VAT due in this period on EC acquisitions	**2**	0.00
Total VAT due (sum of boxes 1 and 2)	**3**	0.00
VAT reclaimed in this period on purchases	**4**	0.00
Net VAT to be paid to Customs or reclaimed by you	**5**	0.00
Total value of sales, excluding VAT	**6**	0.00
Total value of purchases, excluding VAT	**7**	0.00
Total value of EC sales, excluding VAT	**8**	0.00
Total value of EC purchases, excluding VAT	**9**	0.00

Calculate   Adjustments...   Reconcile   Print   Clear   ☐Include Reconciled   Close

6.   Click on the Submit Return icon on the modules toolbar. This icon, and also the HMRC Receipts icon, will only be visible if you have enabled e-VAT when setting up your company preferences.
     A notice will appear warning of the irreversibility of the next stage in the process and penalties for false statements. It asks for confirmation that you wish to continue.

7. Click on Continue.
   A confirmation box will appear presenting the Gateway account user ID, password, company name and VAT registration number that will be used.

8. Click on Submit.
   A message box will appear informing you of possible delays of several minutes in the process.
9. Click on Submit.
   A window will appear informing you whether or not your submission was successful.
10. To make payment online, click on Payment and follow the instructions.
11. Close all windows when finished.

A wide variety of report types have been programmed into Sage 50. This is how to generate a report:

Step by step

1. In the Financial window click on the Reports icon on the Modules toolbar. *The Report Browser window will appear.*

2. Double click on the folder containing the general category of report you want to generate.
   A subfolder will appear listing the types of report that are available.
3. Click on a specific report type within that folder.
   A Criteria box will appear asking for five parameters:
   - *transaction dates (to and from);*
   - *transaction numbers (to and from);*
   - *departments (to and from);*
   - *nominal codes (to and from);*
   - *number of records (an input of 0 is interpreted as 'include all records')*

4. Enter the required details and click on OK.
   A preview of the report will appear.

5. If satisfied, save the report under a suitable name using the Save icon.
6. If a print out is required, use the print icon.
7. Close all windows when finished.

Companies need a system to record goods moving in and out of the stores. The movement of goods may be a result of purchases, sales, purchase returns, sales returns or transfers to the factory as part of larger products (product assemblies), write-offs of obsolete or damaged products or lost or pilfered stock. The system is needed:

- for stock valuation purposes;
- so that profit or loss can be calculated with reasonable accuracy;
- so that a pipeline of sales orders can flow without hiccups;
- so that the products are available to the factory or service department as and when needed.

The supplier's delivery note has traditionally been the source document for booking in and a requisition docket of some kind the source for booking out. Periodical physical stock checks (actually going round and counting the stock) will show up any discrepancies arising from errors or pilferage.

Stock valuation methods
At the end of the accounting period, stocks have to be valued for the balance sheet. Such value is based on the cost price or replacement price, whichever is the lower. The idea is that the asset figures in the accounts should reflect the true values as closely as possible.

If we are valuing the stock at cost price there may have been a number of price changes throughout the year, and if the goods are identical we may not be able to tell which ones cost which amounts. There are three main ways of dealing with this:

- FIFO;
- LIFO;
- Average cost method.

First in first out
FIFO assumes that the remaining stock is the subject of the most recent prices. Suppose a company had purchased 30 televisions, the first 10 at £50, another 10 some months later at £55 and near the end of the year another 10 at £60. Let's suppose, also, that it sold 15 to one customer, an hotelier perhaps, just before the end of the accounting year. Since 30 had been purchased and only 15 sold, there should be 15 left in stock. These 15 would be valued at the prices of the most recently purchased 15; that means all 10 of the most recent purchase at £60 each and five of the previous order at £55 each.

Last in first out
LIFO does the opposite of FIFO. It says that all remaining stock on hand is valued at the earliest purchase price. To value stock according to LIFO, do the same as for FIFO, using the earliest invoices, instead of the most recent.

Average cost method

The average cost method (sometimes referred to as AVCO) requires you to divide the remaining stock (numbers of items) into the total cost of all that stock, each time an item is withdrawn from stock. You then apply the cost figure to the withdrawn stock, and to the stock remaining afterwards. When another withdrawal is made you add the last valuation to the cost of all purchases since. You then divide the total by the actual number of items in stock. Again, you apply this value to the goods withdrawn and to the balance remaining. So, the average value of remaining stock may change continuously.

FIFO is the most commonly used method. It also seems the most realistic, because businesses usually try to sell their oldest stock first.

Advantages of FIFO

- Unrealised profits or losses will not occur, i.e. increases in stock values due to inflation.
- Issuing the oldest items first reduces likelihood of stock perishing.
- Stock valuation will be closer to current prices than with other methods.
- This method is acceptable to HM Revenue and Customs.
- This method complies with SSAP9. This statement of standard accounting practice prescribes that stock should be valued at the lower of cost or net realisable value.

Disadvantages of FIFO

- In inflationary times, costs are understated and profits overstated. This is because the cost of replacing the stock is higher than the cost of the stock used and accounted for. The reverse is true in deflationary times.
- Material issue prices vary so that it is difficult to compare prices over a range.

It is the FIFO method that Sage 50 uses.

		£	£	£
1st purchase	10 @ 50			500
2nd purchase	10 @ 55			550
				1,050
1st withdrawal	2 @ 50			100
Balance	8 @ 50		400	
	10 @ 55		550	950
2nd withdrawal	8 @ 50		400	
	1 @ 55		55	455
Balance	9 @ 55			495

Figure 18. Illustration of stock valuation using FIFO.

Computerising the stock control system

Computerised stock control systems offer many advantages over manual systems:

- faster data processing;
- increased accuracy;
- savings in wages costs;
- continuous analysis to establish economic order quantities;
- automatic reordering made possible;
- *just in time* stock ordering is made feasible, reducing stockholding costs to a minimum;
- more effective control of minimum and maximum levels;
- point of sale stock control facilitated;
- immediate and up-to-date reports on performance of particular stock lines made possible and easy to obtain;
- stock-keeping software can be integrated into the firm's general accounting software.

Viewing stock records in Sage 50

Viewing stock records in Sage 50 is an easy process. This is how to do it:

Step by step

1. Click on Products on the navigation bar.
   The Products window will appear.

2. Scroll to the product record you wish to view and click.
   The record for that product will appear.

3. Click on Close when finished.
4. Repeat the process for any other product records you wish to view.

Viewing transaction histories of particular products

To monitor the quantities and values sold of particular stock lines during the financial year:

Step by step

1. In the Product Record window, click on the Sales tab.

   A window will appear displaying the sale values and the quantities for each month alongside the cost of sale prices, the budget and prior year comparatives.

The sales table shown:

Month	Sales Cost	Actuals	Budgets	Prior Year	Actuals	Budgets	Prior Year
		Sales Value			Quantity Sold		
Late Adj.	184.02	332.59	0.00	0.00	126.00	0.00	0.00
Jan	0.00	0.00	0.00	0.00	0.00	0.00	0.00
Feb	0.00	0.00	0.00	0.00	0.00	0.00	0.00
Mar	0.00	0.00	0.00	0.00	0.00	0.00	0.00
Apr	0.00	0.00	0.00	0.00	0.00	0.00	0.00
May	0.00	0.00	0.00	0.00	0.00	0.00	0.00
Jun	0.00	0.00	0.00	0.00	0.00	0.00	0.00
Jul	0.00	0.00	0.00	0.00	0.00	0.00	0.00
Aug	0.00	0.00	0.00	0.00	0.00	0.00	0.00
Sep	0.00	0.00	0.00	0.00	0.00	0.00	0.00
Oct	0.00	0.00	0.00	0.00	0.00	0.00	0.00
Nov	0.00	0.00	0.00	0.00	0.00	0.00	0.00
Dec	0.00	0.00	0.00	0.00	0.00	0.00	0.00
Future	0.00	0.00	0.00	0.00	0.00	0.00	0.00
Totals	184.02	332.59	0.00	0.00	126.00	0.00	0.00

2. You can view in tabular form or in 2-D or 3-D graphs. To view in the latter formats, click on the Graph tab.
3. Click on Close when finished.

New product record
To make a new product record:

Step by step
1. In the Products window click on the Record icon on the toolbar.
   There are some details that are generated automatically by the system and their fields will not accept a manual input. These items are:
   - *quantity allocated;*
   - *quantity free;*
   - *quantity on order;*
   - *last quantity ordered;*
   - *date last ordered.*
2. Enter a code for the product using the finder arrow and press tab.
3. Enter a description of the product.
4. Enter a category number, if relevant.
5. Enter the nominal ledger codes for sales using the finder arrow.
6. Enter the sales price.
7. Click on the Opening Balance symbol (labelled O/B, but you have to look hard to recognise the letters) at the right of the In Stockfield.
   An Opening Product Setup box will appear.

Opening Product Setup				⊠
Ref	Date	Quantity	Cost Price	
O/BAL	24/02/2010	0.00	0.00	
		Save	Cancel	

8. Check the date is correct and enter the quantity.
9. Click on Save.
10. Click on Close to return to the Products window.

How Sage 50 values the stock
Sage 50 values all stock at the latest price.

Setting opening balances
Stock records will need opening balances to be entered if stock was present prior to setting up the Sage 50 system. Cost price must also be entered, otherwise the system will regard the cost price as zero.

Reorder alerts
If you set reorder levels, the stock records for the products will alert you when stock falls below the reorder level by displaying the record in red in the product window.

Periodical stock checks

Periodically a physical stock-take should be carried out. Once this has started, no transactions that would alter stock levels should be carried out until the stock-take has been completed and the accounts adjusted and reconciled to the stock-take figures.

Search for low stock levels

If there are many stock records in the system, you may wish to speed up the process of viewing by using the Search facility. This filters out all but those stock items that match certain criteria.

Suppose you wanted to search for all products for which there were less than 30 in stock. This is how you would carry out the search:

Step by step

1. In the Products window click on the Search button.
    A Search window will appear.

2. The window has a number of columns. In the 'Join' column, click on the finder arrow and select the 'Where' option from the drop-down menu.
3. Click on the Field column and then, using the finder arrow at the right of the field, select the Quantity in Stock option from the drop-down menu that will appear.
4. In the Conditions column do likewise and, select the 'Is Less Than' option.
5. In the Value Field, use the Calculator icon at the right of the field to enter the quantity (30). Click on Apply.
6. Click on the Search icon (magnifying glass) at the right of the title bar to release the Search function from the list.
7. Click on Close to close the Search window and return to the Products window.

If you're going to make this search regularly, click on Save. This will save you having to go through all the above steps each time.

Product assemblies and bills of materials

A bill of materials is a list of the components required to make a product assembly. To set up a bill of materials:

Step by step

1. In the Products window, select the product record concerned and click.
    A detailed Product Record will appear.

2. Click on the BOM tab.
    Another Product Record window will appear, this one much more simple than the last one.

3. Click on the finder arrow on the first line and select the first component of the product assembly from the drop-down menu.
4. Click on the last column and enter the quantity of this component required for a single assembly.
5. Do the same in the second line for the next component and so on for all the components of the product assembly.
6. Click on Save to store the product assembly details.
7. Click on Refresh if you want to see how many assemblies could be made up from current stock. The figure will appear beside the Refresh button.
8. Click on Close when finished.

You can also check how many completed assemblies are available using the ChkBOM icon on either the modules toolbar or in the Tasks pane.

If your company operates a quantity discount policy, you can set the system up to automatically recognise where a discount will be applicable and apply it to the sales order.

To set up a quantity discount for a product:

Step by step
1. In the Product Record window, click on the Discount A tab.
   The Discount A window for this product will appear.

Product Record - Office Starter Pack			_ □ X

Details | Memo | BOM | Sales | Graph | Activity | Discount | Web

Discount A | Discount B | Discount C | Discount D | Discount E

Discount	Quantity	Discount %	Discounted Value
Level 1	0.00	0.00	0.00
Level 2	0.00	0.00	0.00
Level 3	0.00	0.00	0.00
Level 4	0.00	0.00	0.00
Level 5	0.00	0.00	0.00
Level 6	0.00	0.00	0.00
Level 7	0.00	0.00	0.00
Level 8	0.00	0.00	0.00
Level 9	0.00	0.00	0.00
Level 10	0.00	0.00	0.00

Copy Matrix

Save | Discard | Delete | Previous | Next | Print List | Close

2. Using the finder arrow, enter the quantity to qualify for discount.
3. Using the finder arrow, select the percentage discount that applies for this quantity. *The system calculates the net value and fills in the third column.*
4. If other percentages of discounts apply for different quantities, repeat the process on as many subsequent lines as necessary. These are referred to as levels of discount.
5. Click on Save to store the details.
6. Close all windows when finished.

If the discount structure is identical for different products, you can use the Copy Matrix button to copy the discount structure to another product record and save yourself the time of going through all the steps each time.

Product activity
To view product activity proceed as follows:

Step by step
1. In the Products window, scroll to the product the activity of which you wish to view.
2. Click on the Activity icon on the toolbar.
   The Activity window will appear.

3.   Click on the finder arrow at the right of the Show field.
4.   Select from the menu the date range you wish to view.
5.   Read off the activity for that product during the selected date range.
      The information you can obtain includes:
      • the transaction type code;
      • the date range;
      • the transaction description;
      • the product reference, if any;
      • the cost code, if any;
      • the quantity in;
      • the quantity out;
      • the quantity used;
      • the cost price;
      • the sale price.
      You can also view:
      • the quantity on order;
      • the quantity in stock;
      • the quantity allocated;
      • the quantity available;
6.   To scroll through the products, click on Previous and Next as required.
7.   Click Close when finished.

You need to familiarise yourself with 10 transaction codes. They are:

GI	Goods in
GO	Goods out
AI	Adjustment in
AO	Adjustment out
MI	Movement in
MO	Movement out
DI	Damages in
DO	Damages out
GR	Goods returned
WO	Goods written off

You also need to familiarise yourself with seven terms and their meanings.

Term	Explanation
Quantity available	The quantity in stock minus the quantity already allocated.
Quantity in stock	The sum of all the goods in, adjustments in and movements in, minus the quantity used.
Quantity used	The sum of all the goods out, adjustments out and movements out.
Quantity allocated	The quantity allocated to fill sales orders.
Quantity on order	The quantity on order data that comes direct from the purchase order process.
Sales	The sale price of goods out, adjustments out and goods returned.
Costs	The cost price of goods in, adjustments in, movements in and goods returned transactions.

Product adjustments in

When new stock comes into the stores or stock is taken out of the stores, the adjustments are made by a simple process. To record stock adjustments:

Step by step

1. Click on the In icon on the toolbar of the Products window.
    The Stock Adjustments In window will appear.

2. Enter the product code in the appropriate field.
3. Enter the date.
4. Enter an appropriate reference.
5. Enter the product description in the Details field.
6. Enter the quantity going into the stores.
7. Enter the cost of the new intake, if this is different from that of the last intake (FIFO is used for evaluation, see glossary).
8. Click on Save to store the changes to the stock.
9. Click on Close when finished.

Product adjustments out

When products are taken out of the store there is not so much detail to put in:

Step by step

1. Click on the Out icon on the toolbar of the Products window.
    The Stock Adjustments Out window will appear.

2. Enter the product code and quantity taken out in the appropriate fields.
3. Click on Save to store the changes to the stock.
4. Click on Close when finished.

Sometimes components are transferred from stock to make product assemblies, such as all the individual components required to make a circuit board in a factory. The individual components need to be transferred from the stock records to a record for the assembly they go to make up. This is how to record such product transfers:

Step by step
1. In the Products window click on the Transfer icon on the toolbar.
    The Stock Transfers window will appear.

2. Use the finder arrow in the Product Code field to select the code for the product that has been transferred.
3. Select the relevant product assembly code and click on OK.
4. Check the date and details are correct.
5. Enter the quantity of the product required (if there is insufficient stock the system will tell you).
6. Click on Save.
7. Click on Close when finished.

At the end of the year and perhaps at other selected stages in the year, a physical stock-take should be undertaken. If the levels do not correspond with the records then either some transactions went unrecorded or some stock has been lost or pilfered. To adjust the stock records, click on the Stock – take option in the Products window and enter the adjustment required.

You can quickly check for stock shortfalls at any time by clicking on Shortfalls button on the Product toolbar. This brings up the Shortfall Generator window. You can at any time check which stock items are needed for product assemblies by clicking on the Bill of Materials tab in the relevant product record.

A wide variety of report types to suit most needs are available in Sage 50. To generate a product report proceed as follows:

Step by step

1. In the Products window click on the Reports icon on the toolbar.
    The Report Browser will appear.

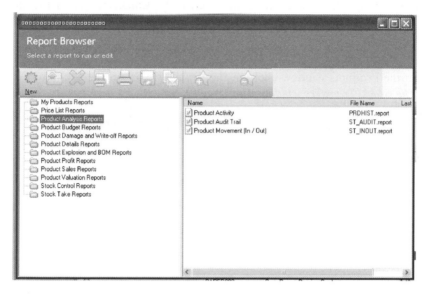

2. Click on the folder containing the general category of the type of report you want to generate.
    A subfolder will appear listing the types of reports that are available.
3. Click on a specific report type within that folder.
4. Select the Preview option.
5. Click on the Generate Report button.
    A Criteria box will appear asking for details such as the date parameters.

6.   When you have filled in the details, click on the OK button.
      The Product Report preview will appear.

7.   Click on Print if a printout is required.
8.   Click on Close when finished.

29 The audit trail

Until recently, company law required all companies to appoint an external auditor. This is no longer a statutory requirement for small companies, but some may still choose to have their accounts audited.

In addition, many clubs and societies are required by their own bylaws to have their accounts externally audited. So what is auditing?

An audit is a check on the accuracy and propriety with which every transaction of an organisation has been recorded. This is done by taking a sample of transactions and following the trail through every stage of recording in the accounts, from the primary record to its effect in the final accounts.

An audit trail is a guide to assist the auditor in this task. It is also a valuable source whenever any cross-checking is required.

Sage 50 offers a variety of options of audit trail formats to provide whatever degree of detail is required. They can be:

- brief;
- summary;
- fully detailed.

In addition, Sage 50 can generate a report of deleted transactions, if required. To view an audit trail:

Step by step

1. Click on the Modules tab.

   A menu of options will appear.

2. Click on the financials option.

   The financials window will appear. Here you will be able to view the audit trail. Deleted transactions appear in red.

Printing out an audit trail

To print out an audit trail:

Step by step

1. Click on the Audit icon on the toolbar.
    The Audit Trail Report box will appear.

2. Click on the appropriate radio button to tell the system whether you want a brief, summary or fully detailed report.
3. Click on Preview in the appropriate column.
4. Click on Run.
    A Criteria Values box will appear.

5. Enter the following details:
    *   date;
    *   transaction number;
    *   customer reference or supplier reference, as appropriate;
    *   number parameters for the report;
    *   whether to exclude deleted transactions.

    If you do not want to include all the records in the report, enter the number of records you do want included. Otherwise, leave this box with the default value of zero and the report will include all records.
6. Click on OK.
    The Audit Trail Report preview will appear.

7. Click on Print.
8. Click on Close when finished.

So far we have seen how Sage 50 does automatically what a manual system does manually. It goes further than that, though. Sage 50 can also do the jobs of the invoice clerk – the clerk in the sales order office who types out the invoices and credit notes. It can also take over the work of the warehouse clerical staff, from processing the paperwork to executing delivery of goods to completing sales orders. It can also do the work of the clerical staff in the buyers' department, creating purchase orders and ordering stock. It can do the work of the warehouse staff in recording the deliveries, and, what is more, when it carries out these tasks the batch processing of paper invoices and credit notes inwards and outwards that was described in earlier chapters doesn't have to be done by the book-keeper at all. The system picks up the details from the sales and warehouse function and does it automatically. If all invoices and credit notes outwards are produced within the system, rather than manually outside the system, and all warehouse processes are dealt with within the system too, you don't need the daybook clerks any more.

Invoicing
This is how invoicing is done with Sage 50.

Sage 50 distinguishes between two basic types of invoice:

- a sales invoice;
- a service invoice.

The differences between the two types of invoice
In the sales invoice process, you input product codes only and the system identifies them with previously entered details, thus saving time. You use one line per item.

However, a service invoice is different as the services provided may be infinitely variable and not so amenable to coding. Here the system invites you to describe the service offered and gives you unlimited space to do so.

If early settlement discounts are offered, there is a facility to include them and not only does Sage 50 calculate them, but it deals with the complex calculations that affect the VAT payable and carries the information through to the VAT Return submission stage, relieving you of the need to deal with this matter at a later date.

Sage 50 generates the invoices as the sales order clerk would do in a traditional office, but faster and almost certainly more accurately, as machines are not subject to the same causes of error as humans are. It then automatically writes up the daybook entries and posts to the ledger.

Where an invoice is going to be repeated regularly, you can instruct the system to remember the details using the Memorise option, and you can quickly recall it when needed again.

Credit notes
Generating credit notes is an identical process.

Generating reports

To keep an eye on things, making sure you have enough stock at all times and that everybody who should have been invoiced has been, you can generate reports on the invoicing activity with a few clicks.

Here's how to generate an invoice for product sales:

Step by step

1. Click on Modules and select the Invoicing option from the drop-down toolbar.
    The Invoicing window will appear.

2. On the toolbar, click on the New/Edit button.
    A Product Invoice window will appear.

3. Change the date if required from that which appears in the Date field. Scroll through the dates using the finder arrow or by means of the direction arrows on your keyboard.
4. Enter the sales order number in the Order No. field.
5. Click on the finder arrow at the right of the A/C field and select the customer account number from the drop-down menu.
   The customer details will be automatically filled in on the invoice.
6. Click on the Product Code field.
   A drop-down product menu will appear.
7. Select from it the product code concerned and the rest of this line will be filled in automatically.
8. Repeat the process for each product to be included in the invoice.
9. If any of the product details need editing for this particular invoice click on the icon at the right of the description field and it will allow you to edit the description.
   There are also three special product codes available for one-off products. Codes S1 and S2 are for products chargeable for VAT and VAT-exempt products respectively and code M is for a two-line message to be added.
10. Click on Save.

If you need to include additional details such as a different delivery address or any special circumstances:

Step by step
1. Click on the Order Details tab.
2. Enter the additional material. This will not be saved to the customer record, as it may be specific to this invoice.

3. Enter the footer details (e.g. carriage details, settlement terms such as 5%, 7 days) by clicking on the Footer Details tab.
4. Enter the carriage details.
5. Enter the settlement terms and any early settlement discount applicable.
6. Click on Save.

VAT details appear in the footer section in the current version of Sage 50. In old versions, it appears in the Details field.

If you have already received payment or even part payment for this invoice, record the details by clicking on the Payments tab.

Printing out the invoices
If you want to print out an invoice:

Step by step
1. In the Product Invoice window click on Print.
   The Report Browser will appear, offering a choice of layouts.

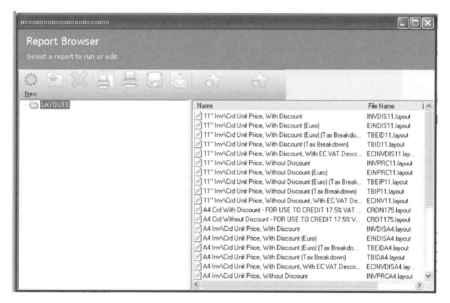

2. Select the one most suitable and click on Preview.
   The preview will appear.

3. If satisfied, click on Print.
    A Print window will appear.

4. Select the number of copies required.
5. Click on OK.
6. Close all windows when finished.

Invoices for services

Invoicing for services is a more or less identical process to invoicing for sales of products. The difference is that you don't have the time-saving facility of clicking on a product code from a menu and letting the system do the rest.

With service invoices, you describe the service in text. There is no limit to the amount of description you can put in, but obviously it is sensible to keep it brief. As your services are not preset categories, there is no automatic linkage to preset nominal ledger accounts. You will have to select a nominal ledger account number to which it is to be posted. To generate a service invoice:

Step by step

1. Click on Modules and select the Invoicing option on the drop-down toolbar.
    The Invoicing window will appear.

2. Click on New/Edit on the toolbar.
    A Product Invoice window will appear.

3. Change the format details to Service, using the finder arrow at the right of the Format field.
4. Change the date if required from that which appears in the Date field. Scroll through the dates using the finder arrow or by means of the direction arrows on your keyboard.
5. Enter the sales order number in the Order No. field.
6. Click on the finder arrow at the right of the A/C field and select the customer account number from the drop-down menu.
   The customer details will then be automatically filled in on the invoice.
7. Type in the description of the service for which you are invoicing.
8. Type in the net price of the service (the VAT and gross will be calculated and entered automatically).
9. Repeat steps 1 to 5 for any other services to be added to the invoice.
10. Enter the footer details (e.g. settlement terms and any early settlement discount applicable, such as 5%, 7 days) by clicking on the Footer Details tab.
11. Click on Save.
12. Close all windows when finished.

If you want to print the invoice, the process is exactly the same as for printing product invoices.

Creating a template invoice

To create a template invoice to save time where identical, or more or less identical, invoices have to be produced frequently, simply enter those details that will be repeated frequently (which may be anything from a few details to almost all details).

Step by step
1. Click on the Memorise button.
   A memorise window will appear.

2. Enter a suitable file reference and description.
3. Click on Save.

Whenever you need to use this template:

1. Click on the Recall button in the Invoice window.
2. Select the most suitable layout from the range of options offered.
3. Click on Load.

You can view a list of template invoices you have saved by clicking on the Recurring button on the toolbar in the Invoicing window.

Automatic generation of recurring invoices

Sage 50 can be set to automatically generate recurring invoices. An example would be invoices for rent, the details of which do not change during the course of a tenancy. Another might be security services to be invoiced monthly on a 12-month contract. To do this, simply enter the required details in the Frequency section of the Memorised and Recurring Invoices window.

These invoices will not be processed without an instruction from the computer operator, but the system will remind you on start-up that you have recurring invoices due for processing. If you wish to process them straight away this is how to do it:

Step by step

1. In the Invoice window click on the Recurring icon on the toolbar.
    The Memorised and Recurring Invoices window will appear.

Memorised and Recurring Invoices			
Reference	Description	Recurring?	Suspended?
Compton	Compton repeat invoice	Yes	No
S D Ent	SD Enterprise repeat	Yes	No

Process | Delete | Edit | Frequency | Print List | Cancel

2. Click on the Process button.
    The Process Recurring Entries window will appear.

Process Recurring Entries					
Show transactions up to:	24/02/2010				
Account	Ref	Date	Description	Amount	Include
COM001	Compton	12/02/2009	Compton rep...	487.80	☑
COM001	Compton	12/06/2009	Compton rep...	487.80	☑
COM001	Compton	12/10/2009	Compton rep...	487.80	☑
COM001	Compton	12/02/2010	Compton rep...	487.80	☑
COM001	Compton	12/12/2009	Compton rep...	487.80	☑
COM001	Compton	12/08/2009	Compton rep...	487.80	☑
COM001	Compton	12/04/2009	Compton rep...	487.80	☑
COM001	Compton	12/12/2008	Compton rep...	487.80	☑
COM001	Compton	12/10/2008	Compton rep...	487.80	☑
SDE001	S D Ent	11/08/2009	SD Enterpr...	4700.00	☑
SDE001	S D Ent	11/10/2009	SD Enterpr...	4700.00	☑
SDE001	S D Ent	11/12/2009	SD Enterpr...	4700.00	☑
SDE001	S D Ent	11/02/2010	SD Enterpr...	4700.00	☑

Process | Cancel

3. Untick the tick box in the Include field for any entries in the list you do not wish to process yet.
4. Click on the Process button.
    A Confirm dialogue box will appear.
5. If you unticked any boxes in step 3, click on the No button in the Confirm window.
    A Process Complete message box will appear.
6. Click on the OK button
7. Click on Cancel to close the window.

Posting to the ledger and updating stock records

You will have now generated the invoices and credit notes. When you wish to post them, you must do so by means of the update function. This is how to do it:

Step by step
1. In the Invoicing window, highlight those invoices and/or credit notes you wish to post to the ledger.
2. Click on the Update icon on the toolbar.
    The Update Ledgers window will appear with radio buttons giving three options:
    ● *Printer;*
    ● *Preview;*
    ● *File.*

3. Check the Preview option.
4. Click on the OK button.
    The update report will be generated.

If you wish to print out the report, click on Print.

A Print Update Ledgers window will appear.

5. Click on OK.
6. Close all windows when finished.

Batch printing of invoices

It may be considered quicker to do all the invoice generating and posting first and then print all the invoices together afterwards, rather than generating and posting each invoice and then printing it out before generating the next one.

It not only may save time, but will also save you having to keep changing mindsets by dealing with all the occurrences of a single stage first and then dealing with all the occurrences of the next stage afterwards. If you choose to do this, then this is how to do batch printing (which is what the process is known as):

Step by step

1. In the Invoicing window, highlight the invoices you wish to print. If there are too many invoices in the list to spot easily the ones you wish to print, you can filter out the ones you want using the Search facility.
2. Click on the Print icon on the toolbar.
   The Report Browser will appear, offering you a choice of layouts.

3. Select the layout required using the finder arrow. There are plenty of standard layouts to choose from, but you can still design your own within the system if you wish.
4. Select preview.
   The preview will appear.
5. If satisfied with the report, click on Print.

The usual print box will appear, asking you to select the page parameters, number of copies and print properties.

6. Enter details as appropriate and click on OK to print out the invoice.
7. Close all windows when finished.

Generating invoicing reports

To generate an invoicing report this is what you do:

Step by step

1. In the Invoicing window click on the Reports icon on the toolbar.
    The Report Browser for invoicing will appear.

2. Double click on the folder containing the general category of report you want to generate.
    A subfolder will appear listing the types of reports that are available.
3. Select a specific report type within that folder.
4. Select the Preview option on the toolbar.
    An Invoice Report Preview window will appear.
5. If you are satisfied with the preview, click on Print.
    The usual print box will appear.
6. Fill in the details as necessary and click on OK to print.
7. Click on Close when finished.

Automatic processing from sales order to delivery and invoice

You can carry out the whole process from sales order to delivery and invoice automatically, thereby cutting out even more manual steps. To do this, you set up a sales order. Stock is allocated, a delivery note is produced when the order is ready to dispatch and an invoice is generated. To set the macro process in motion this is what you do:

Step by step

1. Click on the Modules tab.
2. Click on Sales Order Processing on the drop-down menu.
   The Sales Order Processing window will appear.

3. Click on the New/Edit icon on the toolbar.
4. Change the date if necessary by clicking on the calendar icon at the right-hand side of the Date field.
5. Select the customer's personal account code by clicking on the finder arrow at the right of the A/C field.
   A Product Sales Order window will appear.

6. Select the product code using the finder arrow, which will appear as soon as you click on the first line of the Product Code field.

7. Enter the quantity ordered using the keyboard icon at the right of the Quantity field (unless this detail has been preset on the product record, in which case this detail will be entered automatically). Once a sales order has been dispatched, you cannot reduce the quantity.

8. Repeat the previous two steps for any other items to go on the sales order.

9. If you wish to make any changes to the standard order details, click on the Edit button to the right of the description field.

10. If additional details need to be added, for example a different delivery address, click on the Order Details tab.

11. Enter delivery address, special instructions, customer contact specific to this order, who the order was taken by, customer order number, dispatch date, or any other details which need to be added to the order, including notes for which there is a section on the Order Details page.

12. Click on Save.

13. Footer details such as carriage charges or early settlement discounts offered can be entered on the footer view by clicking on the Footer Details tab.

14. Close all windows when finished.

Allocating stock

After a sales order has been created, stock needs to be allocated to it before it can be dispatched. Here's what to do:

Step by step

1. In the Sales Order Processing window click on the orders to which you wish to allocate stock.
2. Click on the Allocate icon on the toolbar.
3. If there isn't enough stock to fill the order, it will be marked as part complete, as opposed to full.

   A message box will appear giving reasons why the order can't be completed and suggesting a solution, e.g. part fill.

4. If there is enough stock but you don't want to use all of it on this order, you can deliberately part fill it by clicking on the Amend icon on the top row of the Sales Order window.

   An Amend Allocations window will appear.

Amend Allocations

		Order Number	17
Patterson & Graham Garages		Order Date	11/03/2008
The Showroom		Order Value	1137.66
112, 116 James Street		Account Ref	PAT001
West Denton			
East Kilbride			
EK1 7HY			

Product Code	Description	Ordered	Despatched	Outstanding	Allocated	This Despatch
MEM003	DIMM 128mb 100...	2.00	2.00	0.00	0.00	0.00
MOTH001	MTH1000 Motherb...	3.00	3.00	0.00	0.00	0.00
MOUSE003	Mouse Mat - [241 x...	2.00	2.00	0.00	0.00	0.00
PRC003	PCR700 Processor	3.00	3.00	0.00	0.00	0.00
PRN003	JP010 Jet Printer	1.00	1.00	0.00	0.00	0.00

Off Order   Allocate All   Despatch   Previous   Next   Close

5. When you have made the allocation amendments and are satisfied with the instructions you have given, click Allocate All in the Confirm dialogue box.
6. Close all windows when finished.

If afterwards you wish to view the details of any sale, just double click on the particular order in the Sales Order Processing window.

Dispatching sales orders

Once the stock has been allocated to a sales order, it can be dispatched. When this happens the stock records will be updated and an invoice and delivery note generated.

Most of the details of a product invoice generated in the sales order processing routine can be edited, but not the quantity. That is not changeable. To dispatch sales orders:

Step by step

1. In the Sales Order Processing window select the orders you wish to dispatch.
2. Click on the Dispatch icon on the toolbar.
   The Confirm dialogue box will appear to invite you to confirm you wish to create an invoice, update stock records and record the dispatch of the goods.

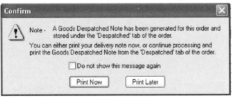

3. Click on Yes.
   An invoice number will be generated automatically by the system when the order is dispatched.
   Another Confirm dialogue box will appear, asking you to confirm whether you wish the delivery note to be produced now or later.

4. Click on the Print Now button, or the Print Later button if you wish to do all your printing in one go (batch printing).
5. If you are printing now, select the delivery note layout you wish to use.
6. Click on the Generate Report button.
7. Click on Print.
8. Close all windows when finished.

Delivery notes can also be generated by clicking on the Generate Delivery Note icon on the toolbar. It won't work, however, if the 'Do not generate' instruction has been set up in the generate delivery note options.

Sales order allocation can be changed right up to the dispatch stage. You may want to do this to complete one customer's order by reducing the allocation to another's order. This may be because one customer's order is more urgent than another's. You can check the stock availability to fill orders by clicking on the Shortfalls icon on the toolbar. If a full allocation is reduced to part complete, the invoice will be changed so that only that part is invoiced.

To amend the allocation to a sales order prior to dispatch this is what you do:

Step by step
1. In the Sales Order Processing window, select the order the allocation of which you wish to amend.
2. Click on the Amend icon on the toolbar.
    The Amend Allocations window will appear.

▣ Amend Allocations						_ □ ✕	
Macolm Hall Associates				Order Number	18		
172 Edison Street				Order Date	17/03/2008		
Chester				Order Value	3319.95		
Cheshire							
CH1 4PL				Account Ref	MAC001		

Product Code	Description	Ordered	Despatched	Outstanding	Allocated	This Despatch
PRN004	JP020 Jet Printer	5.00	5.00	0.00	0.00	0.00
PC002	PC Combo Pack 2	4.00	4.00	0.00	0.00	0.00
TR004	JP020 Jet Printer C...	2.00	2.00	0.00	0.00	0.00
TR003	JP010 Jet Printer C...	2.00	2.00	0.00	0.00	0.00

Off Order	Allocate All	Despatch	Previous	Next		Close

3. Amend the quantity to allocate as required.
4. Close all windows when finished.

Printing batch orders

If you want to print out all order documents at the same time this is what you do:

Step by step
1. Select the orders you wish to print.
2. Click on the Print button.
    A Report Browser will appear offering a choice of formats for the invoices.
3. Select the layout you wish to use.
4. Click on the Preview icon.
5. If you are satisfied with the appearance of the preview, click on Print.
    The usual Print dialogue box will appear.
6. Enter the number of copies you require, and click on OK to print.
7. Close all windows when finished.

Generating sales order reports

To generate a sales order report:

Step by step

1. In the Sales Order Processing Window click on the Reports icon on the toolbar.
    The Report Browser will appear offering a choice of formats.
2. Double click on the folder containing the general category of report you want to generate.
    A subfolder will appear listing the types of reports that are available.
3. Select a specific report type within that folder.
4. Click on the Preview icon.
    A Criteria box will appear.
5. Enter the order number, customer reference and date parameters in the appropriate fields.
6. Click on OK.
    The Sales Order Report preview will appear.
7. Click on Print if a printout is required and follow the usual print process.
8. Close window when finished.

Creating a purchase order

You can do the whole process from purchase order to delivery and update of stock records automatically, thereby cutting out even more manual steps. The first thing that has to be done is to create a purchase order. This is how to do it:

Step by step

1. Click on Modules.
2. Select the Purchase Order Processing option from the drop-down menu.
    The Purchase Order Processing window will appear.

3. Click on the New/Edit icon on the toolbar.
   A Product Purchase Order window will appear.

4. Change the date if necessary by clicking on the calendar icon at the right-hand side of the Date field.
5. Select the supplier's personal account code by clicking on the finder arrow at the right of the A/C field.
   The supplier's details will be filled in automatically.
6. Select the product code using the finder arrow, which will appear as soon as you click on the first line of the Product Code field. If the order is for goods that for one reason or another don't have to be paid for, e.g. display cases supplied by a manufacturer, the product code M should be used.
7. Enter the quantity ordered using the keyboard icon at the right of the Quantity field (unless this detail has been preset on the product record, in which case this detail will be entered automatically).
   Once a purchase order has been dispatched you cannot reduce the quantity. Product quantities can be increased but not decreased after dispatch of the purchase order.
8. Repeat steps 5 and 6 for any other items to go on the purchase order.
9. Click on Save.
10. If you wish to make any changes to the standard order details, click on Edit to the right of the Description field.
11. If additional details need to be added, these can be entered on the order details tab (accessed by clicking on the Order Details tab). Enter any additional details required, for example:

- delivery address;
- carriage charges;
- settlement terms;
- special instructions;
- supplier contact specific to the order;
- name of person who took the order;
- their telephone number;
- the order number;
- dispatch date.

There is also a section in this window for miscellaneous notes.

12. Footer details can be added by clicking on the Footer Details tab.
13. Click on Save.
14. Close all windows when finished.

Regularly used purchase order details can be saved as skeleton purchase orders in just the same way as for sales orders.

The purchase order must now be placed 'on order'. This will allow deliveries to be recorded and the stock updated.

To place a purchase order 'on order' this is what you do:

Step by step

1. In the Purchase Order Processing window, click on the orders you wish to place 'on order'. Use the Search button to filter out orders that meet selected criteria if this would speed things up.
2. Click on the Order icon on the toolbar.
   The Confirm print dialogue box will appear.

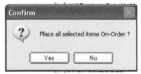

3. Click on Yes if you want to print the selected order, or No if you do not.
   A Confirm dialogue box will appear asking you if you wish to place the selected item on order.

4. Click on Yes.
5. Close all windows when finished.

When the goods are delivered

When a delivery is complete, you can record it by using the Deliver icon on the toolbar of the Purchase Order Processing window. If only a part delivery is made, you need to use the Amend icon, as otherwise the delivery will be recorded as full. To record a full delivery:

Step by step

1. In the Purchase Order Processing window, select the orders for which you wish to record delivery.
2. Click on the Deliver icon on the toolbar.
    A dialogue box will appear asking if you wish to update stock records and record delivery.

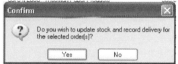

3. Click on Yes.
    Another dialogue box will appear asking if you want to print out a goods received note now or later.

4. Click on Print Now or Print Later as required.
5. If you instruct it to be printed now, a preview will be shown and you must then click on Print and go through the print process which you will be familiar with by now.
    The record in the Purchase Order Processing window will now show the delivery as complete.

5. Close all windows when finished.

When only a part delivery is made

When only a part delivery is made proceed as follows:

Step by step

1. In the Purchase Order Processing window, select the orders for which you wish to record part delivery.
2. Click on the Amend icon on the toolbar.
    An Amend Deliveries window will appear.

Amend Deliveries								
McNally Computer Supplies						Order Number		38
Station Lane Ind Est						Order Date		15/05/2008
Birtley						Order Value		913.57
Chester le Street						Account Ref		MCN001
County Durham								
DH1 3RG								

Product Code	Description	Project Ref	Cost Code	Ordered	Delivered	Outstanding	This Delivery
PC005	PC Combo Pack 5	PROJ008	DESK	1.00	0.00	1.00	1.00

Off Order   Deliver   Previous   Next   Close

3. Enter the quantity actually received.
4. Click on Deliver.
    A dialogue box will appear asking if you wish to update stock records and record delivery.

Confirm

? Do you wish to update stock and record delivery for the selected order(s)?

Yes   No

5. Click on Yes.
6. Close all windows when finished.

The record on the Purchase Order Processing window will now show that the order has only been part completed.

Manually processing purchase orders

The Amend icon can also be used to cancel purchase orders or manually place orders 'on order' as an alternative to the automatic routine. To manually place an order 'on order':

Step by step

1. In the Purchase Order Processing window, select the order you require to manually place 'on order'.
2. Click on the Amend icon on the toolbar.
   The Amend Deliveries window will appear.

Amend Deliveries							

McNally Computer Supplies
Station Lane Ind Est
Birtley
Chester le Street
County Durham
DH1 3RG

Order Number   38
Order Date   15/05/2008
Order Value   913.57
Account Ref   MCN001

Product Code	Description	Project Ref	Cost Code	Ordered	Delivered	Outstanding	This Delivery
PC005	PC Combo Pack 5	PROJ006	DESK	1.00	0.00	1.00	1.00

Order   Deliver   Previous   Next   Close

3. Click on the Order button at the bottom left-hand corner of the window.
4. Close all windows when finished.

Cancelling an order

If you wish to cancel an order this is what you have to do:

Step by step

1. Click on the Amend icon on the toolbar.
2. Click on the Off Order button at the bottom left-hand corner of the window.
   It will then be marked as cancelled.

Printing batch purchase orders

If you want to print out all order documents at the same time proceed as follows:

Step by step

1. In the Purchase Order Processing window, select the orders you wish to print.
2. Click on the Print button on the toolbar.
   A Report Browser window will appear offering a choice of formats.
3. Select the layout you wish to use.
4. Click on the Preview icon.
   The purchase order preview will appear.
5. If you are satisfied with it, click on Print and complete the printing process that you should know well by now.
6. Close all windows when finished.

Generating purchase order reports

To generate a purchase order report:

Step by step

1. In the Purchase Order Processing window click on the Reports icon on the toolbar.
   The relevant Report Browser window will appear.
2. Double click on the folder containing the general category of report you want to generate.
   A subfolder will appear listing the types of reports that are available.

3. Select a specific report type within that folder.
   A criteria box will appear asking for the supplier reference and date parameters and also the number of records you wish to include. If you leave it as zero the system will interpret this as All Records.
4. Enter the details and click on OK.
   A preview of the report will appear.
5. If you are satisfied with it, click on print and complete the printing process.
6. Click on Close when finished.

If your business trades with other EU states, you can produce a report on the trade statistics by clicking on the Intrastat icon on the toolbar.

A wide range of report formats are supplied in Sage 50, but if there isn't one that suits your purpose you can either modify an existing one or create an entirely new one using the Report Wizard. This can be used for various kinds of statutory reports and forms and also for letters and labels. Information can be viewed by pressing the F1 key on your keyboard.

The Report Designer window is a Windows application, complete with a menu bar, desktop and the facility to display several layouts at once. To view the Report Designer desktop proceed as follows:

Step by step
1. Click on the Tools icon on the browser toolbar.
2. Click on the Report Designer option.
   The Report Designer window will appear.

3. In the left-hand pane, double click on a document type folder, e.g. customer, departments or letters.
   A list of preset layouts will appear for that category of document.
4. Select from the list in the left-hand pane the general category of report you require and double click on it.
   A list of specific report types within that category will appear in the right-hand pane.
5. Click on Close when finished.

Creating a report design from scratch
To create a simple report design from scratch proceed as follows:

Step by step
1. Click on Tools on the browser toolbar.
2. Select Report Designer from the drop-down menu.

3. In the Report Designer window, click on File.
   A drop-down menu will appear.

4. Click on New.
5. Click on Report.
   A Document Type window will appear.

6. From the list of document types, click on the general aspect of the business to which your report relates, e.g. Customer.
7. Click on Next.
   The Select Fields window will appear.

This window has two panes. The left-hand pane is for fields available to include in your report. The right-hand pane is for those that are in your report.

Double clicking on certain fields will reveal lower order fields within them, For example, double clicking on the Company field offers subfields like Name, Company Address 1 (first line of address), Company Address 2 (second line), Company Address 3, Company Address 4, and so on.

Select from the left-hand pane the fields you want to include in your report and move them into the right-hand pane by means of the right-facing arrows between the panes. The single arrows move single items and the double arrows move all the items together. You can't highlight a group of items and move them together with the double arrows though; the double arrows symbol moves everything in the pane, which is usually more than you want to move. If you have a group of things to move, you will have to do them one at a time.

You can also move items back using the left-facing arrows.

8. If, for example, you want to make a report of all customers whose accounts are on hold, double click on COMPANY in the left-hand pane to make the following fields available:
   - NAME
   - ADDRESS_1
   - ADDRESS_2
   - ADDRESS_3
   - ADDRESS_4

9. Move each of these into the right-hand pane using the single right-facing arrow. The report type names then appear there together with their category names separated by a dot, e.g. NAME appears as COMPANY. NAME and ADDRESS_1 appears as COMPANY.ADDRESS_1.
10. Double click on SALES_LEDGER in the left-hand pane to reveal the subfields in this area.
11. Highlight SALES_LEDGER.ACCOUNT_ON_HOLD and move it into the right-hand pane using the single arrow.
12. Click on Next.
    The Grouping window will appear, showing how the fields will be grouped in the report. In this example, grouping is unnecessary.
13. Click on Next.
    The Sort window will appear.
14. If you want the information sorted in terms of customer names in alphabetical order, highlight COMPANY.NAME in the left-hand column and move it into the right pane by means of the right-facing arrow.
    A Sort Order dialogue box will appear asking whether you want the information sorted in ascending or descending order.
15. Click on the Ascending button, as it is the most relevant in our example.
16. Click on Next.
    A Totals window will appear.
17. We are not interested in totals in this report, just names of companies whose accounts are On Hold, so leave the right-hand pane empty.
18. Click on Next.
    A Criteria window will appear asking which of a list of details is to be omitted from the report.
19. In our case, since none of the information in the list is needed, move it all into the left-hand pane using the double arrows symbol.
    A window will appear asking you to name your report.
20. Give it a suitable name, such as Accounts on Hold.
21. Click on Finish.
    The preview of the report pro forma will appear.
22. If you are satisfied with it, click on File on the browser.
23. Click on Save.
    A box will appear inviting you to save your report pro forma in a folder called My Customer Reports, where it will be available for use along with all the other pro formas on the system.
24. Close all windows when finished.

The report pro forma generated in this example is a simple one, but once you know how to create a report format from scratch, you can add as much complexity as you wish.

Adapting an existing report

Instead of creating a new report format from scratch, you can modify an existing report layout. This is how you do it:

Step by step

1. Open a report pro forma that is similar to the design you want, e.g. a report on monthly payments to contractors could be adapted to make a report pro forma for payments to commission agents.

2. Click on the Data tab and use this to add or remove variables or features as necessary in order to achieve the new report design you need. The Criteria option, for example, will give you the opportunity to change the details that will be shown on the report.

3. You can change the order that the names appear, for example, they can be ordered by contractor reference number or alphabetically by contractor name. You can change the format of the report, add whole new sections to it and make many other types of change.
4. When you are satisfied with your modifications, click on OK.
5. Click on Save As.
6. Type in a relevant file name.
7. Click on OK.
8. Close the window when finished.

Regardless of the fact that you may have entered many transactions in the electronic books, the balances in the ledger will remain at zero if you have not yet entered the opening balances.

Entoring balances mid-year

It is obviously important to post the opening figures as soon as possible, as without them you have no useful accounts. It may be that for part of the year you have kept the records in a manual system though, and changed to Sage 50 halfway through the year. Your opening figures for the year will have to be entered then. If you have been using a manual system for part of the year you will not have had the facility of having an up-to-date trial balance always on hand. You will have to do some end-of-period accounting or ask your accountant to prepare an up-to-date trial balance, which you can use as a source of your opening figures for Sage 50. If interim profit and loss accounts have been produced, the profit or loss figures will also be needed.

When you enter the opening figures for your nominal ledger or bank account, dual postings are automatically made to the suspense account. If the figures are taken from an accurate trial balance and accurately recorded, then by the time they have all been entered all the debit entries will equal all the credit entries, and so too will the debit and credit counter entries that have been made to the suspense account. It stands to reason that this must be so. The balance of the suspense account will, therefore, be zero.

If this is not so then a balance must have been missed out (error of omission) or a debit misposted as a credit or vice versa (error of commission). You will need to run a new trial balance to check what has been missed or misposted.

Inputting opening figures for VAT

Opening balances are obtainable from the last end-of-year trial balance, and these can be used in aggregate form if the Standard VAT scheme is being used, but it is recommended that outstanding invoices are listed separately in order to better facilitate credit control measures such as age analysis. If the VAT Cash Accounting scheme is in use, it is compulsory that invoices, credit notes and VAT-chargeable journal entries are recorded separately.

Inputting customer opening balances

To set up a customer opening balance proceed as follows:

Step by step
1. On the navigation bar click on the Customers button.
   The Customers window will appear.
2. Select the relevant customer record.
3. On the Modules toolbar in that window, click on the Record icon.
   That customer's record window will appear.
4. Click on the O/B symbol at the right of the Balance field (the letters O/B are not very clear on the symbol).
   The Opening Balance Setup window will appear.

Opening Balance Setup			☒
Ref	Date	Type	Gross
	25/02/2010	Invoice	0.00

[Save]   [Cancel]

5. Enter details of the opening balance itemised in terms of the references, dates, types of transactions and values it represents. As pointed out this can be entered as a lump sum if the Standard VAT scheme is being used, but such aggregation is not recommended.
6. Click on Save.

Inputting opening balances on the nominal ledger

To input opening balances on the nominal ledger this is what you do:

Step by step

1. In the nominal ledger, click on the first account on the list.
2. Click on the Record icon on the Modules toolbar.
    A Nominal Record window will appear.

Nominal Record –

Details | Graphs | Activity | Memo

N/C |

Name

Balance   0.00   ▥   Account Type   Nominal Account

Month	Actuals	To end Dec 2007
B/F	0.00	0.00
Jan	0.00	0.00
Feb	0.00	0.00
Mar	0.00	0.00
Apr	0.00	0.00
May	0.00	0.00
Jun	0.00	0.00
Jul	0.00	0.00
Aug	0.00	0.00
Sep	0.00	0.00
Oct	0.00	0.00
Nov	0.00	0.00
Dec	0.00	0.00
Future	0.00	0.00
Total	0.00	0.00

tp://www.runaware.com/clients/td-support/support.jsp   Window (6) ▼   Allowing Pop-Ups (0) ▼   He

3. Select a nominal ledger account number using the finder arrow at the right of the N/C field.
4. Click the O/B button at the right of the Balance field.
    The Opening Balance Setup dialogue box will appear.

181

5. Set up the opening balance and date by clicking on the symbols at the right of the relevant fields.
6. Enter a suitable reference, e.g. opening balance or O/B.
7. Click on Save.
8. Close all windows when finished.

Inputting bank opening balances on the bank record
To input the opening figures on the bank account:

Step by step
1. In the Bank Accounts window, select the first account on the list and click on the Record icon on the Modules toolbar.
   A Bank Record window will appear.

2. Click the O/B button at the right of the Current Balance field.
   The Opening Balance Setup dialogue box will appear.

3.   Set up the opening balance and date by clicking on the symbols at the right of the relevant fields.
4.   Enter a suitable reference, e.g. opening balance or O/B.
5.   Click on Save.
6.   Close all windows when finished.

Inputting product opening balances

When you create new product records it may be easy to ascertain the stock levels by means of a physical stock-take and enter them as opening balances, but if it is not that simple then opening balances may be entered at a later date. In the latter case, Adjustments In Transactions will be posted and appear on stock reports as Opening Stock quantities.

This is how to enter product opening balances:

Step by step

1.   In the Products window, select the first product for which you seek to enter an opening balance.
2.   Click on the Record icon on the Modules toolbar.
     A Product Record window will appear.

3.   Select a product using the finder arrow at the right of the Product Code field.
4.   Click on the OB symbol at the right of the In Stock field.
     The Opening Product Setup dialogue box will appear.

5. Enter a suitable reference, e.g. opening balance or O/B.
6. Change the date if appropriate using the calendar at the right of the Date field.
7. Select the quantity using the symbol at the right of the Quantity field.
8. Select the cost price using the symbol at the right of the Cost Price field.
9. Click on Save.
10. Close all windows when finished.

You can show a jpg image of a stock item with the stock record if you wish. To do this, click on the Web tab and then, in the image section of the pane, click on Add.

Backing up data

It is important to back up your data regularly to guard against data loss through system error or file corruption. If it happens, you will be able to restore your files, as they were at the last backup. The backup procedure on Sage 50 stores the location of your last backup as the default location and the file name you used as the default file name. This can be changed if required. Sage 50 prompts you to back up your data every time you exit the program. You should back up your data at least once a day.

To back up your data proceed as follows:

Step by step

1. On the browser toolbar, click on the File tab.
2. Click on the Backup option on the drop-down menu.
   A dialogue box will appear asking you if you would like to check your data before backing up.

3. Click on No, unless you particularly want to do so.
   A Backup window will appear.

4.   Select a location for the backup if you do not wish to use the same location as last time. If you are happy to store the backup in the same location as last time, with the same file name, thus overwriting it, click on OK.

Restoring data

If your records happen to suffer data loss or file corruption, you can restore the files to how they were at the last backup, which, ideally, will be no earlier than the last time you exited the program.

When you use the Restore facility on Sage 50, it will overwrite any current version of the same data. The more frequently you back up your data the more up to date will be the restoration and therefore the less data will have to be inputted from scratch. It is important to label restored files correctly, so that you do not replace whole files that may contain only a few errors with the wrong backup files which may contain many. One of the reasons you might lose data is if there is a fire at your place of work. If your backup disks are kept in the same room as your hard disk, they too are likely to be destroyed in any fire that destroys your hard disk. It is wise to keep them in a different and preferably fireproof place.

To restore files from backup disks:

Step by step

1.   On the browser toolbar click on the File tab.
2.   On the drop-down menu click on the Restore option.
     A dialogue box will appear informing you that you will have to close all other windows to run this process. It asks if you wish to do so and warns that unsaved files will be lost.
3.   Click on the Yes button.
     A Restore window will appear.

186

4. Enter the details of the file you want to restore. If the backup file is on a disc or some kind of external storage unit place the disc in the drive or plug in the external storage unit and type the file location into the File field.
5. Click on OK.
6. Click on OK again to confirm the Restore instructions and execute the Restore command.

Checking for input errors should be carried out regularly, particularly when backing up and restoring. To check for input errors:

Step by step
1. On the browser toolbar click on the File tab.
2. Click on the Maintenance option on the drop-down menu.
    The File Maintenance window will appear.

3. Click on the Check Data button.
    If everything is fine, a message box will appear informing you that there are no problems to report.

    If there are problems in the files, a File Maintenance Problems Report window will appear.
4. Scroll though the errors reported and click on the Fix button when a correction is needed.
5. Close all windows when finished.

Mistakes made while inputting a transaction can be corrected by means of the Corrections button on the File Maintenance menu bar, as long as the invoice has not been deleted from the audit trail. This is how to it:

Step by step
1. On the browser toolbar click on the File tab.
2. Select the Maintenance option on the drop-down menu and click.
    A File Maintenance window will appear.

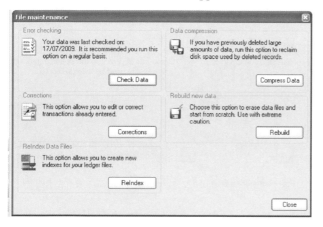

3. Click on the Corrections button.
    The Corrections window will appear.

189

4. Select the invoice you need to correct. If there are a lot of transactions, you can use the Find button to search for the one you need to correct.
5. Click on the Edit Item icon on the toolbar.
   A dialogue box will appear revealing all the details of the transaction.

6. If there are corrections to be made that apply to the whole invoice, make them in the boxes on the main grey area of the window.
7. If there are corrections to be made that apply to just a single item on the invoice, highlight that item in the bottom pane of the window and click on Edit.
   Another Sales Invoice window will appear.

8. Make corrections as necessary by overtyping in the relevant boxes.
9. Click on Close when finished.
10. Click on Save to store your changes.

You cannot amend journal entries using this function. The only way you can amend them is by posting another journal entry with an equal and opposite value to correct the error in the previous journal entry, just the same as in manual book-keeping.

Deleting transactions

A transaction can be deleted as long as it has not been recorded on the VAT Return. Deleted transactions appear in red at the end of the Corrections window. To delete a transaction proceed as follows:

Step by step

1. On the browser toolbar, click on the File tab.
2. Select the Maintenance option on the drop-down menu and click.
   The File Maintenance window will appear.
3. Click on Corrections.
   The Corrections window will appear.

4. Select the transaction you need to correct. If there are a lot of transactions, you can use the Find button to search for the one you need to correct.
5. Click on the Delete icon on the toolbar.
   A dialogue box will appear asking you to check the details to make sure you are deleting the right file.

Number 1214, Bank Payment   ☒

Before deleting this transaction and its associated items, review the information below to make sure you have selected the correct transaction.

Bank Payment Details

Bank	1200	
Reference	DD/STO	
Description	Rent Direct Debit	Posted by MANAGER
Created on	22/06/2008	☐ Bank rec on
Posted on	22/06/2008	VAT Rec. Date / /

Totals

Net	1200.00	Tax	0.00	Paid	1200.00

Information

☑ Paid in full   ☐ Finance charge   ☐ Disputed   ☐ Printed
☐ Opening balance   ☐ DS reconciled   ☐ Revaluation

Foreign currency

Gross	1200.00	Rate	1.000000	Currency	1 Pound Sterling

To view details of a specific item on this Bank Payment, highlight the item and click 'View'.   [View]

No	N/C	Details	Net	T/C	Tax
1214	7100	Rent Direct Debit	1200.00	T9	0.00

[How will this affect my data?]   [Delete]   [Close]

6. When you are satisfied that it is the right file, click on Delete.
    A dialogue box asking you to confirm that you wish to delete this file and warning of the consequences of doing so will appear.

Confirm   ☒

(?) Do you wish to delete this transaction?

[Yes]   [No]

7. If you are sure, click on Yes.
    The file will be deleted and will show on the corrections list in red as a deleted file.
8. Close all windows when finished.

A business may need to apply a single percentage change to a whole area of its financial arrangements, e.g. when credit limits are to be reduced or all prices increased by a fixed percentage. A fixed percentage cut may have to be applied to all items in the budget, company standard discount rates may need to be changed, or reorder quantities changed if, for example, the company is changing to a 'just in time' stock order policy. Global changes may also be useful if you are adjusting your customer credit period to match your supplier credit period. These global changes can quickly and easily be achieved by means of the Global Changes Wizard in Sage 50. This is how you do it:

Step by step
1. On the browser toolbar, click on the Tools tab.
2. Click on the Global Changes option on the drop-down menu.
   The usual message box will appear informing you that you must close other open windows.

3. Click on Next.
   The welcome to Global Changes Wizard window will appear.

4.   Click on Next.
     A list of types of changes will appear.

```
┌─────────────────────────────────────────────────────────────┐
│ Global Changes Wizard                                    [X] │
│                                                              │
│  Global Changes                                              │
│                                                              │
│   Now, select the items you want to make this change to.  Selecting the swap │
│   button with none highlighted will select all items.        │
│   ┌──────────────┬────────────────────────────┐             │
│   │ A/C          │ Name                       │  ┌────────┐ │
│   │ A1D001       │ A1 Design Services         │  │ Swap   │ │
│   │ ABS001       │ ABS Garages Ltd            │  └────────┘ │
│   │ BBS001       │ Bobs Building Supplies      │             │
│   │ BRI001       │ Fred Briant                │  ┌────────┐ │
│   │ BRO001       │ Bronson Inc                │  │ Clear  │ │
│   │ BUS001       │ Business Exhibitions        │  └────────┘ │
│   │ CASH001      │ Cash and Credit Card Sales │             │
│   └──────────────┴────────────────────────────┘             │
│                                                              │
│  ┌────────┐ ┌────────┐     ┌────────┐ ┌────────┐  ┌───────┐ │
│  │ Cancel │ │ Help   │     │ Back   │ │ Next   │  │ Finish│ │
│  └────────┘ └────────┘     └────────┘ └────────┘  └───────┘ │
└─────────────────────────────────────────────────────────────┘
```

5.   Select the type of change that is going to be made.
6.   Click on Next.
     *A window inviting you to select the items (records) to which changes are to
     apply will appear.*

```
┌─────────────────────────────────────────────────────────────┐
│ Global Changes Wizard                                    [X] │
│                                                              │
│  Global Changes                                              │
│                                                              │
│   Enter the type of price change and the amount to change it by below.  Use the rounding │
│   function to link your prices to particular price points.   │
│   Type of change:    [Add amount              ▼]             │
│   Value:             [      0.00 ▣]                          │
│   Rounding Direction: [Round up to        ▼]                │
│                                                              │
│   ⊙ To          [2    ▼] Decimal Places                      │
│   ○ Multiples of  [ 0.00 ▣] plus adjustment  [ 0.00 ▣]      │
│   (e.g. to round to the nearest 0.99, enter a value of 1.00 with an adjustment of -0.01) │
│                                                              │
│  ┌────────┐ ┌────────┐     ┌────────┐ ┌────────┐  ┌───────┐ │
│  │ Cancel │ │ Help   │     │ Back   │ │ Next   │  │ Finish│ │
│  └────────┘ └────────┘     └────────┘ └────────┘  └───────┘ │
└─────────────────────────────────────────────────────────────┘
```

7.   Select the specific items (records) to which the change will apply.
8.   Click on Next.
     A dialogue box asking for the type and value of the change will appear.

9. Select the type of change to be made by means of the finder arrow at the right of the Type of Change field.
10. Enter the value of change in the Value field.
11. Click on Next.

   A message box asking you to check the changes will appear. You can amend the changes using the back arrow if you need to.

12. Click on Next.

   A Global Changes Finished confirmation box will appear.

13. Click on Finish.

   A final warning will appear informing you that the changes cannot be reversed and asking you to confirm that you are sure you want to make them.

14. Click on Yes to complete the process.

You may, for one reason or another, have to import data such as a batch of records, previously stored on a spreadsheet, or other electronic document, such as a Word file. These might, for example, be daybook entries covering the period prior to adopting Sage 50. If such is the case, you will not have to enter each detail manually; Sage 50 can read documents as long as they are written in CSV format (comma separated values). If they are not written in such a format they may be able to be saved in it, using the right software. Even paper documents can be scanned in and interpreted by OCR software and then saved as CSV files for inputting directly to Sage 50.

What is a CSV File?

A CSV file is one that has the following qualities:

- Each unit of data is separated by a comma, e.g. Woodley and Son, 10 boxes of nails, 30.00, 5.25, 35.25 (representing the name of a supplier, details of goods supplied, the net value of the order, the VAT and the gross value).
- There is only one record per line.
- Each record ends with an Enter command.
- Spaces at the beginning and end of a record are ignored.
- If any data units themselves contain commas, which should be shown as commas in the record, then those commas are placed in quotation marks.
- Two consecutive commas are used after dates that could otherwise be misinterpreted by the system.

To import data in this way this is what you do:

Step by step

1. On the browser toolbar, click on the File tab.
2. On the drop-down menu click on the Import option.

A message box will appear asking for confirmation that you wish to close all other windows as required for running this process.

3. Click on Yes.

The Welcome to the Data Import Wizard message box will appear.

Data Import Wizard

Sage 50 Accounts - Data Import

1. Welcome
2. Data type
3. Data source
4. Field mappings
5. Finish

Welcome to the Data Import wizard.

Using this wizard, you can import data from Excel worksheets (*.xls;*.xlsx) and files containing comma-separated values (*.csv).

WARNING: This operation is NOT reversible.

We strongly recommend you take a backup of your data before proceeding.

[Backup...]

[Cancel] [Help]   [Back] [Next] [Finish]

4. Click on Backup and complete the backup procedure by following the instructions.
5. Click on Next.
    A dialogue box will appear asking you to select the relevant data type of the material you want to import.

http://www.runaware.com/launch/run?c_app_id=14543&refid=17370&useproxy=y&width=10 [▼] [Go]

Sage 50 Accounts - Data Import

1. Welcome
2. **Data type**
3. Data source
4. Field mappings
5. Finish

Select the type of data you want to import: ?

Audit Trail transactions
Customer records
Fixed Asset records
Nominal accounts
Product records
Project records
Project-Only transactions
Stock transactions
Supplier records

[Cancel] [Help]   [Back] [Next] [Finish]

6. Select the data type from the list and click on Next.
    A dialogue box will appear asking you to select the format of the data source.

Data Import Wizard

Sage 50 Accounts - Data Import

1 Welcome

2 Data type

3 **Data source**

4 Field mappings

5 Finish

Select the format of the data you will be importing:

○ Comma-separated (*.csv)

○ Excel worksheet (*.xls,*.xlsx)

Select the file to import:

[   ] [Browse...]

☑ First row contains headings   ?

[Cancel]   [Help]   [Back]   [Next]   [Finish]

7.   Check the radio button for Comma separated or Excel worksheet as appropriate.
8.   Click on Next.
     The Field Mappings window will appear.

Data Import Wizard

Sage 50 Accounts - Data Import

1 Welcome

2 Data type

3 Data source

4 **Field mappings**

5 Finish

Map the fields in your data to the fields in Sage 50 Accounts.

Required?	Imported Field	Sage Field
*	Account Reference	Account Reference
*	Account Name	Account Name
	Street 1	Street 1
	Street 2	Street 2
	Town	Town
	County	County
	Postcode	Postcode
	Contact Name	Contact Name
	Telephone Number	Telephone Number

Map file in use: [none]

[Clear Map]   [Load Map...]   [Save Map...]

[Cancel]   [Help]   [Back]   [Next]   [Finish]

9.   If your software dos not recognise the column headings for any particular column in your data source, a mapping table will appear marking the unrecognised columns with an asterisk. When you click on any of these asterisked lines in the Imported Field column, an Imported Field drop-down list invites you to select an appropriate column header which Sage 50 will recognise. Work through the asterisk marked columns (which are confusingly expressed as lines rather than columns in the mapping table) and then click on Save Map.

A select a Data Import Map File window will appear.

10. Enter a suitable file name and a location to which your Data Import Map file should be saved.

11. Click on Save.

    Your Import Map file will be saved in the Company Import Maps folder.

12. Click on Next.

    The Finish window will appear.

When the import has taken place, an Import Results window will appear informing you whether your data import has been successful and listing any files that have not been imported.

13. Close the window when you have seen all you need to see and investigate the reasons why any particular files have failed to be imported.

If a lot of records have been deleted from a file, you can use the compressed data option to recreate the files without the deleted records, thereby freeing up space. To compress a file:

Step by step

1. On the browser toolbar, click on the File tab.
   A drop-down menu will appear.
2. Scroll to the Maintenance option and click.
   The File maintenance window will appear.
3. Click on the Compress Data button.
   The Compress Data Files window will appear.

Compress Data Files

☑ Compress All Data Files

☑ Audit Trail	☑ Products
☑ Sales Ledger	☑ Invoices
☑ Purchase Ledger	☑ Sales Orders
☑ Nominal Ledger	☑ Purchase Orders
☑ Bank Accounts	☑ Fixed Assets
☑ Goods Received Notes	☑ Price Lists
☑ Goods Despatched Notes	☑ Project Ledger
	☑ Diary Events

[Compress] [Close]

4. Tick the boxes of the files you wish to compress and then click on the Compress button.
   The Data Compression Complete message box will appear when finished

Information

ⓘ Data compression complete.

[OK]

5. Click on Close.

If a customer's debt has come to be deemed uncollectable, perhaps due to insolvency or the company has gone into liquidation, or perhaps it has been decided that it would simply cost more to enforce than it is worth, it should be written off. Then it can be removed from the profit calculations. This will result in a more true and accurate record. It will prevent more tax being paid than is due and perhaps enable the firm to recover the VAT that the customer was charged on the invoice and which was paid to HMRC but not recovered from the customer.

Write offs and refunds are treated in the same way in the accounts, since they are essentially the same thing. If a business decides a debt is uncollectable, it refunds the money to the customer's ledger account in order to close it down, for the account cannot be closed if a balance remains on it. If the business subsequently receives information that suggests that the debt has become collectable again, it can reinstate it.

If you are using the Standard VAT scheme, the refund is in full rather than in part and the original invoice has not been removed from the audit trail, then proceed as follows to record a refund:

Step by step

1. In the Customers window, click on the Write-off/Refund option in the Tasks Pane.
   The Write Off, Refund and Returns Wizard window will appear asking you to select the area in which to make the amendment.

2. Select the type of item you want to refund from the list and click on Next. Let's suppose it is a customer invoice. Scroll to this option and click on Next.
   A second Write Off, Refund and Returns Wizard window will appear inviting you to select the customer account concerned.

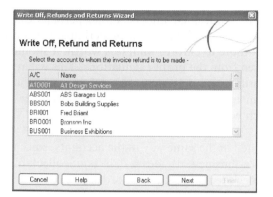

3. Select the account from the list and click on Next.
    A third Write Off, Refund and Returns Wizard window will appear inviting you to select the particular invoices concerned.

4. Select the invoices and click on Next.
    A fourth Write Off, Refund and Returns Wizard window will appear asking you to select the bank account to which the refund is to be paid.

5. Select the customer's account that will be affected by the refund and click on Next.
    A fifth Write Off, Refund and Returns Wizard window will appear asking you to enter the date for the refund and any reference number you wish to use.
6. Enter the required details and click on Next.
    A final Write Off, Refund and Returns Wizard window will appear inviting you to check the details and click on Finish to complete the process.

7. Check the details and click Finish.

Returned cheques

On occasions, hopefully rare ones, the company may find that the cheque a customer has presented has been dishonoured by their bank for lack of funds, or some other reason (e.g. out of date). Providing you are using the Standard VAT scheme, there is a quick way to deal with this. You can't use this method if you use the VAT Cash Accounting scheme. There you have to record it manually using the Journal.

This is how to record a returned/dishonoured cheque:

Step by step
1. In the Tasks pane of the Customers window, click on the Write-off/Refund option.
    A Write Off, Refund and Returns Wizard window containing types of customer refund will appear as before.
2. Click on the Customer Cheque Returns option.
    A Write Off, Refund and Returns Wizard window for selecting the account to which the cheque is to be returned will appear.
3. Select the customer's account and click on Next.
    A Write Off, Refund and Returns Wizard window for selecting the cheque that has been returned will appear.

4. Scroll to the cheque concerned and click on Next.
   A New Write Off, Refund and Returns Wizard window will appear asking you to enter the date for the refund and any reference number you wish to use.

5. Enter the required details and click on Next.
   A final Write Off, Refund And Returns Wizard window will appear asking you to check the details and click on Finish to complete the process.

6. Check the details are correct. Use the Back button to locate any details you wish to change.

7. Click on Finish.

Dealing with contra entries

If a supplier is also a customer, you can offset monies they owe to you against money you owe to them using the Contra Entries option. This is what you do:

Step by step

1. Click on the Tools tab on the browser toolbar.
   A drop-down menu will appear.

2. Click on the Contra Entries option.

The Contra Entries window will appear.

3. Select the customer and supplier ledger accounts concerned using the finder arrows at the right of the relevant fields.
    The Customer and Supplier boxes will then be automatically filled in.
4. Select the outstanding sales invoices from the list.
5. Select the outstanding purchase invoices to which the contra entry is to be applied.
6. If the total values of the sales and purchase invoices selected are not equal, a dialogue box will appear asking if you want to make a part-contra for the lowest amount.

Confirm

The sales balance does not match the purchases balance - Do you want to make a part-contra for the lowest amount ?

| Yes | No |

7. Click on the Yes button to complete the process.

If you are using the VAT Cash Accounting scheme, you will have to ensure that the transactions which are being treated in this way have the same VAT tax code, otherwise you cannot deal with them using this function.

At the end of each month, certain adjustments to the accounts are made, e.g. to account for accruals, prepayments and depreciation. Carrying out these procedures on a monthly basis enables useful financial reports to be produced for management purposes, e.g.:

- profit and loss account;
- balance sheet;
- trial balance;
- budget and comparables report;
- customer statements and age analysis;
- reports of debtors and creditors.

There are a number of items in a typical month-end procedure:

- check prepayments, accruals and depreciation procedures have been set up and processed;
- check that all recurring entries have been set up and processed;
- check all postings have been made;
- reconcile bank account/s;
- ensure all required reports have been printed;
- ensure all necessary journal postings have been made.

When all these checks have been carried out this is how to run the month-end routine:

Step by step

1. If you are running it on the first day after the end of the month, back up your data files.
2. Click on Settings on the browser toolbar.
   A drop-down menu will appear.
3. Select the Change Program Date option and click.
   The usual message box will appear informing you that you must close all other windows to run this procedure and asking you if you wish to do so.
4. Click on Yes.
   The Change Program Date window will appear.

5. Using the calendar icon at the right of the Default Program Date field, select the last day of the month.
6. Click on OK.
7. Click on the Tools tab on the browser toolbar.
   A drop-down menu will appear.

8. Select the Period End option.
   A second submenu will appear.
9. Select the Month End option and click.
   The Month End window will appear.

10. Tick the boxes for the functions you wish to include in the procedure.
11. Click on OK.
    A Confirm window will appear.

12. Click on Yes.
13. Print out the report if desired.

Consolidation

On the Sage 50 multicompany version, you can consolidate the data for several companies into one set of accounts using the Consolidation option, providing they trade in the same currencies.

All month-end procedures must have been completed before you run the year-end procedure, as these contain the adjustments that affect the final figures, e.g. accruals, prepayments and depreciation. In small firms it may be that these adjustments are only carried out at the end of the year, but as they are so easy to do using Sage 50 there is really no justification in leaving the process until then.

When the last month's procedure is run, refrain from clearing the audit trail. To run the year-end procedure proceed as follows:

Step by step
1. Backup your files with at least two copies.
2. Click on Settings on the browser toolbar.
   A drop-down menu will appear.
3. Select the Change Program Date option and click.
   The Change Program Date window will appear.
4. Using the calendar icon at the right of the Default Program Date field, select the last day of the financial year.
5. Click on OK.
6. Click on the Tools tab on the browser toolbar.
   A drop-down menu will appear.
7. Select the Period-end option and click.
   A submenu will appear.
8. Select the Year End option and click.
   The Year End window will appear.

9. If you wish to update your budgeted figures for nominal accounts and the profit and loss account and also the values for each product record, click on the radio buttons labelled Copy Current Year Actuals in both the Nominal and the Stock sections (which are side by side). This will automatically untick the radio buttons labelled Copy Current Year Budgets as you can't have both.
10. Alter the Year End Journals date if needed using the finder arrow at the right of the relevant box.

11. Click on the appropriate output radio button to save to file or print out the report as required.
12. Click on OK to run the end-of-year procedure.
    A message box will appear asking you to confirm you wish to run the procedure, just as it did in the Month End procedure.
13. Click on Yes.
    A Print box will appear.
14. Click on OK.
    A message will appear asking you to ensure your program date is correct before proceeding.

15. Check the date is right and then click on OK to complete the procedure.

A principal goal of accounting is clarity. The accounts should be simple and easy to read. Paid and reconciled transactions can be removed to avoid clutter. Removing these also frees up disk space. To remove paid and reconciled transactions from the audit trail proceed as follows:

Step by step
1. Back up your data files.
2. Click on the Tools tab on the browser toolbar.
    A drop-down menu will appear.
3. Select the Period End option.
    A submenu will appear as before.
4. Select the Clear Audit Trail option and click.
    The Welcome to the Clear Audit Trail Wizard window will appear.

5. Click on Next.
    Another Clear Audit Trail Wizard window warning of the irreversibility of the process will appear.

6. Click on Next.

   A third Clear Audit Trail Wizard window will appear asking you to enter the date up to which you want to remove transactions.

7. Using the calendar icon at the right of the Date field, enter the date up to which you want to remove transactions from the audit trail.
8. Click on Next.

   A fourth Clear Audit Trail Wizard window will appear confirming you are about to clear the audit trail.

9. Click on the Process button.

   A Clear Audit Trail Finished message box will appear.
10. Click on Finish to complete the procedure.

    A preview of the Clear Audit Trail Report will appear.

11. Save and/or print out the report as desired.

Clearing stock records

To avoid unnecessary clutter, you may want to delete from your current stock records any transactions, the records of which are no longer serving any useful purpose other than as a historical record of a previous accounting year. To delete these proceed as follows:

Step by step

1. Back up your files.
2. Click on the Tools tab on the browser toolbar.
   A drop-down menu will appear.
3. Select the Period End option.
   A submenu will appear.
4. Select the Clear Stock option and click.
   A dialogue box will appear. It is the one that always appears after clicking options on the Period End menu, telling you that you can't run the procedure with other windows open and asking you if you wish the program to close them.
5. Click on Yes.
   A Clear Stock dialogue box will appear warning you that clicking on Yes will have permanent effects, reminding you to back up before doing so and asking you for the date before which all stock transaction records are to be cleared.

6.   Having already backed up your data, enter the date parameter required using the calendar icon at the right of the field and click on Yes.
     A second Clear Stock dialogue box will appear reminding you again of the irreversibility of the process and the necessity of backing up your data.

Confirm	☒
? This option is NOT reversable, Ensure you have taken a backup of your data before proceeding. Are you sure you want to continue ? Yes No	

7.   Click on Yes to complete the process.

Your role may require you to chase debts. If so, Sage 50 provides a useful aid in the diary function. You can use this to record who owes money and by when they promised payment. Sage 50 will remind you on that date to check whether they have, in fact, paid, so that you can contact them straight away and thereby keep on top of credit control. To set up such a reminder system this is what you do:

Step by step
1. Click on the Diary button at the bottom of the navigation bar.
    The Diary window will appear.
2. Open the Tasks pane by clicking on the grey bar at the top of the Customers button and dragging down the navigation bar containing all the buttons to reveal the open Tasks pane.

3. In the Links pane of the diary, click on the Chase Debt option.
    The Chase Debt window will appear.

4. Select the customer you are monitoring.
5. Click on the Communication icon on the modules toolbar.

The Customer Communication History window will appear. If relevant, it will have an Over Credit Limit warning superimposed on it.

217

6.   Click on OK on the warning box, if present, and it will disappear, letting you see all of the communication history behind it.
7.   Click on New to bring up a new record window.

8.   When you call the customer to chase the payment, you can record the duration of the telephone conversation using the Telephone Timer. The Notes section of the Customer Communication History window enables you to record the name of the person to whom you spoke and the result of the communication.
9.   Click on Save.

Any new date on or by which payment has been promised will be highlighted in the calendar and a reminder will be given on that day.

The Chase Debt function can be used to print out a report on which customers are over their credit limit or whose accounts are on hold.

The diary can also be used to manage your cash flow by revealing what accounts are due and payable and, if there is insufficient to pay everybody, suggesting who ought to be paid first and how much they should be paid. This is how to do it:

Step by step

1. In the tasks pane of the Diary window, click on the Manage Payments option.

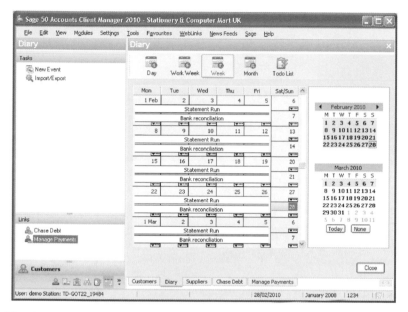

The Manage Payments window will appear.

2. On the browser toolbar, click on the Suggest Payment icon.
    A Suggested Payments window will appear showing which bills are outstanding.

3. Enter the available funds in the relevant box at the top left of the window. If you don't enter a figure the system will tell you what is in the bank current account and ask if it is to assume this amount is to be used.
4. Click on Suggest to see the payments the system recommends.
    The suggested payments will appear in the Payment Amount column.
5. If you agree and wish to make the suggested payments, click on Make Payments.
    The Supplier Payments Bank Accounts window will appear.
6. If there are any disputed accounts among those for which the system is suggesting payment, a message box will appear telling you so. You can then exclude these from consideration for payment by highlighting all the others.

7. When any disputed items have been removed from consideration, re-run the process.
    The Supplier Payments Bank Accounts window will appear again, this time without the disputed items warning.

8. If you are happy to make the payments, click on Pay in Full.
   The Payment column on the first line will be automatically filled in with the amount paid and the cursor will move to the next line.

9. Click on Pay in Full again and so on until the cursor has gone through the complete suggested payments list.
10. Click on Save.
11. Click on Close.

Partnership accounts differ from sole proprietor accounts in the following ways.

- Profit-sharing arrangements will differ from one partnership to another depending on what was agreed when the partnership was set up.
- Changes in shares of goodwill and profits may have to be dealt with in the accounts.
- Separate capital accounts are needed for each partner.
- A profit and loss appropriation account is normally included.

A full explanation of partnerships is provided in my other book *Mastering Book-Keeping* 9th edition, so I will not repeat it here. I will just elaborate on each of the bullet points listed above to the extent that it is necessary and relevant to the task of doing the accounts using Sage 50.

Financial arrangements in partnerships

There are endless types of financial arrangement in partnerships. For example, profits may be shared in proportion to capital invested, or interest may be paid on capital before any residual net profit is shared equally, regardless of capital. Similarly, the partners may agree that interest will be charged on all individual drawings against capital. At the outset, they may decide that each working partner will receive a fixed salary.

Where there is no written partnership agreement, the Partnership Act 1890 (section 24) states that no interest is to be allowed on capital except where provided in excess of any agreement (in which case 5% would be allowed). No interest is to be charged on drawings, no partner will be entitled to a salary, and each will share the profits equally.

Changes in share of goodwill and profit-sharing arrangements

Changes in share of goodwill and profit-sharing arrangements will occur when a new partner joins, when the profit-sharing percentages change because one partner reduces their hours or when a partner retires or dies. These changes are calculated and recorded exactly the same, whether you are using a manual accounting method or a computerised method. The entries are made in the journal in both cases. The only difference is that when you are using a computerised system you don't have to post to the ledger; the system does this automatically.

Separate capital accounts

Since the ownership of the business is shared, it stands to reason that there must be not one but several capital accounts.

The appropriation account

Partnership accounts are normally accompanied by an appropriation account. This is a statement showing how the net profit of the partnership is to be distributed between the partners. It is not needed for the accounts of a sole proprietor, because all the net profit goes to the one proprietor's capital account.

If a partner has drawn money from the business (other than salary), he/she may have to pay interest on it, according to arrangements between the parties. Any such interest payment will have to he deducted from any interest due to them on their capital. Such transactions are shown in the appropriation account.

If a partner has lent money to the partnership, however, this is a very different thing. Any interest payable to that partner would be an expense to the business, not an appropriation of profit. Its proper place would be in the profit and loss account.

After deducting net liabilities of partners (interest on drawings minus interest on capital), we have to show how the rest of the profit will be shared out. We will show an equal split, or an unequal one, depending on the profit-sharing arrangements between the partners.

What you need:

- details of interest rate on capital due to partners;
- details of interest rate payable by partners on drawings;
- details of partners' capitals;
- details of partners' drawings;
- details of partners' salaries and/or fees;
- details of profit-sharing arrangements.

Preparation

Work out the interest on capital, if any, due to each partner. Remember to apply the correct percentage interest rate. Work out the interest payable, if any, by each partner on their drawings, again applying the correct percentage interest rate.

It is easy enough to set up separate capital accounts for each partner. There are plenty of NL codes available within the region reserved for capital accounts – 99 in fact, from code 3000 to 3099.

The appropriation account is not a part of the process in which the net profit of the partnership is calculated. It only explains how it is going to be shared out. Despite the fact that it has traditionally been called an account, all it really needs to be is a statement or report. Sage 50 doesn't have a ready report format for this, but it is an easy matter to simply type the report from scratch.

Once the details of the profit-sharing are calculated, the relevant amounts will be credited to the partners' capital accounts and debited to the profit and loss account by means of journal entries before the balance sheet is compiled. The process of making journal entries is fully dealt with in Chapter 13, so it would be superfluous to repeat it here. The reader should simply refer back. However, an example of the details of the entries that may need to be made are given below.

Journal

Smith Interest on capital account		2,500
Smith Interest on drawings account	500	
Smith Salary account		40,000
Smith Share of profits 50% account		8,000
Jones Interest on capital account		2,100
Jones Interest on drawings account	100	
Jones Salary account		40,000
Jones Share of profits 50% account		8,000
Profit and loss appropriation account	100,000	
	100,600	100,600

An example of journalising these facts using manual methods is given above and the example below shows how they would be journalised using the Sage 50 computerised method.

New partner joining

When a new partner is admitted to a partnership, their acquisition of a share in the existing value of goodwill means that other partners will lose. Those partners who gain should be charged the amount of their gain and those who lose should he compensated for their loss.

Paying for the goodwill acquired

There are a number of ways in which a new partner can pay for their share of goodwill and the accounting processes differ with each. A full explanation of each of these ways is provided in my other book *Mastering Book-Keeping* 9th edition and so they will not be repeated here. Readers who wish to explore them should refer to that book. The main purpose of this book is to show how the processes described in the latter book are carried out using computerised methodology rather than manual methods, and the essential skills that need to be mastered are the same whichever of the methods are chosen. The method I will demonstrate here is that of opening a goodwill account and capitalising the existing goodwill shares, i.e. debit the goodwill account with the total value of the goodwill and post the equivalent value to the credit of the existing partners' capital accounts in the proportions of their existing profit-sharing arrangements.

The goodwill account can then be credited with the total amount to close it down, with the debit entries being posted in equal proportions to all the partners' capital accounts, including the new partner.

This is how you would make the journal entries using Sage 50:

N/C	Name	Dept	Details	T/C	Debit	Credit
0012	Goodwill	0		T9	45000.00	0.00
3031	Capital Account Able	0		T9	0.00	15000.00
3032	Capital Account Bryce	0		T9	0.00	15000.00
3033	Capital Account Collins	0		T9	0.00	15000.00
3031	Capital Account Able	0		T9	11250.00	0.00
3032	Capital Account Bryce	0		T9	11250.00	0.00
3033	Capital Account Collins	0		T9	11250.00	0.00
3034	Capital Account Dean	0		T9	11250.00	0.00
0012	Goodwill	0		T9	0.00	45000.00
					0.00	0.00

Reference: Capital Adjustment Posting Date: 22/03/2010 Balance: 0.00

Total: 90000.00 90000.00

Reverse Journals ☐ Reversing Date 22/03/2010

Save Discard Memorise Recall Print List Close

Changes in profit-sharing ratios for other reasons

The admission of a new partner is not the only circumstance in which profit-sharing ratios may change. They may change because a partner ceases to work full-time or his/her skills cease to be as important as those of the other partners. If a partner agrees to take a smaller percentage of profits, he/she deserves to be compensated for what they have given up. The financial adjustments can be made by the same methods as for changes in profit-sharing as a result of a new partner joining.

Death or retirement of a partner

If a partner dies or retires from the partnership, goodwill has to be accounted for so that the retiring partner, or their estate, if deceased, can be paid a fair value for their share in the business. The process is essentially the same as for a joining partner and once the adjustments to the capitals have been made the goodwill can he written off if desired and the account closed down.

Example

Suppose Bryce is retiring from the partnership of Able, Bryce, Collins and Dean. The value of goodwill has been agreed as £48,000.

The example below shows the journal entries that would properly account for his retirement to ensure he received the full value of his share of the partnership, including the goodwill element.

The example shows the asset of goodwill being created for the purpose of valuing his share and then being written off immediately afterwards.

N/C	Name	Dept	Details	T/C	Debit	Credit
0012	Goodwill	0		T9	48000.00	0.00
3031	Capital Account Able	0		T9	0.00	12000.00
3032	Capital Account Bryce	0		T9	0.00	12000.00
3033	Capital Account Collins	0		T9	0.00	12000.00
3034	Capital Account Dean	0		T9	0.00	12000.00
3031	Capital Account Able	0		T9	16000.00	0.00
3033	Capital Account Collins	0		T9	16000.00	0.00
3034	Capital Account Dean	0		T9	16000.00	0.00
0012	Goodwill	0		T9	0.00	48000.00

Nominal Ledger Journals

Reference: Capital Adjstmnts   Posting Date: 22/03/2010   Balance: 0.00

96000.00   96000.00

Reverse Journals ☐   Reversing Date 22/03/2010

Save   Discard   Memorise   Recall   Print List   Close

46   Accounts of limited companies

The form and extent of the published accounts of limited companies are governed by the Companies Act 1985. They are quite complex and are outside the scope of this book. For a full treatment of companies and their accounts, published and internal, readers should refer to my other book *Mastering Book-Keeping* 9th edition.

This book deals with company accounts up to internal accounts stage, before they reach the publication stage. There are no such legal requirements for these.

Debentures

Some of the net assets of a company may be financed by debentures. These are loans and interest has to be paid on them. Since debentures have to be repaid, we have to show them as liabilities in the balance sheet.

When funds are loaned to the company in return for a debenture (which is a legal charge on assets to the value of the loan) the book entries are made via the journal. The debit entry is made to the bank account, or a fixed asset account if that is the form in which the loan was given to the company. The credit entry is made to the creditor who advanced the funding. Chapter 13 explains how to journalise things, so the process will not be repeated here.

Interest has to be paid on the loan and this can be set up as a recurring journal entry, with the credit entry being posted to the account of the financier who advanced the funding and the debit entry being posted to the loan note interest account. Setting up recurring entries is explained in Chapter 13.

Dealing with corporation tax in the final accounts

It is current orthodox practice to account for corporation tax in the profit and loss account, or income statement as it is increasingly being called. When all the expenses have been deducted from the gross profit, you arrive at a figure of profit before taxation. The computed figure for taxation is then deducted from this to give a figure for profit for the year after taxation. This is presented in the Statement of Changes in Equity.

Retained profits

In the accounts of sole proprietors and partnerships the profit and loss account is closed each year by transferring any balance to the capital account. In the case of limited companies, any undistributed profits stay on the profit and loss account as reserves along with undistributed profits for all previous periods. A company is allowed to retain part of the profits to finance growth. How much is up to the directors. The remainder will be shared between the shareholders in dividends. There will, therefore, be an opening balance on the profit and loss account at the start of each year.

However, to avoid showing a high profit and loss account balance, a company will often transfer some of it to a general reserve account. This is a simple matter of journalising. These reserves, along with paid-up shares, are called shareholders' funds because they are owned by the shareholders.

Share capital

The capital account has its own special treatment in limited company accounts. The capital of limited companies is divided into shares. A share in the capital of the company entitles the shareholder to a share of the profits of the company, just as a partner owning capital in a firm is entitled to profits.

Ordinary and preference shares

Limited companies can have different kinds of shares with different kinds of entitlements attached to them, e.g. ordinary shares and preference shares.

Preference shares receive a fixed rate of dividend (profit share), provided sufficient profit has been made. For example, it might be 10% of the original value of the preference shares.

Ordinary shares have no such limit on their dividend, which can be as high as the profits allow. However, they come second in the queue, so to speak, if the profit is too little to pay dividends to both the preference and ordinary shareholders.

Unless otherwise stated in the company's memorandum of association, preference shares are cumulative. In other words, any arrears of dividend can be carried forward to future years until profits are available to pay them.

Since the Companies Act 1985, a company is allowed to issue redeemable shares, preference and ordinary. These are shares that the company can redeem (buy back) from the shareholder at their request.

When these shares are purchased the records are made by journalising with the debit entry going to the bank and the credit entry going to the share capital accounts.

Dealing with dividends

Dividends on preference shares and ordinary shares should be shown only as a note on the profit and loss account, as it is not actually an expense but rather a distribution of profit. The place where its effect on the finances of the company is shown is in the Statement of Changes in Equity, as it represents some equity leaving the company. However, even there it is important to show only those dividends that have actually been paid and which, therefore, represent funds that have actually left the company.

To calculate the dividends that are to be paid out for each class (preference and ordinary) multiply the number of shares that have been issued by the percentage dividend that is being paid on them. The percentage will be a matter for the directors to decide.

Balance sheets of limited companies

In the balance sheet of a limited company creditors have to be analysed into those falling due for payment within a year and those falling due in more than a year (e.g. long-term loans).

THE INSTITUTE
OF CERTIFIED
BOOKKEEPERS

THE LEVEL II CERTIFICATE IN
COMPUTERISED BOOKKEEPING
FINAL ASSIGNMENT

This final assignment should be completed and returned to the Institute by the date at the bottom of this page. You are advised to obtain proof of posting from The Royal Mail.

Required

Complete the various tasks and send all the required print outs to the Institute at the address below. Ensure that you include your name and enrolment number on each section.

Deadline Date.....................................

(Smart Computers)

The Institute of Certified Bookkeepers
Wolverton Park, Wolverton, Hampshire RG26 5RU

Tel: 0845 060 2345 www.bookkeepers.org.uk

Assessment Criteria

This piece of work will be graded at Distinction, Merit, Pass or Fail.

Pass   To gain a Pass, candidates must achieve between 85-89%, with a minimum of 43 marks on tasks 1-4

Merit   To gain a Merit, candidates must achieve between 90-94% with a minimum of 43 marks on tasks 1-4

Distinction To gain a Distinction, candidates must achieve between 95-100%

Fail   Candidates who achieve less than 85% of the total marks will be failed.

Any error will lead to a reduction in total marks. An error could include posting to the wrong nominal code, VAT being incorrectly coded, incorrect depreciation, accounts coded to the wrong section of the chart of accounts etc.

Note – it is important that you keep your own back-up of your data until you are informed that you have successfully completed this assignment.

Extra Information regarding Rebuilding the Data

You will need to rebuild the files in your system before you can attempt this assignment, as you must remove all data from previous work.

To do, firstly ensure that your files are safely backed-up.

Next you must select the File, Maintenance, Rebuild option. and to avoid problems with the print outs, you should ensure that the following areas remain ticked. Your version of Sage may not replicate the exact screenshot below, but the same principle applies.

If requested, give the year start date as 1 June 2003

Once you have completed this process, you should use the File, Restore option to load the file from the CD.

Important

It is important to select the correct file from the list of files contained on the CD provided, if you are using Sage then you will need to select either Sageback v8 or Sageback v12, depending on the version of Sage you are using, do not select the opening balances file, which is in PDF format, as this may conflict with your Sage program.

You can then complete the tasks in the assignment. Remember to take a final back up at the end of the assignment and keep it safe until you have received your results.

Additional information on the tasks:

Petty Cash

The data file should contain an opening balance in the petty cash account of £150. If it does not, to set up the petty cash account, use the Bank, Transfer option and transfer £150 from the current bank account into the petty cash account as follows and click the save button (see diagram below but change the amount to £150). Note, when using the transfer method, enter the cheque number into the reference box to ensure that you can find this when carrying out the bank reconciliation process later.

You should then process the transactions as per a normal bank payment and at the end of each week, transfer a further amount from the bank account into the petty cash account to restore the balance back to £150.

Bank Reconciliation

To reconcile the bank account, select the Bank, Reconcile option. A list of receipts and payments will appear. Enter the closing bank balance figure from the statement in the appropriate place, click on those transactions that appear in the bank statement to highlight them, and when all have been highlighted you should have a reconciled balance appear at the bottom. Click on the save button to save the changes and then proceed to produce the required report.

Please note that the help menu will assist you with this procedure

To write off the bad debt, issue a credit note to the customer for the full amount, (remember to use VAT code T9 and not T1 in accordance with Customs and Excise Regulations) using the bad debts account as the nominal ledger code. Then, in the bank, customer window and select the customer. This will show all the outstanding invoices and the credit note you have just entered. Click on each line in turn and click the pay in full button. Once all the transactions have been selected you will have made a "dummy" bank payment which will clear out the account and leave the balance in the bad debts account. This will then be transferred to the profit and loss account when the final accounts are produced.

ICB – Level II Final Assignment

Smart Computer Solutions Ltd
Kennedy Industrial Estate
Edinburgh
Scotland
WW5 9FG

Scenario

You work as a bookkeeper for Smart Computer Solutions Ltd., a supplier of computer equipment and stationery for various companies within the Edinburgh areas. The business is registered for value added tax and up to the close of business at the end of this year did all of its accounting using hand written ledgers.

Business is expanding and it is felt that the present system will not cope with the extra paperwork that will be produced. The closing balances have been transferred into a computerised accounts package.

With this assignment is a data disk which contains the accounts you require to complete this assignment. Brought forward balances from the previous year have already been calculated and entered.

This assignment contains a number of tasks which take the form of a set of exercises which require you to either input data to the accounting system or extract information from the accounting system as reports.

Instructions to candidates

You are required to complete the tasks as listed below

Task	Activity	Marks
1	Add new customer and supplier details to the sales ledger	2
2	Input sales invoices and credit notes to the ledger	20
3	Input purchase invoices and credit notes to the ledger	18
4	Input cheques received and paid to the appropriate ledgers	10
5	Input Petty cash paid and monies received	14
6	Deal with writing off of a bad debt in the appropriate ledgers	3
7	Produce a bank reconciliation statement	7
8	Produce a journal for wages and salaries and post to the ledger	8
9	Produce a journal for depreciation and post to the ledger	8
10	Produce the journal entry for closing stock, a trial balance, trading profit and loss account and a balance sheet.	10

Task 1 - New customer and supplier names and addresses

Required

i. Enter the following information for new customers into your accounts package

Company	Account number
Glen Steels Ltd	GL001
Boydston Way	
Hawick	
Scotland	
SC3 9TL	
Company	**Account number**
Hart Instruments	HI001
Iona Place	
Livingstone	
Scotland	
SC4 8MC	

ii. Enter the following information for new suppliers into your accounts package

Company	Account number
Computers Direct	CD001
Carrick Drive	
Irvine	
Scotland	
SC4 5ER	
Company	**Account number**
Tinie Computers	TC001
Crosshouse Road	
Kilmarnock	
Scotland	
SC5 9DF	
Company	**Account number**
Tyme Computers	TC002
Fenwick Road	
Kilmarnock	
Scotland	
SC12 4RT	

iii. Print out the complete customers' name and address list
iv. Print out the complete suppliers' name and address list

Task 2 – Customers' invoices and credit notes for the month of June

Required:

i. You are required to post the following invoices to the customer's ledger (instruction manuals and consumables such as cartridges are to be coded to computer stationery, whilst cables are to be posted to computer hardware)

Company	Description	Nominal Code	Invoice Number	Date	Goods Inc Vat
Glen Steels	Desktop PC		6576	03/00/03	450.00
	Printer				90.00
Hart Instruments	Computer Ink Cartridge		6574	01/06/03	35.00
	Copier/laser paper A4				125.30
Ledra Steels	Invoice sets A4		6575	02/06/03	450.00
	Statements		6578	05/06/03	282.30
	Remittance slips		6580	07/06/03	192.70
Vector Int Ltd	Desktop printer		6585	09/06/03	90.00
	Printer cables				25.00
James Stuart Ltd	Desktop laser printer		6590	15/06/03	500.00
	Printer cables				50.00
Barry Blair & Co	Ink cartridges		6595	19/06/03	38.00
	Screen wipes				12.70
Fastmet plc	Word 2003 software		6600	24/06/03	450.00
	Instruction manual		6602	29/06/03	35.60
Franklin Steels Plc	Macrosoft Pro Office Suite		6605	29/06/03	1,250.00
Forthbridge Metals	Computer stationery		6609	30/06/03	325.75
	Printer Cables		6610	30/06/03	60.00

ii. You are required to post the following credit notes to the customers ledger

Company	Description	Nominal code	Cr Note Number	Date	Goods Inc Vat
Franklin Steels	Macrosoft Pro Office Suite		Cr6606	29/06/03	1,250.00
Forthbridge Metals	Computer stationery		Cr6611	30/06/03	325.75

iii. Print out a detailed customer activity report
iv. Print out an aged debtor's analysis (summary)

Task 3 – Suppliers' invoices for the month of June

Required:

i. Post the following invoices to the suppliers ledger

Company	Description	Invoice Number	Date	Goods	Vat	Total
Tyme	Desktop computers	2835	01/06/03	350.00	61.25	411.25
Computers	Stationery to order	2846	03/06/03	112.00	19.60	131.60
Tinie	Ink cartridges	6028	06/06/03	135.80	23.77	159.57
Computers	Stationery pack	6029	09/06/03	91.35	15.99	107.34
Computers	Computers to order	8972	09/06/03	225.00	39.38	264.38
Direct	Invo desktop printers	8992	15/06/03	180.00	31.50	211.50
	Computer cables	9123	29/06/03	75.00	13.12	88.12
Jedo Estates	Rent of unit for June	R6712	30/06/03	346.20	60.59	406.79
Icon Advertising	Advert in Computers Weekly	2296	12/06/03	75.00	13.12	88.12
Silverdale	Macrosoft Pro Software	3297	19/06/03	450.00	78.75	528.75
Computers	Copier/laser paper A4	4621	25/06/03	149.30	26.13	175.43
Computer Stationery	Digicards A4	4308	10/06/03	290.00	50.75	340.75
Level 9	Invoice sets	8829	21/06/03	136.91	23.96	160.87
Computer Stationery	Statements	9136	29/06/03	140.38	24.57	164.95
Saturn garage	Petrol and oil for June	9385	29/06/03	295.60	51.73	347.33
Johnstone & Partners Chartered Accountants	Audit fees for 2002/2003	3136	27/06/03	500.00	87.50	587.50

ii. Post the following credit notes to the suppliers ledger

Company	Description	Credit Note No	Date	Goods	Vat	Total
Silverdale Computers	Macrosoftware	Cr78	29/06/03	100.00	17.50	117.50
Level 9 Computer Stationery	Stationery	Cr 75	21/06/03	35.00	6.12	41.12

iii. Print out a detailed supplier activity report
iv. Print out an aged creditors analysis (summary)

Task 4 - Cheques received and paid out by Smart Computers

Required:

i.   Post the following cheques to the customers ledger

Customer	Account number	Inv No	Value
Glen Steels 17 June 2003	GL001	6576	450.00
Ledra Steels 19 June 2003	LS001	6578	282.30
James Stuart 24 June 2003	JS001	6572	528.75
Barry Blair 25 June 2003	BB001	6573	264.38
Forthbridge Metals 29 June 2003	FM001	6568	205.92

ii.   Post the following cheques paid to the suppliers ledger

Customer	Account number	Cheque No	Value
Tyme Computers 5 June 2003		32153	411.25
Icon Advertising Agency 11 June 2003		32155	468.21
Computer stationery 22 June 2003		32158	544.40
Saturn Garage 27 June 2003		32159	229.42
Johnstone & Partners 30 June 2003		32160	587.50

iii.   Print out a list of bank receipts and payments

Task 5 - Petty Cash Summary for the Month of June

Required:

i. Post the following petty cash payments and receipts to the ledger. The company uses the imprest system for petty cash and starts each week with £150. 00. (At the end of each week, the balance on the petty cash account is made up by transferring funds from the bank account.)

Date	Description	Voucher No	Nominal code	£	
3 June	Bought postage stamps	5421		4.65	
4 June	Bought petrol	5422		25.00	inc VAT *
5 June	Bought tea, coffee	5423		3.50	
8 June	Paid window cleaner	5424		35.00	
Weekly total (ch no 32154)					
Date	Description	Voucher No	Nominal code	£	
10 June	Bought postage stamps	5425		5.52	
11 June	Bought rail ticket for Sales Director	5426		17.56	
12 June	Bought envelopes	5427		14.95	*inc VAT
13 June	Paid office cleaner	5428		45.00	
14 June	Bought A4 writing pads	5429		11.65	inc VAT*
Weekly total (ch no 32156)					
Date	Description	Voucher No	Nominal code	£	
16 June	Paid window cleaner	5430		35.00	
17 June	Bought postage stamps	5431		5.25	
18 June	Paid office cleaner	5432		45.00	
19 June	Bought petrol	5433		25.01	inc VAT*
20 June	Flowers for reception area	5434		9.45	inc VAT*
Weekly total (ch no 32157)					
Date	Description	Voucher No	Nominal code	£	
24 June	Paid car hire charge	5435		38.52	*inc VAT
25 June	Purchased A4 writing pad	5436		3.06	*inc VAT
26 June	Bought tea, coffee, milk, sugar	5437		5.63	
26 June	Bought 12 HB pencils	5438		4.99	*inc VAT
27June	Paid office cleaner	5439		45.00	
27 June	Paid parcel post "Red Star"	5440		12.36	inc VAT*
Weekly total (ch no 32161)					

* VAT at the rate of 17.5 %

ii. Print out a copy of the petty cash account receipts and payments

Task 6 – Producing a statement and writing off a bad debt

You have received the following letter, which requires your attention.

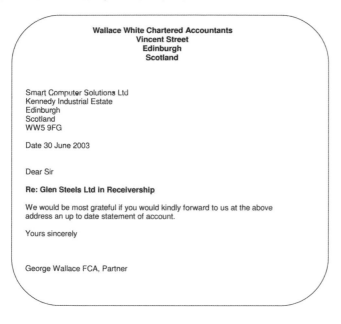

Wallace White Chartered Accountants
Vincent Street
Edinburgh
Scotland

Smart Computer Solutions Ltd
Kennedy Industrial Estate
Edinburgh
Scotland
WW5 9FG

Date 30 June 2003

Dear Sir

Re: Glen Steels Ltd in Receivership

We would be most grateful if you would kindly forward to us at the above address an up to date statement of account.

Yours sincerely

George Wallace FCA, Partner

Required:

i.   Print out a statement of account for Glen Steels Ltd, showing the outstanding balance on 30 June.

ii. Make the appropriate journal entries to write off the outstanding balance and print out the appropriate entries in the audit trail

iii. Print out a copy of the detailed customer activity for Glen Steels Ltd to show the zero balance.

Task 7 – Bank Reconciliation Statement

The following bank statement has been received

The Scottish Bank plc
Birkenhall House
Stuart Street
Edinburgh

Account of Smart Computer Solutions Ltd **Statement Date:** 30 June 2003
Account Number 90563244 **Statement No:** 105
Sort Code 22-33-44

Date	Details	Debits	Credits	Balance
2003				
1 June	Brought forward			4000.00
9 June	Cheque 32153	411.25		
11 June	Cheque 32154	68.15		
	Cheque 32156	94.68		3425.92
19 June	Sundry receipt		732.30	
20 June	Cheque 32157	119.71		4038.51
27 June	Sundry receipt		528.75	4567.26

Required:

i.   Complete a bank reconciliation procedure as at 30 June 2003
ii. Print out a list of unreconciled payments and receipts as at 30 June 2003

Task 8 - Wages and Salaries

Required:

i.   Set up the following accounts into the appropriate areas in your nominal ledger for voluntary donations that are deducted from wages and salaries and are due to be sent to the appropriate organisation:

      1. National Savings
      2. Oxfam

ii. Enter the following wages and salaries for the Month of June using the journal

	Dr entry	Cr entry	
Staff salaries	3580.00		
Tax deductions		1759.00	
Employee NICs owed to National Insurance		456.00	
National Savings		75.00	voluntary deduction
Oxfam		85.00	voluntary deduction
Net pay		1205.00	
Employer NICs	198.00		
Employer NICs owed to National Insurance		198.00	

iii. Print out a copy of the audit trail entries for the above transactions

Task 9 – Depreciation

Mr Twaite, the chief accountant has prepared the following information for inclusion into the accounts for the month of June

Depreciation of fixed assets

Plant and machinery	50.00	Office equipment	150.00
Furniture and fixtures	20.00	Motor vehicles	600.00

Required:

i.   Enter the relevant figures for the depreciation of fixed assets
ii. Print out the relevant audit trail entries for these transactions

Task 10 - Entering closing stock and producing final accounts

Required:

i.   Please enter the closing stock figure: Closing stock as at 30 June £6,500.00
ii. Produce the following reports:

- VAT return for the month of June 2003
- Trial Balance report at the 30 June 2003
- Trading Profit and Loss Account for the month ending 30 June 2003
- Balance Sheet as at the close of business on 30 June 2003

This is the end of this final assignment

I/D 109

Qualification
LEVEL 1 Certificate in Computerised Book-keeping
(Qualification Accreditation No: **500/3160/0**)

Examination
Single Unit: Basics of business record keeping using Accounting software

JUNE 2009

QUESTION PAPER

Time Allowed: 1 hour 30 minutes

Suite 30, 40 Churchill Square, Kings Hill, West Malling, Kent ME19 4YU
Tel: 0844 330 3527, Fax: 0844 330 3514, email:education@iab.org.uk

IAB Level 1 I/D 109 Question Paper

INTERNATIONAL ASSOCIATION OF BOOK-KEEPERS

QUALIFICATION TITLE:
IAB LEVEL 1 CERTIFICATE IN COMPUTERISED BOOK-KEEPING

Unit Title:
Basics of business record keeping using Accounting software

General Information and Instructions

1   You must enter your **Candidate Number, Student Number, Name of Centre, Date of Examination** and **Software used** on the front cover provided.

2   Time Allowed: ONE HOUR AND THIRTY MINUTES.

3   Printing may be carried out after completion of the one hour and thirty minutes examination time.

4   All written answers should be in pen or word processed.

5   The use of silent non-programmable calculators is permitted.

6   NOTE - This Question Booklet has information and data printed on both sides of the pages.

7   The practical data input and printing of reports account for 90 marks, the remaining 10 marks cover Tasks 11 - 13.

8   Answers to Tasks 11 - 13 and the printouts taken at Task 14 should be firmly stapled into the Answer Booklet provided.

SCENARIO

Amy Millar started business on 1st June 2009, trading as Bride's Made. The business sells wedding dresses and children's bridesmaid dresses.

SALES

Sales are recorded in two accounts:-

-   One for sales of wedding dresses
-   A second account for sales of bridesmaid dresses.

PURCHASES

There are two Purchase accounts:-

-   One for the purchase of wedding dresses
-   A second to reflect the purchase of bridesmaid dresses.

Note: The Account numbers given throughout this paper are appropriate to Sage Accounting software – if you are using a different package, use appropriate numbers/names and ensure you have indicated on the cover page the name of the software you have used.

You have one hour and thirty minutes to complete the following tasks (with the exception of printing reports, which may be carried out after completion of the one hour and thirty minutes):

Task 1

a) Set the financial year start date as June 2009 and set the program date as 30th June 2009.

b) Enter the name of the business as:

    'Bride's Made'. (This should be followed by your candidate number)

c) Enter Bride's Made address as:

    5 Wychwood Village
    Weston
    Cheshire
    CW2 5FH

Note: this paper has been produced using 17.5% as the standard rate of VAT.

Task 2

Set up the following accounts in the nominal ledger.

ACCOUNT NUMBER	DESCRIPTION
3000	Capital
3001	Drawings
4000	Sales – Wedding Dresses
4001	Sales – Bridesmaid Dresses
5000	Purchases – Wedding Dresses
5001	Purchases – Bridesmaid Dresses
5003	Packaging – Tissue Paper
7000	Wages
7505	Magazines
8205	Refreshments

Task 3

Set up the following Supplier account details.

A/C REFERENCE	SUPPLIER	ADDRESS
GALLIERS	Galliers Wedding Dresses	10 Walnut Street Hough Crewe CW2 5JT
SOPHIES	Sophie's Bridal Gowns	The Village Green Audlem Cheshire CW5 7GF
WEDDING	Wedding Belles	15 Alkington Hall Barns Nantwich Cheshire CW1 5DS

245

Task 4

Enter the following purchase invoices onto the system. The invoice number should be used as the reference.

<table>
<tr><td colspan="5" align="center">Galliers Wedding Dresses
10 Walnut Street
Hough
Crewe
CW2 5JT</td></tr>
<tr><td colspan="2">Bride's Made
5 Wychwood Village
Weston
Cheshire
CW2 5FH</td><td colspan="3" align="center">INVOICE</td></tr>
<tr><td colspan="2">Invoice Date: 1st June 2009</td><td colspan="3" align="right">Invoice No: 502</td></tr>
</table>

Details	Unit Price £	VAT Rate	£
10 Wedding Dresses – various sizes	250.00	17.5%	2500.00
10 Wedding Dresses – Designer	700.00	17.5%	7000.00
	Sub Total		9500.00
	VAT @ 17.5%		1662.50
	Invoice Total		11162.50

Coding | Supplier A/C | GALLIERS
NominalA/C | 5000

<table>
<tr><td colspan="4" align="center">Sophie's Bridal Gowns
The Village Green
Audlem
Cheshire
CW5 7GF</td></tr>
<tr><td colspan="2">Bride's Made
5 Wychwood Village
Weston
Cheshire
CW2 5FH</td><td colspan="2" align="center">Invoice</td></tr>
<tr><td colspan="2">Invoice Date: 4th June 2009</td><td colspan="2" align="center">Invoice No: S150</td></tr>
</table>

Details		Unit Price £	£
25 Bridesmaid Dresses – Children's		200.00	5000.00
	Sub Total		5000.00
	VAT zero rated		
	Invoice Total		5000.00

Coding | Supplier A/C | SOPHIES
Nominal A/C | 5001

Wedding Belles		
15 Alkington Hall Barns		
Nantwich		
Cheshire		
CW1 5DS		

Bride's Made		
5 Wychwood Village	Invoice	
Weston		
Cheshire		
CW2 5FH		

Invoice Date: 6th June 2009		Invoice No: W025	
Details		Unit Price £	£
15 Wedding Dresses – American Ivory		550.00	8250.00
		Sub Total	8250.00
		VAT @ 17.5%	1443.75
		Invoice Total	9693.75

Coding	Supplier A/C	WEDDING
	Nominal A/C	5000

Galliers Wedding Dresses		
10 Walnut Street		
Hough		
Crewe		
CW2 5JT		

Bride's Made		
5 Wychwood Village	Invoice	
Weston		
Cheshire		
CW2 5FH		

Invoice Date: 7th June 2009		Invoice No: 647	
Details		Unit Price £	£
20 Wedding Dresses – White		335.00	6700.00
10 Wedding Dresses – Cream		335.00	3350.00
		Sub Total	10050.00
		VAT @ 17.5%	1758.75
		Invoice Total	11808.75

Coding	Supplier A/C	GALLIERS
	Nominal A/C	5000

247

<table>
<tbody>
<tr><td colspan="3" align="center">**Sophie's Bridal Gowns**
The Village Green
Audlem
Cheshire
CW5 7GF</td></tr>
</tbody>
</table>

Bride's Made 5 Wychwood Village Weston Cheshire CW2 5FH	Invoice	
Invoice Date: 8th June 2009	Invoice No: S198	

Details	Unit Price £	£
5 Wedding Dresses	445.00	2225.00
	Sub Total	2225.00
	VAT @ 17.5%	389.38
	Invoice Total	2614.38

Coding | Supplier A/C | SOPHIES
Nominal A/C | 5000

Task 5

Enter the following purchase credit note onto the system. The credit note number should be used as the reference.

<table>
<tbody>
<tr><td colspan="3" align="center">**Wedding Belles**
15 Alkington Hall Barns
Nantwich
Cheshire
CW1 5DS</td></tr>
</tbody>
</table>

Bride's Made 5 Wychwood Village Weston Cheshire CW2 5FH	CREDIT NOTE	
Credit Note Date: 10th June 2009	Credit Note No: CR601	

Details	Unit Price £	£
2 Damaged Wedding Dresses	550.00	1100.00
	Sub Total	1100.00
	VAT @ 17.5%	192.50
	Credit Note Total	1292.50

Coding | Supplier A/C | WEDDING
Nominal A/C | 5000

Task 6

Set up the following Customer account details.

A/C Reference	CUSTOMER	ADDRESS
JOSEPH	Josephine's Brides	15 High Street Audlem Cheshire CW4 8HG
ISOBEL	Isobella's	7 The Barns Nantwich Cheshire CW1 7DF

Task 7

Enter the following customer invoices. The invoice number should be used as the reference.

Bride's Made 5 Wychwood Village Weston Cheshire CW2 5FH	DATE: 8TH JUNE 2009 INVOICE REF: B001

DATE: 8TH JUNE 2009
INVOICE REF: B001

TO   Josephine's Brides
     15 High Street
     Audlem
     Cheshire
     CW4 8HG

INVOICE

Qty	Description	Unit price	Line total
5	Wedding Dresses	320.00	1600.00
5	Wedding Dresses – Designer	975.00	4875.00
		SUBTOTAL	6475.00
		VAT @ 17.5%	1133.13
		TOTAL	7608.13

CODING	Customer A/C	JOSEPH
	Nominal A/C	4000

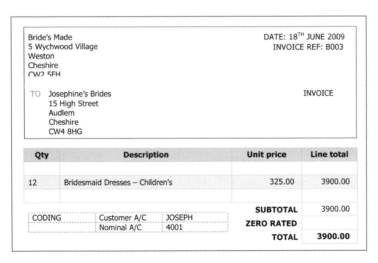

Bride's Made
5 Wychwood Village
Weston
Cheshire
CW2 5FH

DATE: 12TH JUNE 2009
INVOICE REF: B002

TO   Isobella's
      7 The Barns
      Nantwich
      Cheshire
      CW1 7DF

INVOICE

Qty	Description	Unit price	Line total
8	Wedding Dresses – American Ivory	750.00	6000.00
5	Wedding Dresses – White	495.00	2475.00
2	Wedding Dresses – Cream	495.00	990.00
		SUBTOTAL	9465.00
		VAT @ 17.5%	1656.38
		TOTAL	**11121.38**

CODING   Customer A/C   ISOBEL
          Nominal A/C   4000

Bride's Made
5 Wychwood Village
Weston
Cheshire
CW2 5FH

DATE: 18TH JUNE 2009
INVOICE REF: B003

TO   Josephine's Brides
      15 High Street
      Audlem
      Cheshire
      CW4 8HG

INVOICE

Qty	Description	Unit price	Line total
12	Bridesmaid Dresses – Children's	325.00	3900.00
		SUBTOTAL	3900.00
		ZERO RATED	
		TOTAL	**3900.00**

CODING   Customer A/C   JOSEPH
          Nominal A/C   4001

250

Task 8

Amy has set up a Standing Order to pay business telephone costs (Nominal code 7502). It is to be paid on the 10th of each month, starting in June 2009 and is £105 per month (£89.36 plus £15.64 VAT). Set this up as a Recurring Entry with the reference S/O1 and post it for June.

Task 9

Enter the following transactions for the month of June. Ensure each one has a unique reference number.

Date	Reference	Account	Details
1st June	BR1	3000	Amy paid £30,000.00 into the business bank account as her capital. (Tax code T9)
2nd June	001		Amy drew cheque 001 for £175.00 for petty cash.
3rd June	PC1	5003	Paid £52.00 including VAT from petty cash for tissue paper, using petty cash voucher PC1. (Tax code T1)
4th June	PC2	8205	Paid £10.00 from petty cash for refreshments (zero rated Tax code T0), using petty cash voucher PC2.
10th June	002	GALLIERS	Paid Supplier, cheque 002 for £11162.50 to pay their invoice number 502 in full.
12th June	003	WEDDING	Paid Supplier, cheque 003 for £8401.25 to pay their invoice W025 in full and less credit note CR601.
19th June	004	7000	Amy drew cheque 004 for £225.00 to pay staff wages. This is outside the scope of VAT. (Tax code T9)
22nd June	005	3001	Amy drew cheque 005 for £250.00 to cover her personal expenses. This is outside the scope of VAT. (Tax code T9)
25th June	2501	JOSEPH	Amy received cheque number 2501 for £7608.13 from Josephine's Brides to pay her invoice B001 in full.
29th June	3524	ISOBEL	Amy received cheque number 3524 for £5000.00 from Isobella's in part payment of her invoice B002.
30th June	PC3	7505	Paid £75.00 from petty cash for magazines for customers to take away, using petty cash voucher PC3. This is zero rated for VAT. (Tax code T0)

251

Task 10

Amy has received the following Bank Statement for June 2009 which you should now reconcile to the computer Bank records.

CHESHIRE BANK LTD

Account Number: 10563478

Amy Millar
T/A Bride's Made
5 Wychwood Village
Weston
Cheshire
CW2 5FH

STATEMENT OF ACCOUNT
Sheet No. 1
Sort Code: 12-26-25

Telephone: 01270 125647

30th June, 2009

Date	Details	Payments	Receipts	Balance
1 June	Counter Credit		30000.00	30000.00
2 June	001	175.00		29825.00
10 June	Standing Order	105.00		29720.00
13 June	002	11162.50		18557.50
15 June	003	8401.25		10156.25
22 June	004	225.00		9931.25
22 June	005	250.00		9681.25
26 June	Counter Credit		7608.13	17289.38

IAB Level 1 I/D 109 Question Paper

Answers to Tasks 11 - 13 should be word processed or written on the sheet at the back of this Question Paper. Please detach the sheet and include it with your printouts.

Task 11

From your computer system, state how much will be required to restore the petty cash balance to £175.00?

2 marks

Task 12

Amy is concerned about data kept on the computer; briefly explain two ways in which you would keep it confidential and secure.

4 marks

Task 13

Accuracy in book-keeping is vital. Briefly explain
- one check you would make while entering the data, and
- one check, other than Bank Reconciliation, you would make later.

4 marks

Task 14

Print the following reports at the end of June.
- Summary Audit Trail
- Trial Balance
- Customers Address List
- Suppliers Address List
- Detailed Aged Debtors Analysis
- Detailed Aged Creditors Analysis
- Nominal Activity Report for both categories of Sales.

THIS IS THE END OF THE QUESTION PAPER

Qualifications for business

Exam I/D 109

MODEL ANSWERS

Qualification:
**LEVEL 1 CERTIFICATE IN COMPUTERISED
BOOK-KEEPING**
(Qualification Accreditation Number 500/3160/0)

June 2009

Suite 30, 40 Churchill Square, Kings Hill, West Malling, Kent ME19 4YU
Email: education@iab.org.uk website: www.iab.org.uk

I/D 109

June 2009 Level 1 Cert CB – Bride's Made

Task 11

From your computer system, state how much will be required to restore the petty cash balance to £175.00?

£137.00

2 marks

Task 12

Amy is concerned about data kept on the computer; briefly explain two ways in which you would keep it confidential and secure.

- **Have a password on the computer to prevent unauthorised access**
- **Take regular back-ups and keep one off site**
- **Keep the office locked**
- **Never leave the computer unattended – install a timer which requires the password to be re-entered if the computer is left for more than a few minutes**

2 x 2 marks

Task 13

Accuracy in book-keeping is vital. Briefly explain
- one check you would make while entering the data, and
- one check, other than Bank Reconciliation, you would make later.

- **Check all amounts and references have been entered correctly**
- **Check the batch totals agree**

- **Check the Audit Trail for any omissions on details or references**
- **Ensure the nominal codes have been changed on the Trial Balance to represent the correct type of sales or purchases**

2 x 2 marks

Date: 23/04/2009
Time: 12:20:54

Page: 1

L1 CertCB - Bride's Made
Audit Trail (Summary)

Date From:	01/01/1980		Customer From:	
Date To:	31/12/2019		Customer To:	ZZZZZZZZ
Transaction From:	1		Supplier From:	ZZZZZZZZ
Transaction To:	99999999		Supplier To:	ZZZZZZZZ
Dept From:	0		N/C From:	
Dept To:	999		N/C To:	99999999
Exclude Deleted Tran:	No			

No	Type	Date	A/C	N/C	Dept	Ref	Details	Net	Tax	T/C	Pd	Paid	V	B	Bank Rec. Date
1	PI	01/06/2009	GALLIERS	5000	0	S02	Purchases - Wedding Dresses	9,500.00	1,662.50	T1	Y	11,162.50	N	-	
2	PI	04/06/2009	SOPHIES	5001	0	S150	Purchases - Bridesmaids Dresses	5,000.00	0.00	T0	N	0.00	N	-	
3	PI	06/06/2009	WEDDING	5000	0	W025	Purchases - Bridesmaids Dresses	8,250.00	1,443.75	T1	Y	9,693.75	N	-	
4	PI	07/06/2009	GALLIERS	5000	0	647	Purchases - Wedding Dresses	10,050.00	1,758.75	T1	N	0.00	N	-	
5	PI	08/06/2009	SOPHIES	5000	0	S198	Purchases - Wedding Dresses	2,225.00	389.38	T1	N	0.00	N	-	
6	PC	10/06/2009	WEDDING	5000	0	CR601	2 Damaged Wedding Dresses	1,100.00	192.50	T1	Y	1,292.50	N	-	
7	SI	08/06/2009	JOSEPH	4000	0	B001	Sales - Wedding Dresses	6,475.00	1,133.13	T1	Y	7,608.13	N	-	
8	SI	12/06/2009	ISOBEL	4000	0	B002	Sales - Wedding Dresses	9,465.00	1,656.38	T1	N	5,000.00	N	-	
9	SI	18/06/2009	JOSEPH	4001	0	B003	Sales - Bridesmaid Dresses	3,900.00	0.00	T0	N	0.00	N	-	
10	BP	10/06/2009	1200	7502	0	S/01	Telephone	89.36	15.64	T1	Y	105.00	N	R	30/06/2009
11	BR	01/06/2009	1200	3000	0	BR1	Capital Introduced	30,000.00	0.00	T9	Y	30,000.00	-	R	30/06/2009
12	JC	02/06/2009	1200	1200	0	001	Petty Cash	175.00	0.00	T9	Y	175.00	-	R	30/06/2009
13	JD	02/06/2009	1230	1230	0	001	Petty Cash	175.00	0.00	T9	Y	175.00	-	N	
14	CP	03/06/2009	1230	5003	0	PC1	Tissue Paper	44.26	7.74	T1	Y	52.00	N	N	
15	CP	04/06/2009	1230	8205	0	PC2	Refreshments	10.00	0.00	T9	Y	10.00	N	N	
16	PP	10/06/2009	GALLIERS	1200	0	002	Purchase Payment	11,162.50	0.00	T9	Y	11,162.50	-	R	30/06/2009
17	PP	12/06/2009	WEDDING	1200	0	003	Purchase Payment	8,401.25	0.00	T9	Y	8,401.25	-	R	30/06/2009
18	BP	19/06/2009	1200	7000	0	004	Staff Wages	225.00	0.00	T9	Y	225.00	-	R	30/06/2009
19	BP	22/06/2009	1200	3001	0	005	Drawings	250.00	0.00	T9	Y	250.00	-	R	30/06/2009
20	SR	25/06/2009	JOSEPH	1200	0	2501	Sales Receipt	7,608.13	0.00	T9	Y	7,608.13	-	R	30/06/2009
21	SR	29/06/2009	ISOBEL	1200	0	3524	Sales Receipt	5,000.00	0.00	T9	Y	5,000.00	-	N	
22	CP	30/06/2009	1230	7505	0	PC3	Magazines	75.00	0.00	T0	Y	75.00	N	N	

IAB Level 1 I/D 109 Model Answers

L1 CertCB - Bride's Made

Aged Creditors Analysis (Detailed)

Date From:	01/01/1980		Supplier From:	
Date To:	30/06/2009		Supplier To:	ZZZZZZZZ

Include future transactions: No
Exclude later payments: No

** NOTE: All report values are shown in Base Currency, unless otherwise indicated **

A/C:	GALLIERS	Name:	Galliers Wedding Dresses	Contact:			Tel:			

No:	Type	Date	Ref	Details	Balance	Future	Current	Period 1	Period 2	Period 3	Older
4	PI	07/06/2009	647	Purchases - Wedding 1	11,808.75	0.00	11,808.75	0.00	0.00	0.00	0.00
				Totals:	11,808.75	0.00	11,808.75	0.00	0.00	0.00	0.00

Turnover: 19,550.00
Credit Limit £   0.00

A/C:	SOPHIES	Name:	Sophie's Bridal Gowns	Contact:			Tel:			

No:	Type	Date	Ref	Details	Balance	Future	Current	Period 1	Period 2	Period 3	Older
2	PI	04/06/2009	S150	Purchases - Bridesmai	5,000.00	0.00	5,000.00	0.00	0.00	0.00	0.00
5	PI	08/06/2009	S198	Purchases - Wedding I	2,614.38	0.00	2,614.38	0.00	0.00	0.00	0.00
				Totals:	7,614.38	0.00	7,614.38	0.00	0.00	0.00	0.00

Turnover: 7,225.00
Credit Limit £   0.00

| | | | | Grand Totals: | 19,423.13 | 0.00 | 19,423.13 | 0.00 | 0.00 | 0.00 | 0.00 |

Date: 23/04/2009
Time: 12:20:08

L1 CertCB - Bride's Made

Customer Address List

Page: 1

Customer From:
Customer To: ZZZZZZZZ

A/C	Name & Address	Contact Name	Telephone	Fax
ISOBEL	Isobella's 7 The Barns Nantwich Cheshire CW1 7DF			
JOSEPH	Josephine's Brides 15 High Street Audlem Cheshire CW4 8HG			

Date: 23/04/2009
Time: 12:22:26

L1 CertCB - Bride's Made

Aged Debtors Analysis (Detailed)

Page: 1

Date From:	01/01/1980	Customer From:	
Date To:	30/06/2009	Customer To:	ZZZZZZZZ
Include future transactions:	No		
Exclude later payments:	No		

** NOTE: All report values are shown in Base Currency, unless otherwise indicated **

A/C: ISOBEL   Name: Isobella's   Contact: Tel:

No	Type	Date	Ref	Details	Balance	Future	Current	Period 1	Period 2	Period 3	Older
8	SI	12/06/2009	B002	Sales - Wedding Dress	6,121.38	0.00	6,121.38	0.00	0.00	0.00	0.00
				Totals:	6,121.38	0.00	6,121.38	0.00	0.00	0.00	0.00

Turnover: 9,465.00
Credit Limit £   0.00

A/C: JOSEPH   Name: Josephine's Brides   Contact: Tel:

No	Type	Date	Ref	Details	Balance	Future	Current	Period 1	Period 2	Period 3	Older
9	SI	18/06/2009	B003	Sales - Bridesmaid Dr	3,900.00	0.00	3,900.00	0.00	0.00	0.00	0.00
				Totals:	3,900.00	0.00	3,900.00	0.00	0.00	0.00	0.00

Turnover: 10,375.00
Credit Limit £   0.00

| | | | | **Grand Totals:** | 10,021.38 | 0.00 | 10,021.38 | 0.00 | 0.00 | 0.00 | 0.00 |

IAB Level 1 I/D 109 Model Answers

L1 CertCB - Bride's Made

Nominal Activity

Page: 1

Date From:		01/01/1980							N/C From:	4000		
Date To:		30/06/2009							N/C To:	4001		

Transaction From: 1
Transaction To: 99999999

N/C:	4000		Name:	Sales - Wedding Dresses				Account Balance:			15,940.00 CR

No	Type	Date	Account	Ref	Details	Dept	T/C	Value	Debit	Credit	V	B
7	SI	08/06/2009	JOSEPH	B001	Sales - Wedding Dresses	0	T1	6,475.00		6,475.00	N	-
8	SI	12/06/2009	ISOBEL	B002	Sales - Wedding Dresses	0	T1	9,465.00		9,465.00	N	-
							Totals:	15,940.00		15,940.00		
							History Balance:	15,940.00		15,940.00		

N/C:	4001		Name:	Sales - Bridesmaid Dresses				Account Balance:			3,900.00 CR

No	Type	Date	Account	Ref	Details	Dept	T/C	Value	Debit	Credit	V	B
9	SI	18/06/2009	JOSEPH	B003	Sales - Bridesmaid Dresses	0	T0	3,900.00		3,900.00	N	-
							Totals:	3,900.00		3,900.00		
							History Balance:	3,900.00		3,900.00		

IAB Level 1 I/D 109 Model Answers

L1 CertCB - Bride's Made

Supplier Address List

Page: 1

Supplier From:
Supplier To: ZZZZZZZZ

A/C	Name	Contact	Telephone	Fax
GALLIERS	Galliers Wedding Dresses 10 Walnut Street Hough Crewe CW2 5JT			
SOPHIES	Sophie's Bridal Gowns The Village Green Audlem Cheshire CW5 7GF			
WEDDING	Wedding Belles 15 Alkington Hall Barns Nantwich Cheshire CW1 5DS			

IAB Level 1 I/D 109 Model Answers

L1 CertCB - Bride's Made

Period Trial Balance

To Period: Month 1, June 2009

N/C	Name	Debit	Credit
1100	Debtors Control Account	10,021.38	
1200	Bank Current Account	22,289.38	
1230	Petty Cash	38.00	
2100	Creditors Control Account		19,423.13
2200	Sales Tax Control Account		2,789.51
2201	Purchase Tax Control Account	5,085.26	
3000	Capital		30,000.00
3001	Drawings	250.00	
4000	Sales - Wedding Dresses		15,940.00
4001	Sales - Bridesmaid Dresses		3,900.00
5000	Purchases - Wedding Dresses	28,925.00	
5001	Purchases - Bridesmaid Dresses	5,000.00	
5003	Packaging - Tissue Paper	44.26	
7000	Wages	225.00	
7502	Telephone	89.36	
7505	Magazines	75.00	
8205	Refreshments	10.00	
	Totals:	72,052.64	72,052.64

I/D 110

International Association of Book-keepers

Level 2 Certificate in Computerised Book-keeping

JUNE 2009

Qualification Accreditation Number 500/3079/6

Question Paper

Candidates Instructions:

- **Time allowed: 2 hours**
- **Candidates should answer all Tasks**
- **All written answers should be written in pen or word -processed**

Suite 30, 40 Churchill Square, Kings Hill, West Malling, Kent ME19 4YU
Tel: 0844 330 3527, Fax: 0844 330 3514, email:education@iab.org.uk

IAB Level 2 I/D 110 Question Paper

INTERNATIONAL ASSOCIATION OF BOOK-KEEPERS

QUALIFICATION TITLE:
IAB LEVEL 2 CERTIFICATE IN COMPUTERISED BOOK-KEEPING

Unit Title:
Book-keeping to Trial Balance using Accounting Software

General Information and Instructions

1   You must enter your **Candidate Number, Student Number, Name of Centre, Date of Examination** and **Software used** on the front cover provided.

2   Time Allowed: TWO HOURS

3   Printing may be carried out after completion of the two hours examination time.

4   All written answers should be in pen or word processed.

5   The use of silent non-programmable calculators is permitted.

6   NOTE - This Question Booklet has information and data printed on both sides of the pages.

7   The practical data input and printing of reports (Tasks 1 and 3) account for 90 marks, the remaining 10 marks cover Task 2.

8   Answers to Task 2 and the printouts taken at Task 3 should be firmly stapled into the Answer Booklet provided.

SCENARIO

Kate Guzowski started in business on 1st June 2009 trading as *Kate's Hair Supplies*. The business sells hair products and magazines and will be trading on both a credit and cash basis.

The business will be registered for VAT (Standard Accounting).

Sales will be divided into 2 categories – sales of hair products and sales of magazines. The latter is VAT zero rated.

Purchases will be divided into 2 categories – purchases of hair products and purchases of magazines. The latter is VAT zero rated.

Required:

TASK 1

You are to assume the role of Accounts Assistant and carry out the instructions in the order that they are given using a commercial accounting software package.

Kate Guzowski is relying on you to process the data accurately. You should ensure that every transaction has a unique reference.

The name and address of the business is:

> **Kate's Hair Supplies**
> **Broad Street**
> **Birmingham**
> **B1 5KE**

Enter this information into your accounting program and, after the name "Kate's Hair Supplies", add your Examination Entry number.

Set up the financial year start date.

Note: this paper has been produced using 17.5% as the standard rate of VAT. You should ensure that your accounting software package has been set up for this correctly.

Set up the following Nominal Accounts, using an account reference relevant to the package you are using:

Nominal Account.	*Nominal Code.*
Capital	
Drawings	
Sales – Hair Products	
Sales – Magazines	
Purchases – Hair Products	
Purchases – Magazines	

Set up the following Credit Customer Accounts, using an appropriate customer account reference:

Boyds Hair Design 15 Metchley Lane Harborne Birmingham B33 6FD	*Valente Ltd* Unit 20 Wainwright Street Aston Birmingham B6 5TD
Retro Hair Birmingham Road Sutton Coldfield B15 4DE	*Sajna Hair & Beauty* High Street Birmingham B1 6DD

Set up the following Credit Supplier Accounts, using an appropriate supplier account reference:

Aveda Hair Upper Mall West Bullring Birmingham B5 4BP	*Mohdajaib* 321 Wellington Road Handsworth Birmingham B20 2QL
Wella 125 Broad Street Birmingham B1 5KH	*Shine Hairdressers* 7 The Quay Broad Street Birmingham B1 6DE

266

Kate Guzowski financed her business as follows:

Date	Details
1 June	Kate Guzowski introduced £10,000 worth of fixtures and fittings into the business and £15,000 of her own savings to her newly opened business bank account with the Birmingham Bank.
3 June	A loan was taken out for £20,000 from the Birmingham Bank. It too was paid into the business bank account. Kate Guzowski arranged to repay the loan by standing order at the rate of £500 per month with £400 being the loan repayment and the balance being the interest. Repayments are to be made on the 26th of each month, starting on 26th June 2009. Set this up and process the first payment at the appropriate time.

A Cheque Log was set up (extract below) which lists all cheques paid out of the bank current account.

From the Cheque Log for the first week of June, you are required to enter the following details into the system:

CHEQUE LOG

Date	Cheque no	Payee	Details	Net £	VAT £	Gross £	✓
2 June	100001	Broad Street Property	Property rental	1,000.00	175.00	1,175.00	
5 June	100002	Shop Insurance Co.	Shop Insurance	750.00	Exempt	750.00	
7 June	100003	Shop Accessories Ltd.	Shop Fixtures	300.00	52.50	352.50	
9 June	100004	Computer World	Computer	1,100.00	192.50	1,292.50	
11 June	100005	Petty Cash	Set up Petty Cash Float	350.00	-	350.00	

During June, Kate Guzowski sent out the following sales invoices and credit note to her customers. A cash discount is offered to selected customers to encourage prompt payment.

Enter the following sales invoices and credit note:

INVOICE.	**Kate's Hair Supplies** **Broad Street** **Birmingham** **B1 5KE**	
	Telephone: 0121 313 5566	
Invoice To: Boyds Hair Design 15 Metchley Lane Harborne Birmingham B33 6FD	**Invoice No.**	**KH 01**
	Invoice Date	01.06.09

	VAT Rate	**Net**
10 x 500ml bottles of shampoo	17.5%	**£50.00**
10 x 500ml bottles of conditioner	17.5%	**£50.00**
5 magazines	Zero	**£ 6.25**
		£106.25
	VAT	**£ 17.50**
	Invoice Total	**£123.75**

Terms: 30 days nett
VAT Reg. No. 315 4769 639

INVOICE.	**Kate's Hair Supplies** **Broad Street** **Birmingham** **B1 5KE**	
	Telephone: 0121 313 5566	
Invoice To: Sajna Hair & Beauty High Street Birmingham B1 6DD	**Invoice No.**	**KH 02**
	Invoice Date	05.06.09

	VAT Rate	**Net**
90 cans of hairspray	17.5%	**£315.00**
10 magazines	Zero	**£12.50**
		£327.50
	VAT	**£55.12**
	Invoice Total	**£382.62**

Terms: 30 days nett
VAT Reg. No. 315 4769 639

INVOICE.	Kate's Hair Supplies Broad Street Birmingham B1 5KE	
	Telephone: 0121 313 5566	
Invoice To:	Invoice No.	KH 03
Valente Ltd Unit 20 Wainwright Street Aston Birmingham B6 5TD		
	Invoice Date	10.06.09

	VAT Rate	Net
10 GHD straighteners	17.5%	£1200.00
15 magazines	Zero	£18.75
50 bottles of shine serum	17.5%	£199.50
		£1,418.25
	VAT	£237.56
	Invoice Total	£1,655.81

Terms: 3% cash discount for payment within 14 days
VAT Reg. No. 315 4769 639

INVOICE.	Kate's Hair Supplies Broad Street Birmingham B1 5KE	
	Telephone: 0121 313 5566	
Invoice To:	Invoice No.	KH 04
Retro Hair Birmingham Road Sutton Coldfield B15 4DE		
	Invoice Date	15.06.09

	VAT Rate	Net
50 bottles of 500ml conditioner	17.5%	£250.00
50 bottles of 500ml shampoo	17.5%	£250.00
5 magazines	Zero	£6.25
		£506.25
	VAT	£84.88
	Invoice Total	£591.13

Terms: 3% cash discount for payment within 14 days
VAT Reg. No. 315 4769 639

269

INVOICE.	Kate's Hair Supplies Broad Street Birmingham B1 5KE		
	Telephone: 0121 313 5566		
Invoice To: Boyds Hair Design 15 Metchley Lane Harborne Birmingham B33 6FD	**Invoice No.**		**KH 05**
	Invoice Date		16.06.09
	VAT Rate		**Net**
15 x 500ml bottles of shampoo	17.5%		**£75.00**
15 x 500ml bottles of conditioner	17.5%		**£75.00**
20 magazines	Zero		**£25.00**
			£175.00
	VAT		**£26.25**
	Invoice Total		**£201.25**
Terms: 30 days nett VAT Reg. No. 315 4769 639			

INVOICE.	Kate's Hair Supplies Broad Street Birmingham B1 5KE		
	Telephone: 0121 313 5566		
Invoice To: Sajna Hair & Beauty High Street Birmingham B1 6DD	**Invoice No.**		**KH 06**
	Invoice Date		25.06.09
	VAT Rate		**Net**
30 x magazines	Zero		**£37.50**
50 cans of hairspray	17.5%		**£336.00**
			£373.50
	VAT		**£58.80**
	Invoice Total		**£432.30**
Terms: 30 days nett VAT Reg. No. 315 4769 639			

270

CREDIT NOTE.	Kate's Hair Supplies Broad Street Birmingham B1 5KE		
	Telephone: 0121 313 5566		
Credit To: Boyd's Hair Design 15 Metchley Lane Harborne Birmingham B33 GFD	Credit Note No.		KH CN-1
	Credit Note Date		27.06.09
	VAT Rate		**Net**
5 x 500ml bottles of shampoo – leaked	17.5%		**£25.00**
			£25.00
	VAT		**£4.37**
	Total		**£29.37**
VAT Reg. No. 315 4769 639			

During June, Kate's Hair Supplies received the following purchase invoices and credit note from their suppliers. Kate's Hair Supplies are offered a cash discount by some of their suppliers to encourage them to pay promptly.

You are required to enter the following purchase invoices and credit note as appropriate:

INVOICE.	Aveda Hair		
	Upper Mall West		
	Bullring		
	Birmingham		
	B5 4BP		
Invoice To:		**Invoice No.**	*AH 234*
Kate's Hair Supplies			
Broad Street			
Birmingham			
B1 5KE			
		Invoice Date	01.06.09
		VAT Rate	**Net**
100 x 500ml bottles of shampoo		17.5%	**£350.00**
100 x 500ml bottles of conditioner		17.5%	**£350.00**
			£700.00
		VAT	**£120.05**
		Invoice Total	**£820.05**

Terms: Cash Discount of 2% for payment within 30 days.
VAT Reg. No. 668 6385 17

INVOICE.	Mohdajaib		
	321 Wellington Road		
	Handsworth		
	Birmingham		
	B20 2QL		
Invoice To:		**Invoice No.**	M004
Kate's Hair Supplies		**Invoice Date**	01.06.09
Broad Street			
Birmingham			
B1 5KE			
		VAT Rate	**Net**
50 hair magazines		Zero	**£49.50**
250 cans of ultrahold hairspray		17.5%	**£625.00**
50 GHD straighteners		17.5%	**£5,250.00**
			£5,924.50
		VAT	**£1,028.12**
		Invoice Total	**£6,952.62**

Terms: 30 days nett.
VAT Reg. No. 352 7388 93

INVOICE.	Shine Hairdressers 7 The Quay Broad Street Birmingham B1 6DE		
Invoice To: Kate's Hair Supplies Broad Street Birmingham B1 5KE		**Invoice No.** **Invoice Date**	SH 2434 05.06.09
		VAT Rate	**Net**
150 bottles of shine serum		17.5%	**£375.00**
			£375.00
		VAT	£63.65
		Invoice Total	£438.65
Terms: Cash Discount of 3% for payment within 30 days. VAT Reg. No. 271 5839 57			

INVOICE.	_Wella_ _125 Broad Street_ _Birmingham_ _B1 5KH_		
Invoice To: Kate's Hair Supplies Broad Street Birmingham B1 5KE		**Invoice No.** **Invoice Date**	W 509 12.06.09
		VAT Rate	**Net**
100 bottles of 500ml shampoo		17.5%	**£400.00**
100 bottles of 500ml conditioner		17.5%	**£400.00**
			£800.00
		VAT	£140.00
		Invoice Total	£940.00
Terms: 30 days nett. VAT Reg. No. 621 7453 84			

273

INVOICE.

Mohdajaib
321 Wellington Road
Handsworth
Birmingham
B20 2QL

Invoice To:
Kate's Hair Supplies
Broad Street
Birmingham
B1 5KE

| | **Invoice No.** | M009 |
| | **Invoice Date** | 15.06.09 |

	VAT Rate	**Net**
25 hair magazines	Zero	**£24.75**
50 cans of ultrahold hairspray	17.5%	**£125.00**
10 GHD straighteners	17.5%	**£1,050.00**
		£1,199.75
	VAT	**£205.63**
	Invoice Total	**£1,405.38**

Terms: 30 days nett.
VAT Reg. No. 352 7388 93

CREDIT
NOTE

Shine Hairdressers
7 The Quay
Broad Street
Birmingham
B1 6DE

Credit To:
Kate's Hair Supplies
Broad Street
Birmingham
B1 5KE

| | **Credit Note No.** | SH CN056 |
| | **Credit Note Date** | 15.06.09 |

	VAT Rate	**Net**
5 bottles of shine serum – damaged bottles	17.5%	**£12.50**
		£12.50
	VAT	**£2.19**
	Credit Note Total	**£14.69**

VAT Reg. No. 271 5839 57

During June, Kate Guzowski has spent cash and has provided the following authorised petty cash vouchers that require entering onto the system.

Petty Cash Voucher No. PCV 01 Date 02.06.09	VAT Rate: 17.5%
Expense Details.	Amount including VAT (where applicable)
Premises repairs *(receipt attached)*	£35.00
Signed **Kate Guzowski**	Total £35.00

Petty Cash Voucher No. PCV 02 Date 04.06.09	VAT Rate: Zero
Expense Details	Amount including VAT (where applicable)
Refreshments *(receipt attached)*	£19.75
Signed **Kate Guzowski**	Total £19.75

Petty Cash Voucher No. PCV 03 Date 12.06.09	VAT Rate: 17.5%
Expense Details	Amount including VAT (where applicable)
Printing *(receipt attached)*	£18.40
Signed **Kate Guzowski**	Total £18.40

275

Petty Cash Voucher No. PCV 04 Date 21.06.09	VAT Rate: 17.5%
Expense Details	Amount including VAT (where applicable)
Second hand office desk *(receipt attached)*	£55.00
Signed *Kate Guzowski*	Total £55.00

Petty Cash Voucher No. PCV 05 Date 23.06.09	VAT Rate: 17.5%
Expense Details	Amount including VAT (where applicable)
Repairs to shop door *(receipt attached)*	£27.50
Signed *Kate Guzowski*	Total £27.50

Petty Cash Voucher No. PCV 06 Date 27.06.09	VAT Rate : Zero
Expense Details	Amount including VAT (where applicable)
Shop cleaning *(receipt attached)*	£25.00
Signed *Kate Guzowski*	Total £25.00

276

During the month the following cheques were received from Credit Customers and paid into the business bank account.

Date		Cheque Received £
06 June	Cheque (no 638256) received from Boyds Hair Design in full settlement of our invoice KH 01	123.75
10 June	Cheque (no 634279) received from Sajna Hair & Beauty in part payment of our invoice KH 02	200.00
22 June	Cheque (no 534278) received from Retro Hair in full settlement of our invoice KH 04 having taken the discount offered	575.94
30 June	Cheque (no 638301) received from Boyds Hair Design in full settlement of our invoice KH 05 less our credit note KH CN-1	171.88

Cash Sales.

During June, Kate Guzowski informs you that she has made the following cash sales (including VAT where appropriate) to members of the public at a trade show. All takings from cash sales were paid directly into the bank on 22nd June.

Sales of Hair Products	£120.00
Sales of Magazines	£145.00
TOTAL	**£265.00**

277

During June Kate Guzowski made payments as follows. Complete the Cheque Log for the remaining cheque payments.

You have already entered the ticked cheques from the Cheque Log.

CHEQUE LOG.

Date	Cheque no.	Payee	Details	Net £	VAT £	Gross £	✓
2 June	100001	Broad Street Property	Property rental	1,000.00	175.00	1,175.00	✓
5 June	100002	Shop Insurance Co.	Shop Insurance	750.00	Exempt	750.00	✓
7 June	100003	Shop Accessories Ltd.	Shop Fixtures	300.00	52.50	352.50	✓
9 June	100004	Computer World	Computer	1,100.00	192.50	1,292.50	✓
11 June	100005	Petty Cash	Set up Petty cash float	350.00	-	350.00	✓
11 June	100006	Mohdajaib	Paid invoice M004			6,952.62	
14 June	100007	Aveda Hair	Paid invoice AH 234 taking advantage of the discount offered			806.05	
18 June	100008	Shine Hairdressers	Paid invoice SH 2434 taking advantage of the discount offered and less credit note SH CN056			412.71	
23 June	100009	Wella	Payment on account			500.00	
24 June	100010	Printers Ltd	Printing of posters	100.00	17.50	117.50	
30 June	100011	Kate Guzowski	Drawings	500.00	-	500.00	

MONTHLY WAGES.

The wages for June have been calculated as follows:

- 30 June – Total Net Wages paid to the staff from the business bank account by BACS were £1,750.00

- Kate Guzowski does not intend to pay the June Income Tax and NICs to HM Revenue & Customs until 19th July.

They have been calculated as follows and should be entered by Journal Entries.

Income Tax deducted	£194.00
Employees' NIC deducted	£213.00
Employer's NIC	£232.00

278

MONTH-END ADJUSTMENT.

Kate Guzowski has been notified by Sajna Hair & Beauty that they have gone into liquidation. Process the outstanding amount on Sajna Hair & Beauty's account as a bad debt.

BANK STATEMENT

The Bank Statement for June has now been received; reconcile it to your computer records.

BIRMINGHAM BANK PLC	**Statement of Account**	
Account Number	**Sort Code:**	40-67-46
63428965		
Account Name:	**Telephone:**	0121 500 6000
	Facsimile:	0121 500 6001
Kate Guzowski		
T/A Kate's Hair Supplies	**Sheet No. 1.**	
Broad Street		
Birmingham		
B1 5KE	**June 2009**	

Date	Details	Payments £	Receipts £	Balance £
1 June	Counter Credit		15,000.00	15,000.00
3 June	Tfr – Birmingham Bank Loan a/c		20,000.00	35,000.00
6 June	100001	1,175.00		33,825.00
9 June	100002	750.00		33,075.00
9 June	Counter Credit		123.75	33,198.75
11 June	100003	352.50		32,846.25
11 June	100004	1,292.50		31,553.75
11 June	100005	350.00		31,203.75
13 June	Counter Credit		200.00	31,403.75
16 June	100106	6,952.62		24,451.13
24 June	Counter Credit		575.94	25,027.07
24 June	100107	806.05		24,221.02
24 June	Counter Credit		265.00	24,486.02
26 June	Tfr – Birmingham Bank Loan a/c	500.00		23,986.02
27 June	100008	412.71		23,573.31
26 June	100009	500.00		23,073.31
30 June	BACS	1,750.00		21,323.31

TASK 2

Answers to Task 2 should be word processed or written on the sheet at the back of this Question Paper. Please detach the sheet and include it with your printouts.

After completing the book-keeping for June, Kate Guzowski asks you to explain the following:-

i.   How much does Kate owe to her supplier Wella at 30th June 2009?

(2 marks)

ii.   How could Kate ensure her business would be up and running again, if the computer was stolen from the office?

(4 marks)

iii.   Explain which of the reports you have printed would be most useful to Kate on a day to day basis and why?

(4 marks)

TASK 3

Print the following reports at the end of the month:

This task may be carried out after completion of the two hour examination time.

     a. Address lists for customers and suppliers
     b. Customer Statement for Valente Ltd
     c. Trial Balance
     d. Summary Audit Trail
     e. Detailed Aged Debtors and Creditors Analyses
     f. Nominal Activity reports for each category of Sales and Purchases
     g. Nominal Activity reports of the Bank and Cash Transactions
     h. Reconciled and Unreconciled Bank Transactions

280

Qualifications for business

Exam I/D 110

MODEL ANSWERS

Qualification:
LEVEL 2 CERTIFICATE IN COMPUTERISED
BOOK-KEEPING
(Qualification Accreditation Number 500/3079/6)

June 2009

Suite 30, 40 Churchill Square, Kings Hill, West Malling, Kent ME19 4YU
Email: education@iab.org.uk website: www.iab.org.uk

I/D 110
June 2009 Level 2 Cert CB – Kate's Hair Supplies

TASK 2

Answers to Task 2 should be word processed or written on the sheet at the back of this Question Paper. Please detach the sheet and include it with your printouts.

After completing the book-keeping for June, Kate Guzowski asks you to explain the following:-

i.   How much does Kate owe to her supplier Wella at 30th June 2009?

Kate owes Wella £440 at 30th June 2009

2 marks

ii. How could Kate ensure her business would be up and running again, if the computer was stolen from the office?

- **Take regular back-ups of her work**
- **Keep a separate back-up off site**
- **Keep software off site**
- **Have a second computer at home with the information stored (not sure this is necessary – if software and backups are off site, it would be quick to purchase another computer, if the need arose.)**
- **Take regular reports and keep on file**

(2 points = 4 marks)
4 marks

iii. Explain which of the reports you have printed would be most useful to Kate on a day to day basis and why?

- **Aged Debtors as Kate can see how much her customers owe her**
- **Aged Creditors as Kate can see how much she owes her suppliers**
- **Details of Bank Account/Balance**

(2 points = 4 marks)
4 marks

Date: 25/04/2009
Time: 15:26:54

Date From: 01/01/1980
Date To: 31/12/2019

Transaction From: 1
Transaction To: 99999999

Dept From: 0
Dept To: 999

Exclude Deleted Tran: No

L2 CertCB - Kate's Hair Supplies
Audit Trail (Summary)

Customer From: / Customer To:
Supplier From: / Supplier To: ZZZZZZZ / ZZZZZZZ
N/C From: / N/C To: 9999999

Page: 1

No	Type	Date	A/C	N/C	Dept	Ref	Details	Net	Tax	T/C	Pd	Paid	Y	B	Bank Rec. Date
1	JD	01/06/2009	0040	0040	0	JV1	Fixtures & Fittings	10,000.00	0.00	T9	Y	10,000.00	-	R	30/06/2009
2	JD	01/06/2009	1200	1200	0	JV1	Capital	15,000.00	0.00	T9	Y	15,000.00	-	R	30/06/2009
3	JC	01/06/2009	3000	3000	0	JV1	Capital Introduced	25,000.00	0.00	T9	Y	25,000.00	-	-	
4	BR	03/06/2009	1200	2300	0	BR1	Loan	20,000.00	0.00	T9	Y	20,000.00	-	R	30/06/2009
5	BP	02/06/2009	1200	7100	0	100001	Rent	1,000.00	175.00	T1	Y	1,175.00	N	R	30/06/2009
6	BP	05/06/2009	1200	7104	0	100002	Shop Insurance	750.00	0.00	T2	Y	750.00	N	R	30/06/2009
7	BP	07/06/2009	1200	0040	0	100003	Shop Fixtures	300.00	52.50	T1	Y	352.50	N	R	30/06/2009
8	BP	09/06/2009	1200	0030	0	100004	Computer	1,100.00	192.50	T1	Y	1,292.50	N	R	30/06/2009
9	JC	11/06/2009	1200	1200	0	100005	Petty Cash	350.00	0.00	T9	Y	350.00	-	R	30/06/2009
10	JD	11/06/2009	1230	1230	0	100005	Petty Cash	350.00	0.00	T9	Y	350.00	N	-	
11	SI	01/06/2009	BOYDS	4000	0	KH 01	Sales - Hair Products	100.00	17.50	T1	Y	117.50	N	-	
12	SI	01/06/2009	BOYDS	4001	0	KH 01	Sales - Magazines	6.25	0.00	T0	Y	6.25	N	-	
13	SI	05/06/2009	SAJNA	4000	0	KH 02	Sales - Hair Products	315.00	55.12	T1	Y	370.12	N	-	
14	SI	05/06/2009	SAJNA	4001	0	KH 02	Sales - Magazines	12.50	0.00	T0	Y	12.50	N	-	
15	SI	10/06/2009	VALENTE	4000	0	KH 03	Sales - Hair Products	1,399.50	237.56	T1	N	0.00	N	-	
16	SI	10/06/2009	VALENTE	4001	0	KH 03	Sales - Magazines	18.75	0.00	T0	N	0.00	N	-	
17	SI	15/06/2009	RETRO	4000	0	KH 04	Sales - Hair Products	500.00	84.88	T1	Y	584.88	N	-	
18	SI	15/06/2009	RETRO	4001	0	KH 04	Sales - Magazines	6.25	0.00	T0	Y	6.25	N	-	
19	SI	16/06/2009	BOYDS	4000	0	KH 05	Sales - Hair Products	150.00	26.25	T1	Y	176.25	N	-	
20	SI	16/06/2009	BOYDS	4001	0	KH 05	Sales - Magazines	25.00	0.00	T0	Y	25.00	N	-	
21	SI	25/06/2009	SAJNA	4001	0	KH 06	Sales - Magazines	37.50	0.00	T0	Y	37.50	N	-	
22	SI	25/06/2009	SAJNA	4000	0	KH 06	Sales - Hair Products	336.00	58.80	T1	Y	394.80	N	-	
23	SC	27/06/2009	BOYDS	4000	0	KH CN-1	Damaged goods	25.00	4.37	T1	Y	29.37	N	-	
24	PI	01/06/2009	AVEDA	5000	0	AH 234	Purchases - Hair Products	700.00	120.05	T1	Y	820.05	N	-	
25	PI	01/06/2009	MOHDAJ	5001	0	M004	Purchases - Magazines	49.50	0.00	T0	Y	49.50	N	-	
26	PI	01/06/2009	MOHDAJ	5000	0	M004	Purchases - Hair Products	5,875.00	1,028.12	T1	Y	6,903.12	N	-	
27	PI	05/06/2009	SHINE	5000	0	SH 2434	Purchases - Hair Products	375.00	63.65	T1	Y	438.65	N	-	
28	PI	12/06/2009	WELLA	5000	0	W 509	Purchases - Hair Products	800.00	140.00	T1	N	0.00	N	-	
29	PI	15/06/2009	MOHDAJ	5001	0	M009	Purchases - Magazines	24.75	0.00	T0	N	0.00	N	-	
30	PI	15/06/2009	MOHDAJ	5000	0	M009	Purchases - Hair Products	1,175.00	205.63	T1	N	0.00	N	-	
31	PC	15/06/2009	SHINE	5000	0	SH CN056	Damaged bottles	12.50	2.19	T1	Y	14.69	N	-	
32	CP	02/06/2009	1230	7803	0	PCV 01	Premises repairs	29.79	5.21	T1	Y	35.00	N	Y	

283

Date: 25/04/2009
Time: 15:26:54

L2 CertCB - Kate's Hair Supplies
Audit Trail (Summary)

Page: 2

No	Type	Date	A/C	N/C	Dept	Ref	Details	Net	Tax	T/C	Pd	Paid	V	B	Bank Rec. Date
33	CP	04/06/2009	1230	8205	0	PCV 02	Refreshments	19.75	0.00	T0	Y	19.75	N	N	
34	CP	12/06/2009	1230	7500	0	PCV 03	Printing	15.66	2.74	T1	Y	18.40	N	N	
35	CP	21/06/2009	1230	0030	0	PCV 04	Office Desk	46.81	8.19	T1	Y	55.00	N	N	
36	CP	23/06/2009	1230	7803	0	PCV 05	Premises repairs	23.40	4.10	T1	Y	27.50	N	N	
37	CP	27/06/2009	1230	7801	0	PCV 06	Cleaning	25.00	0.00	T0	Y	25.00	N	N	
38	SR	06/06/2009	BOYDS	1200	0	638256	Sales Receipt	123.75	0.00	T9	Y	123.75	-	R	30/06/2009
39	SR	10/06/2009	SAJNA	1200	0	634279	Sales Receipt	200.00	0.00	T9	Y	200.00	-	R	30/06/2009
40	SR	22/06/2009	RETRO	1200	0	534278	Sales Receipt	575.94	0.00	T9	Y	575.94	-	R	30/06/2009
41	SD	22/06/2009	RETRO	4009	0	534278	Sales Discount	15.19	0.00	T9	Y	15.19	-	-	
42	SR	30/06/2009	BOYDS	1200	0	638301	Sales Receipt	171.88	0.00	T9	Y	171.88	-	N	
43	BR	22/06/2009	1200	4000	0	CS1	Sales - Hair Products	102.13	17.87	T1	Y	120.00	N	R	30/06/2009
44	BR	22/06/2009	1200	4001	0	CS1	Sales - Magazines	145.00	0.00	T0	Y	145.00	N	R	30/06/2009
45	PP	11/06/2009	MOHDAJ	1200	0	100006	Purchase Payment	6,952.62	0.00	T9	Y	6,952.62	-	R	30/06/2009
46	PP	14/06/2009	AVEDA	1200	0	100007	Purchase Payment	806.05	0.00	T9	Y	806.05	-	R	30/06/2009
47	PD	14/06/2009	AVEDA	5009	0	100007	Purchase Discount	14.00	0.00	T9	Y	14.00	-	-	
48	PP	18/06/2009	SHINE	1200	0	100008	Purchase Payment	412.71	0.00	T9	Y	412.71	-	R	30/06/2009
49	PD	18/06/2009	SHINE	5009	0	100008	Purchase Discount	11.25	0.00	T9	Y	11.25	-	-	
50	PA	23/06/2009	WELLA	1200	0	100009	Payment on Account	500.00	0.00	T9	N	0.00	-	R	30/06/2009
51	BP	24/06/2009	1200	7500	0	100010	Printing	100.00	17.50	T1	Y	117.50	N	N	
52	BP	26/06/2009	1200	2300	0	STO1	Capital Repayment	400.00	0.00	T9	Y	400.00	-	R	30/06/2009
53	BP	26/06/2009	1200	7903	0	STO1	Loan Interest	100.00	0.00	T2	Y	100.00	N	R	30/06/2009
54	BP	30/06/2009	1200	3001	0	100011	Drawings	500.00	0.00	T9	Y	500.00	-	N	
55	JC	30/06/2009	1200	1200	0	JV2	Net Wages	1,750.00	0.00	T9	Y	1,750.00	-	R	30/06/2009
56	JD	30/06/2009	7000	7000	0	JV2	Gross Wages	2,157.00	0.00	T9	Y	2,157.00	-	-	
57	JD	30/06/2009	7006	7006	0	JV2	Employer's NIC	232.00	0.00	T9	Y	232.00	-	-	
58	JC	30/06/2009	2210	2210	0	JV2	Liability to HMRC	639.00	0.00	T9	Y	639.00	-	-	
59	SC	30/06/2009	SAJNA	8100	0	BADDBT	Bad Debt Write Off	614.92	0.00	T9	Y	614.92	-	-	

284

L2 CertCB - Kate's Hair Supplies
Customer Address List

Customer From:
Customer To: ZZZZZZZZ

A/C	Name & Address	Contact Name	Telephone	Fax
BOYDS	Boyds Hair Design 15 Metchley Lane Harborne Birmingham B33 6FD			
RETRO	Retro Hair Birmingham Road Sutton Coldfield B15 4DE			
SAJNA	Sajna Hair & Beauty High Street Birmingham B1 6DD			
VALENTE	Valente Ltd Unit 20 Wainwright Street Aston Birmingham B6 5TD			

L2 CertCB - Kate's Hair Supplies
Broad Street
Birmingham
B1 5KE

L2 CertCB - Kate's Hair Supplies
Broad Street
Birmingham
B1 5KE

To:

Valente Ltd
Unit 20 Wainwright Street
Aston
Birmingham
B6 5TD

A/c Ref.	VALENTE
Date:	30/06/2009
Page:	1

From:

Valente Ltd
Unit 20 Wainwright Street
Aston
Birmingham
B6 5TD

A/c Ref.	VALENTE
Date:	30/06/2009
Page:	1

NOTE All values are shown in **Pound Sterling**

Date:	Ref.	Details	Debit	Credit
10/06/09	KH 03	Sales - Hair Products	1,637.06*	
10/06/09	KH 03	Sales - Magazines	18.75*	

NOTE All values are shown in **Pound Sterling**

Date:	Details	Debit	Credit
10/06/09	Sales - Hair Products	1,637.06	
10/06/09	Sales - Magazines	18.75	

Current	Period 1	Period 2	Period 3	Older
£ 1,655.81	£ 0.00	£ 0.00	£ 0.00	£ 0.00

Amount Due	
£	1,655.81

Amount Due	
£	1,655.81

Date: 25/04/2009
Time: 15:25:46

L2 CertCB - Kate's Hair Supplies
Aged Creditors Analysis (Detailed)

Page: 1

Date From:	01/01/1980
Date To:	30/06/2009

Supplier From:	
Supplier To:	ZZZZZZZZ

Include future transactions: No
Exclude later payments: No

** NOTE: All report values are shown in Base Currency, unless otherwise indicated **

A/C: MOHDAJ   Name: Mohdajaib   Contact: Tel:

No:	Type	Date	Ref	Details	Balance	Future	Current	Period 1	Period 2	Period 3	Older
29	PI	15/06/2009	M009	Purchases - Magazines	1,405.38	0.00	1,405.38	0.00	0.00	0.00	0.00
				Totals:	1,405.38	0.00	1,405.38	0.00	0.00	0.00	0.00

Turnover: 7,124.25
Credit Limit £ 0.00

A/C: WELLA   Name: Wella   Contact: Tel:

No:	Type	Date	Ref	Details	Balance	Future	Current	Period 1	Period 2	Period 3	Older
28	PI	12/06/2009	W 509	Purchases - Hair Produ	940.00	0.00	940.00	0.00	0.00	0.00	0.00
50	PA	23/06/2009	100009	Payment on Account	-500.00	0.00	-500.00	0.00	0.00	0.00	0.00
				Totals:	440.00	0.00	440.00	0.00	0.00	0.00	0.00

Turnover: 800.00
Credit Limit £ 0.00

	Grand Totals:	1,845.38	0.00	1,845.38	0.00	0.00	0.00	0.00

Date: 25/04/2009

Time: 15:23:45

Page: 1

L2 CertCB - Kate's Hair Supplies

Aged Debtors Analysis (Detailed)

Date From: 01/01/1980
Date To: 30/06/2009

Customer From:
Customer To: ZZZZZZZZ

Include future transactions: No
Exclude later payments: No

** NOTE: All report values are shown in Base Currency, unless otherwise indicated **

A/C: VALENTE **Name:** Valente Ltd

Contact:

Tel:

No	Type	Date	Ref	Details	Balance	Future	Current	Period 1	Period 2	Period 3	Older
15	SI	10/06/2009	KH 03	Sales - Hair Products	1,655.81	0.00	1,655.81	0.00	0.00	0.00	0.00
				Totals:	1,655.81	0.00	1,655.81	0.00	0.00	0.00	0.00

Turnover: 1,418.25
Credit Limit £ 0.00

	Balance	Future	Current	Period 1	Period 2	Period 3	Older
Grand Totals:	1,655.81	0.00	1,655.81	0.00	0.00	0.00	0.00

288

Date: 25/04/2009

Time: 15:28:45

L2 CertCB - Kate's Hair Supplies

Nominal Activity

Page: 1

Date From:	01/01/1980	N/C From:	1200
Date To:	30/06/2009	N/C To:	1200

Transaction From:	1
Transaction To:	99999999

N/C: 1200   **Name:** Bank Current Account   **Account Balance:** 20,877.69 DR

No	Type	Date	Account	Ref	Details	Dept	T/C	Value	Debit	Credit	V	B
2	JD	01/06/2009	1200	JV1	Capital	0	T9	15,000.00	15,000.00	-	-	R
4	BR	03/06/2009	1200	BR1	Loan	0	T9	20,000.00	20,000.00	-	-	R
5	BP	02/06/2009	1200	100001	Rent	0	T1	1,175.00		1,175.00	N	R
6	BP	05/06/2009	1200	100002	Shop Insurance	0	T2	750.00		750.00	N	R
7	BP	07/06/2009	1200	100003	Shop Fixtures	0	T1	352.50		352.50	N	R
8	BP	09/06/2009	1200	100004	Computer	0	T1	1,292.50		1,292.50	N	R
9	JC	11/06/2009	1200	100005	Petty Cash	0	T9	350.00		350.00	-	R
38	SR	06/06/2009	BOYDS	638256	Sales Receipt	0	T9	123.75	123.75		-	R
39	SR	10/06/2009	SAJNA	634279	Sales Receipt	0	T9	200.00	2C0.00		-	R
40	SR	22/06/2009	RETRO	534278	Sales Receipt	0	T9	575.94	575.94		-	R
42	SR	30/06/2009	BOYDS	638301	Sales Receipt	0	T9	171.88	171.88		-	R
43	BR	22/06/2009	1200	CS1	Sales - Hair Products	0	T1	120.00	120.00		N	R
44	BR	22/06/2009	1200	CS1	Sales - Magazines	0	T0	145.00	145.00		N	R
45	PP	11/06/2009	MOHDAJ	100006	Purchase Payment	0	T9	6,952.62		6,952.62	-	R
46	PP	14/06/2009	AVEDA	100007	Purchase Payment	0	T9	806.05		806.05	-	R
48	PP	18/06/2009	SHINE	100008	Purchase Payment	0	T9	412.71		412.71	-	R
50	PA	23/06/2009	WELLA	100009	Payment on Account	0	T9	500.00		500.00	-	R
51	BP	24/06/2009	1200	100010	Printing	0	T1	117.50		117.50	N	R
52	BP	26/06/2009	1200	STO1	Capital Repayment	0	T9	400.00		400.00	-	R
53	BP	26/06/2009	1200	STO1	Loan Interest	0	T2	100.00		100.00	N	R
54	BP	30/06/2009	1200	100011	Drawings	0	T9	500.00		500.00	-	R
55	JC	30/06/2009	1200	JV2	Net Wages	0	T9	1,750.00		1,750.00	-	R

	Totals:	36,336.57	20,877.69	15,458.88
	History Balance:	20,877.69		

Date: 25/04/2009
Time: 15:30:56

L2 CertCB - Kate's Hair Supplies
Nominal Activity

Page: 1

| Date From: | 01/01/1980 | N/C From: | 1230 |
| Date To: | 30/06/2009 | N/C To: | 1230 |

Transaction From: 1
Transaction To: 99999999

N/C: 1230   Name: Petty Cash   Account Balance: 169.35 DR

No	Type	Date	Account	Ref	Details	Dept	T/C	Value	Debit	Credit	V	B
10	JD	11/06/2009	1230	100005	Petty Cash	0	T9	350.00	350.00	-	N	
32	CP	02/06/2009	1230	PCV 01	Premises repairs	0	T1	35.00		35.00	N	N
33	CP	04/06/2009	1230	PCV 02	Refreshments	0	T0	19.75		19.75	N	N
34	CP	12/06/2009	1230	PCV 03	Printing	0	T1	18.40		18.40	N	N
35	CP	21/06/2009	1230	PCV 04	Office Desk	0	T1	55.00		55.00	N	N
36	CP	23/06/2009	1230	PCV 05	Premises repairs	0	T1	27.50		27.50	N	N
37	CP	27/06/2009	1230	PCV 06	Cleaning	0	T0	25.00		25.00	N	N

Totals: 350.00 180.65

History Balance: 169.35

Date: 25/04/2009
Time: 15:28:06

L2 CertCB - Kate's Hair Supplies

Nominal Activity

Page: 1

Date From: 01/01/1980
Date To: 30/06/2009

N/C From: 5000
N/C To: 5001

Transaction From: 1
Transaction To: 99999999

N/C: 5000 **Name:** Purchases - Hair Products

Account Balance: 8,912.50 DR

No	Type	Date	Account	Ref	Details	Dept	T/C	Value	Debit	Credit	V	B
24	PI	01/06/2009	AVEDA	AH 234	Purchases - Hair Products	0	T1	700.00	700.00		N	-
26	PI	01/06/2009	MOHDAJ	M004	Purchases - Hair Products	0	T1	5,875.00	5,875.00		N	-
27	PI	05/06/2009	SHINE	SH 2434	Purchases - Hair Products	0	T1	375.00	375.00		N	-
28	PI	12/06/2009	WELLA	W 509	Purchases - Hair Products	0	T1	800.00	800.00		N	-
30	PI	15/06/2009	MOHDAJ	M009	Purchases - Hair Products	0	T1	1,175.00	1,175.00		N	-
31	PC	15/06/2009	SHINE	SH CN056	Damaged bottles	0	T1	12.50		12.50	N	-

Totals: 8,925.00 12.50

History Balance: 8,912.50

N/C: 5001 **Name:** Purchases - Magazines

Account Balance: 74.25 DR

No	Type	Date	Account	Ref	Details	Dept	T/C	Value	Debit	Credit	V	B
25	PI	01/06/2009	MOHDAJ	M004	Purchases - Magazines	0	T0	49.50	49.50		N	-
29	PI	15/06/2009	MOHDAJ	M009	Purchases - Magazines	0	T0	24.75	24.75		N	-

Totals: 74.25

History Balance: 74.25

291

Date: 25/04/2009   **L2 CertCB - Kate's Hair Supplies**   **Page:** 1

Time: 15:27:32

Nominal Activity

| Date From: | 01/01/1980 | | N/C From: | 4000 |
| Date To: | 30/06/2009 | | N/C To: | 4001 |

| Transaction From: | 1 |
| Transaction To: | 99999999 |

N/C: 4000   **Name:** Sales - Hair Products   **Account Balance:** 2,877.63 CR

No	Type	Date	Account	Ref	Details	Dept	T/C	Value	Debit	Credit	V	B
11	SI	01/06/2009	BOYDS	KH 01	Sales - Hair Products	0	T1	100.00		100.00	N	-
13	SI	05/06/2009	SAJNA	KH 02	Sales - Hair Products	0	T1	315.00		315.00	N	-
15	SI	10/06/2009	VALENTE	KH 03	Sales - Hair Products	0	T1	1,399.50		1,399.50	N	-
17	SI	15/06/2009	RETRO	KH 04	Sales - Hair Products	0	T1	500.00		500.00	N	-
19	SI	16/06/2009	BOYDS	KH 05	Sales - Hair Products	0	T1	150.00		150.00	N	-
22	SI	25/06/2009	SAJNA	KH 06	Sales - Hair Products	0	T1	336.00		336.00	N	-
23	SC	27/06/2009	BOYDS	KH CN-1	Damaged goods	0	T1	25.00	25.00		N	-
43	BR	22/06/2009	1200	CS1	Sales - Hair Products	0	T1	102.13		102.13	N	R

| | | | | | | | **Totals:** | | 25.00 | 2,902.63 | | |
| | | | | | | | **History Balance:** | | | 2,877.63 | | |

N/C: 4001   **Name:** Sales - Magazines   **Account Balance:** 251.25 CR

No	Type	Date	Account	Ref	Details	Dept	T/C	Value	Debit	Credit	V	B
12	SI	01/06/2009	BOYDS	KH 01	Sales - Magazines	0	T0	6.25		6.25	N	-
14	SI	05/06/2009	SAJNA	KH 02	Sales - Magazines	0	T0	12.50		12.50	N	-
16	SI	10/06/2009	VALENTE	KH 03	Sales - Magazines	0	T0	18.75		18.75	N	-
18	SI	15/06/2009	RETRO	KH 04	Sales - Magazines	0	T0	6.25		6.25	N	-
20	SI	16/06/2009	BOYDS	KH 05	Sales - Magazines	0	T0	25.00		25.00	N	-
21	SI	25/06/2009	SAJNA	KH 06	Sales - Magazines	0	T0	37.50		37.50	N	-
44	BR	22/06/2009	1200	CS1	Sales - Magazines	0	T0	145.00		145.00	N	R

| | | | | | | | **Totals:** | | | 251.25 | | |
| | | | | | | | **History Balance:** | | | 251.25 | | |

IAB Level 2 I/D 110 Model Answers

L2 CertCB - Kate's Hair Supplies
Bank Statement - Reconciled and Un-reconciled

Page:

Date From : 01/01/1980
Date To : 30/06/2009

** NOTE: All values shown on this report are shown in the Bank Account's operating Currency **

Bank Code : 1200   **Bank Name :** Bank Current Account

Reconciled Transactions

No	Type	Date	Ref	Details	Debit	Credit	Balance	Running Bal.
2	JD	01/06/2009	JV1	Capital	15,000.00		15,000.00	15,000.00
5	BP	02/06/2009	100001	Rent		1,175.00	13,825.00	13,825.00
4	BR	03/06/2009	BR1	Loan	20,000.00		33,825.00	33,825.00
6	BP	05/06/2009	100002	Shop Insurance		750.00	33,075.00	33,075.00
38	SR	06/06/2009	638256	Sales Receipt	123.75		33,198.75	33,198.75
7	BP	07/06/2009	100003	Shop Fixtures		352.50	32,846.25	32,846.25
8	BP	09/06/2009	100004	Computer		1,292.50	31,553.75	31,553.75
39	SR	10/06/2009	634279	Sales Receipt	200.00		31,753.75	31,753.75
9	JC	11/06/2009	100005	Petty Cash		350.00	31,403.75	31,403.75
45	PP	11/06/2009	100006	Purchase Payment		6,952.62	24,451.13	24,451.13
46	PP	14/06/2009	100007	Purchase Payment		806.05	23,645.08	23,645.08
48	PP	18/06/2009	100008	Purchase Payment		412.71	23,232.37	23,232.37
40	SR	22/06/2009	534278	Sales Receipt	575.94		23,808.31	23,808.31
43	BR	22/06/2009	CS1	Sales - Hair Products	120.00		23,928.31	23,928.31
44	BR	22/06/2009	CS1	Sales - Magazines	145.00		24,073.31	24,073.31
50	PA	23/06/2009	100009	Payment on Account		500.00	23,573.31	23,573.31
52	BP	26/06/2009	STO1	Capital Repayment		400.00	23,173.31	23,173.31
53	BP	26/06/2009	STO1	Loan Interest		100.00	23,073.31	23,073.31
55	JC	30/06/2009	JV2	Net Wages		1,750.00	21,323.31	21,323.31
				Reconciled Total :	36,164.69	14,841.38	21,323.31	

Non-Reconciled Transactions

No	Type	Date	Ref	Details	Debit	Credit	Balance	Running Bal.
51	BP	24/06/2009	100010	Printing		117.50	-117.50	21,205.81
42	SR	30/06/2009	638301	Sales Receipt	171.88		54.38	21,377.69
54	BP	30/06/2009	100011	Drawings		500.00	-445.62	20,877.69
				Non-Reconciled Total :	171.88	617.50	-445.62	
				Bank Balance :	36,336.57	15,458.88	20,877.69	

293

		L2 CertCB - Kate's Hair Supplies			**Page:**	1

Date: 25/04/2009

Time: 15:25:10

Supplier Address List

Supplier From:

Supplier To: ZZZZZZZZ

A/C	Name	Contact	Telephone	Fax
AVEDA	Aveda Hair Upper Mall West Bullring Birmingham B5 4BP			
MOHDAJ	Mohdajaib 321 Wellington Road Handsworth Birmingham B20 2QL			
SHINE	Shine Hairdressers 7 The Quay Broad Street Birmingham B1 6DE			
WELLA	Wella 125 Broad Street Birmingham B1 5KH			

IAB Level 2 I/D 110 Model Answers

L2 CertCB - Kate's Hair Supplies
Period Trial Balance

To Period: Month 1, June 2009

N/C	Name	Debit	Credit
0030	Office Equipment	1,146.81	
0040	Fixtures & Fittings	10,300.00	
1100	Debtors Control Account	1,655.81	
1200	Bank Current Account	20,877.69	
1230	Petty Cash	169.35	
2100	Creditors Control Account		1,845.38
2200	Sales Tax Control Account		493.61
2201	Purchase Tax Control Account	2,013.00	
2210	Liability to HMR&C		639.00
2300	Loans		19,600.00
3000	Capital Introduced		25,000.00
3001	Drawings	500.00	
4000	Sales - Hair Products		2,877.63
4001	Sales - Magazines		251.25
4009	Discounts Allowed	15.19	
5000	Purchases - Hair Products	8,912.50	
5001	Purchases - Magazines	74.25	
5009	Discounts Taken		25.25
7000	Gross Wages	2,157.00	
7006	Employers N.I.	232.00	
7100	Rent	1,000.00	
7104	Premises Insurance	750.00	
7500	Printing	115.66	
7801	Cleaning	25.00	
7803	Premises Expenses	53.19	
7903	Loan Interest Paid	100.00	
8100	Bad Debt Write Off	614.92	
8205	Refreshments	19.75	
	Totals:	50,732.12	50,732.12

Qualifications for business

Exam ID 111

International Association of Book-keepers

Level 3 Diploma in Computerised Accounting

JUNE 2009
Question Paper

Qualification Accreditation Number 500/3023/1

Unit Accreditation Number J/103/1549

Candidates Instructions:

- **Time allowed: 2 hours and 30 minutes**

- **Candidates should answer all Tasks**

- **All written answers should be written in pen or word-processed**

International Association of Book-keepers, Suite 30, 40 Churchill Square, Kings Hill,
West Malling, Kent ME19 4YU
Tel: 0844 330 3527 e-mail: education@iab.org.uk

IAB Level 3 ID 111 Question Paper

INTERNATIONAL ASSOCIATION OF BOOK-KEEPERS

QUALIFICATION TITLE:
IAB LEVEL 3 DIPLOMA IN COMPUTERISED ACCOUNTING

Unit Title:
Accounting and advanced book-keeping using Accounting software

General Information and Instructions

1   You must enter your **Candidate Number, Student Number, Name of Centre, Date of Examination** and **Software used** on the front cover provided.

2   Time Allowed: **TWO HOURS AND 30 MINUTES**

3   Printing may be carried out after completion of the two hours and 30 minutes examination time.

4   All written answers should be in pen or word processed.

5   The use of silent non-programmable calculators is permitted.

6   NOTE - This Question Booklet has information and data printed on both sides of the pages.

7   The practical data input and printing of reports (Tasks 1 and 3) account for 90 marks, the remaining 10 marks cover Task 2.

8   Answers to Task 2 and the printouts taken at Task 3 should be firmly stapled into the Answer Booklet provided.

Scenario

You carry out the book-keeping for a wholesale business selling Health Foods and Supplements, run by Anton Skornia and his wife Alison. The business is called **Skornia's Health Products** and is operated as a partnership.

The business is registered for VAT (Standard Accounting) and trades on both a credit and cash basis.

Sales are divided into 2 categories – Supplements and Health Foods. The latter is VAT zero rated. Purchases are divided into 2 categories – Supplements and Health Foods, the latter being VAT zero rated.

Note: this paper has been produced using 17.5% as the standard rate of VAT. You should ensure that your software package has been set up for this correctly.

Required

TASK 1

You are required to set up the accounts on a commercial accounting package of your choice at the start of their new financial year on 1st January 2009. Enter this information into your accounting programme. After the name 'Skornia's Health Products' add your examination entry number.

Process the transactions for the month of January, taking into account the additional information provided and ensuring that every transaction has a unique reference number.

The following customer accounts are held in the Sales Ledger
- Country Kitchen
- County Stores
- Gentleman's Gym Ltd.

Outstanding at 31st December 2008

Customer	Invoice No.	Date	Gross amount
Country Kitchen	AS 786	21.11.2008	£2,052.95
	AS 804	15.12.2008	£896.63
County Stores	AS 787	22.11.2008	£3,505.80
	Payment on Account	25.11.2008	£3,000.00
Gentleman's Gym Ltd.	AS 805	10.12.2008	£1,085.62
	Credit Note ASC 043	Issued 14.12.2008	£1,850.62

298

The following supplier accounts are held in the Purchase Ledger

- Edwards & Son Health Foods
- Smith Bros
- Parr's Performance Supplements Ltd.

Outstanding at 31st December 2008:

Supplier	Invoice No.	Date	Gross amount
Edwards & Son Health Foods	E 1003	26.11.2008	£785.40
	E 1036	10.12.2008	£927.50
Smith Bros	SB 407	14.12.2008	£1,835.34
Parr's Performance Supplements Ltd.	PP 1978	19.11.2008	£929.17
	PP 2007	22.12.2008	£1,006.24

The Accountant has provided details of some Nominal Ledger Account Balances as at 31st December 2008:

	Debit £	Credit £
Stock	3,800.00	
Debtors Control Account	2,690.38	
Bank Current Account		1,056.98
Petty Cash	200.00	
Creditors Control Account		5,483.65
VAT Liability	152.80	
PAYE/NIC Liability		514.76
	6,843.18	7,055.39

Additional Information

1. You have been advised that Anton's wife, Alison, has made a loan to the business – the Accountant will later give you details of the amount of the loan; however, you have been told it is repayable at a rate of £500 per month, £380 of which is the capital repayment. The repayments are made by Standing Order on 25th of each month.

2. The gas, electricity and telephone bills are all received in March, June, September and December.
   - The annual total gas and electricity expenditure for 2008 was £3,240 and is expected to rise by £360 in 2009.
   - Telephone is expected to be £450 per month

3. Depreciation
   - Motor vehicles 25% on a straight line basis.
   - Computer and office equipment is depreciated over 10 years based on cost.
   - Freehold premises are to be depreciated at 4% per annum based on cost.
   - No depreciation is charged on assets in the year of sale. A full year's depreciation is charged on a month by month basis in the year of purchase.

The paperwork has been batched and the January transactions, set out below, should now be entered, taking into account any additional information provided.

SALES:

Date	Details
03 Jan	Raised invoice AS 840 to Country Kitchen. This was for Supplements £2,089.56, Health Foods £4,891.34 plus VAT £358.35 (total £7,339.25). The invoice was subject to a 2% settlement discount if paid within 14 days.
09 Jan	Raised invoice AS 841 Gentleman's Gym Ltd. This was for Supplements £895.31 plus VAT £156.67 (total £1,051.98).
12 Jan	Raised invoice AS 842 to a new customer, The Healthy Way. This was for Health Foods £1,098.35.

PURCHASES:

Date	Details
02 Jan	Received invoice SB 427 from Smith Bros. This was for Supplements £1,735.02, Health Foods £2,986.20 plus VAT £303.62 (total £5,024.84)
09 Jan	Received invoice PP 2027 from Parr's Performance Supplements Ltd. This was for Supplements £1,084.32 plus VAT £189.75 (total £1,274.07)
12 Jan	Received invoice E 1098 from Edwards & Son Health Foods. This was for Health Foods £1,093.76. The invoice was subject to a 3% settlement discount if paid within 10 days.

PURCHASE RETURNS:

Date	Details
23 Jan	Received Credit Note SBC 12 from Smith Bros. This was for Supplements £30.00 plus VAT £5.25 (total £35.25).

The PAYING IN BOOK revealed:

Date	Details
15 Jan	Received the VAT refund of £152.80 from HMRC by BACS.
16 Jan	Received cheque 340 from Country Kitchen for £9,252.58. This was for invoices AS 786 and AS 840, which were paid in full, taking account of the discount offered.
20 Jan	Received cheque 208 from Gentleman's Gym. This was for £250.00. It was to clear their account as it stands at present. As there was a mistake on our part with the credit note, we agreed to write off the difference as a goodwill gesture.
24 Jan	Banked £509.60. This was cash sales covering Supplements £308.40 (including VAT), the balance being for Health Foods.

The CHEQUE BOOK revealed:

Date	Details
01 Jan	Raised cheque 236 for £50 for Petty Cash.
02 Jan	Raised cheque 237 for business rates. This was for £3,600.00 and covered the period for three months ended 31 March 2009.
15 Jan	Paid £514.76 to HMRC. This was in settlement of the PAYE/NIC liability. The payment was made 'on line' using internet banking, using a unique reference number.
21 Jan	Raised cheque 238 for £1,060.95, payable to Edwards & Son Health Foods, in full settlement of invoice E 1098, taking advantage of the discount offered.
29 Jan	Was advised by our bank that a cheque for £20.00, relating to cash sales of Health Foods had been returned as 'refer to drawer'.

PETTY CASH vouchers revealed:

Date	Details
02 Jan	Paid £60, including VAT on PCV 1. This was for diesel for the delivery vehicle.
08 Jan	Paid £20, exempt from VAT on PCV 2 for postages.
15 Jan	Paid £14.40, including VAT on PCV 3. This was for carriage inwards on deliveries of purchases.
28 Jan	Paid £15, on PCV 4 for refreshments for a management meeting. This was zero rated for VAT.

302

The Accountant has now provided the complete list of opening balances at 31st December 2008. Work out the adjustments required to bring your opening balances into line with the figures below and make the entries onto the system.

	Debit £	Credit £
Motor Vehicles at Cost	18,000.00	
Motor Vehicle Depreciation		6,800.00
Computer & Office Equipment at Cost	12,800.00	
Computer & Office Equipment Depreciation		3,200.00
Freehold Premises	15,000.00	
Loan from wife		20,000.00
Stock	3,800.00	
Debtors Control Account	2,690.38	
Bank Current Account		1,056.98
Petty Cash	200.00	
Creditors Control Account		5,483.65
VAT Liability	152.80	
PAYE/NIC Liability		514.76
Capital Account – Anton		32,341.90
Capital Account – Alison	16,754.11	
	69,397.29	69,397.29

Required

When you have made these adjustments the Accountant has asked you to edit the chart of accounts, to ensure the Partners' Capital Accounts and Mrs Skornia's loan account are clearly shown.

NB At the present time, Partners' Current Accounts are not kept in the books.

OTHER INFORMATION

Date	Details
1 Jan	Alison introduced her car to the business. This was valued at £6,000.00
30 Jan	Drew cheque 239. This was to reimburse the Petty Cash float and increase it to £320.00
30 Jan	The January wages and salaries were prepared: Net Wages £903.89 Employees NIC £142.90 Employers NIC £202.12 Employees Tax £198.56 Deductions for staff pensions £125.00 The net wages were paid by BACS and the tax and NIC will be sent to HM Revenue & Customs on 15 February and should be posted as a journal.
31 Jan	Anton took his drawings of £800.00, using cheque number 240.
31 Jan	Alison took Supplements at a selling price of £80, including VAT. She also took Health Foods valued at a cost of £120.00. It was the firm's practice to make a gross margin of 25% on sale of Health Foods.
31 Jan	It was agreed that £5,000.00 of the balance on Alison's Capital Account should be offset against Alison's loan account. This was done by Journal Entry after the adjustment for drawings above.
31 Jan	It is the firm's practice to only show the total VAT liability in the accounts. Prepare and post a Journal to transfer the balances on the VAT Sales Tax Account and VAT Purchase Tax Account to a single VAT Liability Account.
31 Jan	The partners decided to create a provision for doubtful debts equal to 2% of the Debtors figure at the end of January.
31 Jan	It was found that £10 of the diesel purchased using PCV 1 was for Alison's daughter's car. This is private and the adjustment should be made by Journal entry.
31 Jan	Stock was valued at £4,000.00
31 Jan	Process the adjustments at the end of January.

PLEASE TURN OVER

TASK 2

Answers to Task 2 should be word processed or written on the sheet at the back of this Question Paper. Please detach the sheet and include it with your printouts.

a) A friend has suggested that the partners could control the business better if they produced an annual budget broken down on a month by month basis.

Explain how they could do this with the accounting package you have used and the benefits it will bring for the business owners.

(4 Marks)

b) A friend has suggested to Anton that he and his wife have separate Capital and Current Accounts, rather than the present set up. Give **two** advantages of this suggestion. **(4 Marks)**

c) Print out the Chart of Accounts and indicate on it where you would expect to find the Current Accounts. **(2 Marks)**

TASK 3

Print the following as at 31st January 2009

This task may be carried out after completion of the two and a half hour examination time.

- Trial Balance
- Summary Audit Trail
- Nominal Activity reports for each category of sales, purchases, bank current account and petty cash accounts.
- Detailed Aged Debtors and Creditors Analyses
- VAT Return for the month of January
- Profit & Loss Account for the month ended 31 January 2009.
- Balance Sheet as at 31 January 2009.

Marking Scheme
June 2009 – Skornia's Health Products

Printouts	Check printouts are those asked for. If not:	
	• If the work can be marked from those provided:	Deduct 3 marks for first, 1 mark for each additional missing/wrong printout.
	○ Missing/wrong printouts	
	○ Wrongly dated printouts	
	• Audit Trail –	
	○ Default dates	No penalty
	○ If "Date from" is 1 January (so b/fwd transactions not on AT)	Deduct 3
	• Other reports:	
	○ If "Date from" is default	No penalty
	○ If "Date to" is incorrect	Deduct 3
	• If complete (or nearly complete) Nominal Ledger Activity is submitted	Deduct 3
	• If Aged Analyses are Summary rather than Detailed	Deduct 1 for each report
		Maximum deduction for printouts of 5
	• If the work cannot be marked from those provided.	Treat transactions as missing
Set up	• If set for VAT Cash Accounting – you can tell this because the Sales Receipts and Purchase Payments are split into net and VAT	Deduct 3 marks, but, assuming total of each SR and PP is correct, no further penalty.
Check Trial Balance	• If Financial Year not set correctly, i.e. January is not Month 1.	Deduct 5 marks.
	• Inappropriately named Nominal Accounts	Deduct 1 mark each **(Max 3 Marks)**
	• Accounts mis-spelt	No penalty
	• If "Sales-xxxxxx" and "Sales-xxxxxx" are missing the word "Sales"	Deduct 1
	• Purchases, as for Sales	Deduct 1
	• If the value split between the two Sales and/or two Purchases Accounts is incorrect	Deduct 3 for first incorrect transaction +1+1 **(max 5 for Sales + 5 for Purchases)**
Check Aged Analyses	• If allocation incorrect, e.g. remaining matching credit note and part of invoice	Deduct 1 each

Following full Moderation

Check Balance Sheet	• **Editing – should be** Partners capital accounts in Financed by – if omitted	Deduct 1 each
Check Audit Trail (or other reports as easiest)	• If opening entries not set at 31 December	Deduct 5 marks
	• References missing	Deduct 1 mark each
	• Where Recurring entry or Journal reference is wrong, treat both parts as one transaction • Reference "not unique", i.e. a relevant "word", e.g. "Capital", "Loan", "January" etc.	Deduct 1 Deduct 1 mark each to a max of 2 **Max deduction for references 5 marks – however, where a candidate has entered nothing for the majority of the reference fields, deduct a further 5 marks.**
	• Details inappropriate (including so long it runs into figures) or missing • Details mis-spelt	Deduct 1 marks each No penalty **Max deduction for details 5 marks – however, where a candidate has entered nothing for the majority of the details fields, deduct a further 5 marks.**
	• **Incorrect :** - Customer or Supplier - Nominal account used - Part of Chart of Accounts, i.e. error of principle - Incorrect month or year in date - Incorrect values (net or VAT)	Deduct 3 marks each time **If transaction linked** and consistent treatment, deduct 1 further mark each to **a maximum of 5 marks**
	• Payments on Account treated as Sales Receipts or Purchase Payments (or vice versa) • If VAT given in paper and it is entered incorrectly (even by 1p)	Deduct 2 each time **Deduct 3 marks for the first item +1 +1 to a maximum deduction 5 for Sales and 5 for Purchases**
	• Manual calculation of VAT (where gross amount is given) may result in 1p difference • More than one error in one transaction	Accept Deduct 5 (3 + 2)

Discounts	• Discount allowed and discount received must be treated as two separate items.	Deduct 3 marks for first time and 1 mark thereafter for Discount allowed. Same for Discount received.
Loan repayments	• Treat the interest and capital element as one transaction.	If not split, deduct 3 marks.
	• The capital repayment can be deducted from the initial advance or shown separately without penalty.	
	• If shown in the wrong section of chart of accounts	Deduct 3 marks.
	• If posted at the start	No penalty
	• Both Nominal Codes wrong	Deduct 4 marks
	• Missing altogether	Deduct 4 marks
Journal entries	Treat as one transaction	
	• Reversal	Deduct 3 marks
	• One wrong Nominal Code	Deduct 3 marks
	• Both Nominal Codes wrong	Deduct 4 marks
	• Codes and values wrong	Deduct 4 marks
		Maximum deduction 5 marks
Wages	• If net wages shown in liabilities section.	Deduct 3 marks.
	• If liability shown in expenses section.	Deduct 3 marks.
	• If employers NI not shown as a separate expenses.	Deduct 1 mark.
	• If net wages correct but Tax and NICs omitted altogether	Deduct 4 marks
		Maximum deduction 6 marks
End of Month Postings - errors	• Errors in amounts, nominal code, reversal etc. or missing entries	Deduct 3 marks each time.
	• Depreciation – own figure based on TB Asset value	No penalty
	• If opening and closing stock netted off in the trading account	Deduct 2 marks
	• Provision for Doubtful Debts – If postings are correct but the debit is to Bad Debts, instead of Bad Debt Provision	Deduct 1
	• If credit is in Debtors Control A/C	Deduct 1
	• The calculation of depreciation may be up to 2p different	No penalty
	• If depreciation credited to cost of asset account	Deduct 1 mark in each case
	Balance Sheet	
	• If adjustment to names on chart of account not carried out as requested	Deduct 1 mark each time, **(Maximum 3 for BS)**

Incomplete Papers	Where transactions are missing or papers have not been completed – count transactions on the **QUESTION PAPER** (not lines on the Audit Trail)	
	• Missing invoice, credit note, receipt, payment OR discount	Deduct 3 marks
	• Loan Repayment	Deduct 4 marks
	• Payment/receipt AND discount	Deduct 4 marks
	• Returned Cheque	Deduct 4 marks
	• Missing Goods for own use	Deduct 5 marks
	• Missing Wages, Tax & NICs and Pension	Deduct 6 marks
	• Missing VAT Transfer	Deduct 4 marks
	• Missing Provision for Doubtful Debts	Deduct 4 marks
	• Correction – fuel for own use	Deduct 4 marks
	• Stock Adjustment	Deduct 4 marks
	• End of month Accruals, Prepayments and Depreciation not processed	Deduct up to 8 (i.e. 6 postings = deduct 3 for the first and 1 for each subsequent omission)
Items specific to this paper	• **Payment on account in opening balances**	
	- Can be entered as SA or SC	No penalty
	- **Order of Opening Balances – if they are all entered at the start**	Deduct 3 marks
	• **"Goodwill Gesture" – should be treated as a discount – if posted to an expense account, appropriately named**	No penalty
	• **If posted as Intangible asset**	Deduct 3 marks
	• **Separate "Cash Sales" account, correctly posted**	No penalty
	- **PCV1 – Carriage Inward, should be cost of sales (5100)**	
	- If posted to Overheads	Deduct 2 marks
	- **PCV4 – Refreshments**	
	- If posted to Subsistence	Deduct 2 marks
	• **Introduction of new Vehicle:**	
	- if no attempt	Deduct 4 marks
	- if some attempt but incorrect	Deduct 3 marks
	Bad Debt write off – if debited to N/C 4001	Deduct 3 marks?
	GOODS FOR OWN USE	We would normally deduct a maximum of 5 for Goods for own use. However, in this paper the Journal correction is also goods for own use and, if candidates get the first wrong, they are likely to get both wrong. Therefore, I am suggesting –5 for each, but capped at –8 in total.

309

	Diesel for daughters use	Accept either £8.51 + £1.49, or £8.52 + £1.48
	- **VAT should be posted to N/C 2202. If posted to 2201**	Deduct 1 mark
	- **If VAT not split off**	Deduct 3 marks
	- **If £10 repaid to Petty Cash rather than debited to Capital or Drawings**	No penalty
	Wages – Pension	
	- Should be debited to Wages, credited to Pension Liability account	No penalty
	- If debit in account of its own in 7-thousands	
	- If liability combined with Tax & NICs	Deduct 3 marks
	- If omitted	Above all to be included in maximum deduction of 6
	VAT transfer of balances – own figures accepted	
	- If figures incorrect	Deduct 3 marks
	- If not carried out	Deduct 4 marks
	VAT Codes	
	- Loan repayment – Capital T9, Interest T2	Deduct 2 marks maximum
	- Daughter's Fuel Journal correction – if incorrect	Deduct 2 marks maximum – maximum deduction for Journal correct = 5
Partners Drawings	- If Partners Current Accounts set up in correct sections and posted to correctly	**No penalty**
	- If only one Drawings account set up but then posted to correctly	**Deduct 3 marks + 1 mark on TB for Account name**
	- If Capital and/or Current Accounts set up in wrong section of Chart of Accounts	**Deduct 5 marks (-3, -1, -1)**

IAB Level 3 Diploma Marking Scheme

L3 DipCA-June 2009-Skornia's Health Products
Period Trial Balance

To Period: Month 1, January 2009

N/C	Name	Debit	Credit
0010	Freehold Property	15,000.00	
0011	Freehold Premises Depreciation		50.00
0030	Computer & Office Equipment	12,800.00	
0031	Computer & Office Equipment Depreciation		3,306.67
0050	Motor Vehicles	21,000.00	
0051	Motor Vehicles Depreciation		7,300.00
1001	Stock	4,000.00	
1100	Debtors Control Account	2,500.78	
1101	Provision for Doubtful Debts		50.02
1103	Prepayments	2,400.00	
1200	Bank Current Account	1,479.00	
1230	Petty Cash	320.00	
2100	Creditors Control Account		11,747.31
2109	Accruals		750.00
2202	VAT Liability		75.14
2210	PAYE/NIC Liability		543.58
2212	Pension Liability		125.00
2300	Loan - Alison		14,620.00
3000	Capital Account - Anton		31,541.90
3001	Capital Account - Alison	6,004.11	
4000	Sales-Supplements		3,315.43
4001	Sales-Health Foods		6,350.89
4009	Discounts Allowed	176.60	
5000	Purchases-Supplements	2,789.34	
5001	Purchases-Health Foods	4,079.96	
5009	Discounts Taken		32.81
5100	Carriage	12.26	
5200	Opening Stock	3,800.00	
5201	Closing Stock		4,000.00
7000	Gross Wages	1,370.35	
7006	Employers N.I.	202.12	
7103	General Rates	1,200.00	
7200	Gas/Electricity	300.00	
7300	Fuel and Oil	42.54	
7501	Postage and Carriage	20.00	
7502	Telephone	450.00	
7903	Loan Interest Paid	120.00	
8000	Freehold Depreciation	50.00	
8003	Vehicle Depreciation	500.00	
8004	Comp.& Office Equipment Depreciation	106.67	
8100	Bad Debt Write Off	20.00	
8102	Bad Debt Provision	50.02	
8205	Refreshments	15.00	
	Totals:	**83,808.75**	**83,808.75**

End of Report

Date: 20/06/2009
Time: 10:49:22

L3 DipCA-June 2009-Skornia's Health Products

Audit Trail (Summary)

Page: 1

Date From:	01/01/1980		Customer From:	
Date To:	31/12/2019		Customer To:	ZZZZZZZZ
Transaction From:	1		Supplier From:	
Transaction To:	99,999,999		Supplier To:	ZZZZZZZZ
Dept From:	0		N/C From:	
Dept To:	999		N/C To:	99999999
Exclude Deleted Tran:	No			

No	Type	Date	A/C	N/C	Dept	Ref	Details	Net	Tax	T/C	Pd	Paid	V	B	Bank Rec. Date
1	SI	21/11/2008	COUNTRY	9998	0	AS 786	Opening Balance	2,052.95	0.00	T9	Y	2,052.95	-	-	
2	SI	15/12/2008	COUNTRY	9998	0	AS 804	Opening Balance	896.63	0.00	T9	N	0.00	-	-	
3	SI	22/11/2008	COUNTY	9998	0	AS 787	Opening Balance	3,505.80	0.00	T9	N	0.00	-	-	
4	SC	25/11/2008	COUNTY	9998	0	PoA	Opening Balance	3,000.00	0.00	T9	N	0.00	-	-	
5	SI	10/12/2008	GG	9998	0	AS 805	Opening Balance	1,085.62	0.00	T9	Y	1,085.62	-	-	
6	SC	14/12/2008	GG	9998	0	ASC 043	Opening Balance	1,850.62	0.00	T9	Y	1,850.62	-	-	
7	PI	26/11/2008	EDWARD	9998	0	E1003	Opening Balance	785.40	0.00	T9	N	0.00	-	-	
8	PI	10/12/2008	EDWARD	9998	0	E1036	Opening Balance	927.50	0.00	T9	N	0.00	-	-	
9	PI	14/12/2008	SMITH	9998	0	SB 407	Opening Balance	1,835.34	0.00	T9	N	0.00	-	-	
10	PI	19/11/2008	PARR	9998	0	PP 1978	Opening Balance	929.17	0.00	T9	N	0.00	-	-	
11	PI	22/12/2008	PARR	9998	0	PP 2007	Opening Balance	1,006.24	0.00	T9	N	0.00	-	-	
12	JD	31/12/2008	1001	1001	0	J1	Stock @ 31 Dec 08	3,800.00	0.00	T9	Y	3,800.00	-	-	
13	JC	31/12/2008	1290	1200	0	J1	Bank @ 31 Dec 08	1,056.98	0.00	T9	Y	1,056.98	-	N	
14	JD	31/12/2008	1230	1230	0	J1	PC @ 31 Dec 08	200.00	0.00	T9	Y	200.00	-	N	
15	JD	31/12/2008	2202	2202	0	J1	VAT @ 31 Dec 08	152.80	0.00	T9	Y	152.80	-	-	
16	JC	31/12/2008	2210	2210	0	J1	PAYE/NIC @ 31 Dec 08	514.76	0.00	T9	Y	514.76	-	-	
17	JC	31/12/2008	9998	9998	0	J1	Incomplete TB Bal.	2,581.06	0.00	T9	Y	2,581.06	-	-	
18	SI	03/01/2009	COUNTRY	4000	0	AS 840	Supplements	2,089.56	358.35	T1	Y	2,447.91	N	-	
19	SI	03/01/2009	COUNTRY	4001	0	AS 840	Health Foods	4,891.34	0.00	T0	Y	4,891.34	N	-	
20	SI	09/01/2009	GG	4000	0	AS 841	Supplements	895.31	156.67	T1	Y	1,051.98	N	-	
21	SI	12/01/2009	HEALTHY	4001	0	AS 842	Health Foods	1,098.35	0.00	T0	N	0.00	N	-	
22	PI	02/01/2009	SMITH	5000	0	SB427	Supplements	1,735.02	303.62	T1	N	0.00	N	-	
23	PI	02/01/2009	SMITH	5001	0	SB427	Health Foods	2,986.20	0.00	T0	N	0.00	N	-	
24	PI	09/01/2009	PARR	5000	0	PP 2027	Supplements	1,084.32	189.75	T1	N	0.00	N	-	
25	PI	12/01/2009	EDWARD	5001	0	E 1098	Health Foods	1,093.76	0.00	T0	N	1,093.76	N	-	
26	PC	23/01/2009	SMITH	5000	0	SBC 12	Supplements	30.60	5.25	T1	N	0.00	N	-	
27	BR	15/01/2009	1200	2202	0	BR1	VAT Refund	152.80	0.00	T9	Y	152.80	-	N	
28	SR	16/01/2009	COUNTRY	1200	0	340	Sales Receipt	9,252.58	0.00	T9	Y	9,252.58	-	-	
29	SD	16/01/2009	COUNTRY	4009	0	340	Sales Discount	139.62	0.00	T9	Y	139.62	-	-	
30	SR	20/01/2009	GG	1200	0	208	Sales Receipt	250.00	0.00	T9	Y	250.00	-	N	

IAB Level 3 Diploma Marking Scheme

Date: 20/06/2009
Time: 10:49:22

L3 DipCA-June 2009-Skornia's Health Products

Audit Trail (Summary)

No	Type	Date	A/C	N/C	Dept	Ref	Details	Net	Tax	T/C	Pd	Paid	V	B	Bank Rec. Date
31	SD	20/01/2009	GG	4009	0	208	Sales Discount	36.98	0.00	T9	Y	36.98	-	-	
32	BR	24/01/2009	1200	4000	0	BR2	Cash Sales-Supplements	262.47	45.93	T1	Y	308.40	N	N	
33	BR	24/01/2009	1200	4001	0	BR3	Cash Sales-Health Foods	201.20	0.00	T0	Y	201.20	N	N	
34	JC	01/01/2009	1200	1200	0	236	Bank to PC	50.00	0.00	T9	Y	50.00	-	N	
35	JD	01/01/2009	1230	1230	0	236	Bank to PC	50.00	0.00	T9	Y	50.00	-	N	
36	BP	02/01/2009	1200	7103	0	237	Business Rates	3,600.00	0.00	T9	Y	3,600.00	-	N	
37	BP	15/01/2009	1200	2210	0	IB1	HMRC Tax/NI	514.76	0.00	T9	Y	514.76	-	N	
38	PP	21/01/2009	EDWARD	1200	0	238	Purchase Payment	1,060.95	0.00	T9	Y	1,060.95	-	N	
39	PD	31/01/2009	EDWARD	5009	0	238	Purchase Discount	32.81	0.00	T9	Y	32.81	-	-	
40	BP	29/01/2009	1200	8100	0	BD1	CS Chq-RTD	20.00	0.00	T9	Y	20.00	-	-	
41	CP	02/01/2009	1230	7300	0	PCV1	Diesel	51.06	8.94	T2	Y	60.00	N	N	
42	CP	08/01/2009	1230	7501	0	PCV2	Postages	20.00	0.00	T2	Y	20.00	N	N	
43	CP	15/01/2009	1230	5100	0	PCV3	Carriage Inwards	12.26	2.14	T1	Y	14.40	N	N	
44	CP	28/01/2009	1230	8205	0	PCV4	Refreshments	15.00	0.00	T9	Y	15.00	N	-	
45	JD	31/12/2008	0050	0050	0	J2	MV @ 31 Dec 08	18,000.00	0.00	T9	Y	18,000.00	-	-	
46	JC	31/12/2008	0051	0051	0	J2	MV Depsn @ 31 Dec 08	6,800.00	0.00	T9	Y	6,800.00	-	-	
47	JD	31/12/2008	0030	0030	0	J2	Comp & OE @ 31 Dec 08	12,800.00	0.00	T9	Y	12,800.00	-	-	
48	JC	31/12/2008	0031	0031	0	J2	Comp & OE @ 31 Dec 08	3,200.00	0.00	T9	Y	3,200.00	-	-	
49	JD	31/12/2008	0010	0010	0	J2	Premises @ 31 Dec 08	15,000.00	0.00	T9	Y	15,000.00	-	-	
50	JC	31/12/2008	2300	2300	0	J2	O/S Loan @ 31 Dec 08	20,000.00	0.00	T9	Y	20,000.00	-	-	
51	JD	31/12/2008	3000	3000	0	J2	Anton A/C @ 31 Dec 08	32,341.90	0.00	T9	Y	32,341.90	-	-	
52	JD	31/12/2008	3001	3001	0	J2	Alison A/C @ 31 Dec 08	16,754.11	0.00	T9	Y	16,754.11	-	-	
53	JC	31/12/2008	9998	9998	0	J2	Clear Suspense	212.21	0.00	T9	Y	212.21	-	-	
54	JC	01/01/2009	0050	0050	0	J3	Car introduced-Alison	6,000.00	0.00	T9	Y	6,000.00	-	-	
55	JC	01/01/2009	3001	3001	0	J3	Car introduced-Alison	6,000.00	0.00	T9	Y	6,000.00	-	-	
56	JC	30/01/2009	1200	1200	0	239	Restore+increase PC	179.40	0.00	T9	Y	179.40	-	N	
57	JD	30/01/2009	1230	1230	0	239	Restore+increase PC	179.40	0.00	T9	Y	179.40	-	N	
58	BP	30/01/2009	1200	7000	0	BACS1	Net Wages Jan	903.89	0.00	T9	Y	903.89	-	N	
59	JD	30/01/2009	7000	7000	0	J4	Employees NIC Jan	142.90	0.00	T9	Y	142.90	-	-	
60	JD	30/01/2009	7006	7006	0	J4	Employers NIC Jan	202.12	0.00	T9	Y	202.12	-	-	
61	JD	30/01/2009	7000	7000	0	J4	Employees Tax Jan	198.56	0.00	T9	Y	198.56	-	-	
62	JC	30/01/2009	2210	2210	0	J4	Total Tax & NI Jan	543.58	0.00	T9	Y	543.58	-	-	
63	JD	30/01/2009	7000	7000	0	J4	Pension deductions Jan	125.00	0.00	T9	Y	125.00	-	-	
64	JC	30/01/2009	2212	2212	0	J4	Pension deductions Jan	125.00	0.00	T9	Y	125.00	-	-	
65	BP	31/01/2009	1200	3000	0	240	Anton-Drgs	800.00	0.00	T9	Y	800.00	-	N	
66	JC	31/01/2009	4000	4000	0	J5	Alison-Goods own use	68.09	0.00	T1	Y	68.09	N	-	
67	JC	31/01/2009	2200	2200	0	J5	Alison-Goods own use-VAT	11.91	0.00	T1	Y	11.91	N	-	
68	JC	31/01/2009	4001	4001	0	J5	Alison-Goods own use	160.00	0.00	T0	Y	160.00	N	-	
69	JD	31/01/2009	3001	3001	0	J5	Alison-Goods own use	240.00	0.00	T9	Y	240.00	-	-	

Date: 20/06/2009
Time: 10:49:22

L3 DipCA-June 2009-Skornia's Health Products

Audit Trail (Summary)

Page: 3

No	Type	Date	A/C	N/C	Dept	Ref	Details	Net	Tax	T/C	Pd	Paid	V	B	Bank Rec. Date
70	JD	31/01/2009	2300	2300	0	J6	Offset from Capital A/C	5,000.00	0.00	T9	Y	5,000.00	-	-	
71	JC	31/01/2009	3001	3001	0	J6	Offset Loan	5,000.00	0.00	T9	Y	5,000.00	-	-	
72	JD	31/01/2009	2200	2200	0	J7	Trf to N/C 2202	572.86	0.00	T9	Y	572.86	-	-	
73	JC	31/01/2009	2201	2201	0	J7	Trf to N/C 2202	499.20	0.00	T9	Y	499.20	-	-	
74	JC	31/01/2009	2202	2202	0	J7	Trf from N/C 2200/2201	73.66	0.00	T9	Y	73.66	-	-	
75	JC	31/01/2009	1101	1101	0	J8	Provision for DD-2%	50.02	0.00	T9	Y	50.02	-	-	
76	JD	31/01/2009	8102	8102	0	J8	Provision for DD-2%	50.02	0.00	T9	Y	50.02	-	-	
77	JD	31/01/2009	3001	3001	0	J9	Fuel-Alison's daughter	10.00	0.00	T9	Y	10.00	-	-	
78	JC	31/01/2009	7300	7300	0	J9	Fuel-Alison's daughter	8.52	0.00	T1	Y	8.52	N	-	
79	JC	31/01/2009	2202	2202	0	J9	Fuel-Alison's daughter-VAT	1.48	0.00	T1	Y	1.48	N	-	
80	JD	31/01/2009	5200	5200	0	J10	Stock @ 1 Jan 09	3,800.00	0.00	T9	Y	3,800.00	-	-	
81	JC	31/01/2009	5201	5201	0	J10	Stock @ 31 Jan 09	4,000.00	0.00	T9	Y	4,000.00	-	-	
82	JD	31/01/2009	1001	1001	0	J10	Change in Stock Jan	200.00	0.00	T9	Y	200.00	-	-	
83	BP	25/01/2009	1200	2300	0	SO1	Alison-Loan Repayment	380.00	0.00	T9	Y	380.00	-	N	
84	BP	25/01/2009	1200	7903	0	SO1	Alison-Loan Interest	120.00	0.00	T2	Y	120.00	-	N	
85	JD	31/01/2009	7200	7200	0	ACCRUE	Gas/Electricity	300.00	0.00	T9	Y	300.00	-	-	
86	JC	31/01/2009	2109	2109	0	ACCRUE	Gas/Electricity	300.00	0.00	T9	Y	300.00	-	-	
87	JD	31/01/2009	7502	7502	0	ACCRUE	Telephone	450.00	0.00	T9	Y	450.00	-	-	
88	JC	31/01/2009	2109	2109	0	ACCRUE	Telephone	450.00	0.00	T9	Y	450.00	-	-	
89	JC	31/01/2009	7103	7103	0	PREPAY	Rates	3,600.00	0.00	T9	Y	3,600.00	-	-	
90	JD	31/01/2009	1103	1103	0	PREPAY	Rates	3,600.00	0.00	T9	Y	3,600.00	-	-	
91	JD	31/01/2009	7103	7103	0	PREPAY	Rates	1,200.00	0.00	T9	Y	1,200.00	-	-	
92	JC	31/01/2009	1103	1103	0	PREPAY	Rates	1,200.00	0.00	T9	Y	1,200.00	-	-	
93	JC	31/01/2009	0031	0031	0	DEPREC	Comp.& Off.Equipment	106.67	0.00	T9	Y	106.67	-	-	
94	JD	31/01/2009	8004	8004	0	DEPREC	Comp.& Off.Equipment	106.67	0.00	T9	Y	106.67	-	-	
95	JC	31/01/2009	0011	0011	0	DEPREC	Freehold Premises	50.00	0.00	T9	Y	50.00	-	-	
96	JD	31/01/2009	8000	8000	0	DEPREC	Freehold Premises	50.00	0.00	T9	Y	50.00	-	-	
97	JC	31/01/2009	0051	0051	0	DEPREC	Motor Vehicles	500.00	0.00	T9	Y	500.00	-	-	
98	JD	31/01/2009	8003	8003	0	DEPREC	Motor Vehicles	500.00	0.00	T9	Y	500.00	-	-	

End of Report

IAB Level 3 Diploma Marking Scheme

Nominal Activity

Date From:	01/01/1980		N/C From:	
Date To:	31/01/2009		N/C To:	99999999
Transaction From:	1			
Transaction To:	99,999,999			

N/C: 1200   **Name:** Bank Current Account   **Account Balance:**   1,479.00 DR

No	Type	Date	Account	Ref	Details	Dept	T/C	Value	Debit	Credit	V	B
13	JC	31/12/2008	1200	J1	Bank @ 31 Dec 08	0	T9	1,056.98		1,056.98	-	N
27	BR	15/01/2009	1200	BR1	VAT Refund	0	T9	152.80	152.80		-	N
28	SR	16/01/2009	COUNTRY	340	Sales Receipt	0	T9	9,252.58	9,252.58		-	N
30	SR	20/01/2009	GG	208	Sales Receipt	0	T9	250.00	250.00		-	N
32	BR	24/01/2009	1200	BR2	Cash Sales-Supplements	0	T1	308.40	308.40		N	N
33	BR	24/01/2009	1200	BR2	Cash Sales-Health Foods	0	T0	201.20	201.20		N	N
34	JC	01/01/2009	1200	236	Bank to PC	0	T9	50.00		50.00	-	N
36	BP	02/01/2009	1200	237	Business Rates	0	T9	3,600.00		3,600.00	-	N
37	BP	15/01/2009	1200	IB1	HMRC Tax/NI	0	T9	514.76		514.76	-	N
38	PP	21/01/2009	EDWARD	238	Purchase Payment	0	T9	1,060.95		1,060.95	-	N
40	BP	29/01/2009	1200	BD1	CS Chq-RTD	0	T9	20.00		20.00	-	N
56	JC	30/01/2009	1200	239	Restore-increase PC	0	T9	179.40		179.40	-	N
58	BP	30/01/2009	1200	BACS1	Net Wages Jan	0	T9	903.89		903.89	-	N
65	BP	31/01/2009	1200	240	Anton-Drgs	0	T9	800.00		800.00	-	N
83	BP	25/01/2009	1200	SO1	Alison-Loan Repayment	0	T9	380.00		380.00	-	N
84	BP	25/01/2009	1200	SO1	Alison-Loan Interest	0	T2	120.00		120.00	N	N
							Totals:		10,164.98	8,685.98		
							History Balance:		1,479.00			

N/C: 1230   **Name:** Petty Cash   **Account Balance:**   320.00 DR

No	Type	Date	Account	Ref	Details	Dept	T/C	Value	Debit	Credit	V	B
14	JD	31/12/2008	1230	J1	PC @ 31 Dec 08	0	T9	200.00	200.00		-	N
35	JD	01/01/2009	1230	236	Bank to PC	0	T9	50.00	50.00		-	N
41	CP	02/01/2009	1230	PCV1	Diesel	0	T1	60.00		60.00	N	N
42	CP	08/01/2009	1230	PCV2	Postages	0	T2	20.00		20.00	N	N
43	CP	15/01/2009	1230	PCV3	Carriage Inwards	0	T1	14.40		14.40	N	N
44	CP	28/01/2009	1230	PCV4	Refreshments	0	T0	15.00		15.00	N	N
57	JD	30/01/2009	1230	239	Restore+increase PC	0	T9	179.40	179.40		-	N
							Totals:		429.40	109.40		
							History Balance:		320.00			

N/C: 4000   **Name:** Sales-Supplements   **Account Balance:**   3,315.43 CR

No	Type	Date	Account	Ref	Details	Dept	T/C	Value	Debit	Credit	V	B
18	SI	03/01/2009	COUNTRY	AS 840	Supplements	0	T1	2,089.56		2,089.56	N	-
20	SI	09/01/2009	GG	AS 841	Supplements	0	T1	895.31		895.31	N	-
32	BR	24/01/2009	1200	BR2	Cash Sales-Supplements	0	T1	262.47		262.47	N	N
66	JC	31/01/2009	4000	J5	Alison-Goods own use	0	T1	68.09		68.09	N	-
							Totals:			3,315.43		
							History Balance:			3,315.43		

315

IAB Level 3 Diploma Marking Scheme

L3 DipCA-June 2009-Skornia's Health Products

Nominal Activity

N/C:	4001		Name:	Sales-Health Foods				Account Balance:		6,350.89 CR	

No	Type	Date	Account	Ref	Details	Dept	T/C	Value	Debit	Credit	V	B
19	SI	03/01/2009	COUNTRY	AS 840	Health Foods	0	T0	4,891.34		4,891.34	N	-
21	SI	12/01/2009	HEALTHY	AS 842	Health Foods	0	T0	1,098.35		1,098.35	N	-
33	BR	24/01/2009	1200	BR2	Cash Sales-Health Foods	0	T0	201.20		201.20	N	N
68	JC	31/01/2009	4001	J5	Alison-Goods own use	0	T0	160.00		160.00	N	-
							Totals:			6,350.89		
							History Balance:			6,350.89		

N/C:	5000		Name:	Purchases-Supplements				Account Balance:		2,789.34 DR	

No	Type	Date	Account	Ref	Details	Dept	T/C	Value	Debit	Credit	V	B
22	PI	02/01/2009	SMITH	SB427	Supplements	0	T1	1,735.02	1,735.02		N	-
24	PI	09/01/2009	PARR	PP 2027	Supplements	0	T1	1,084.32	1,084.32		N	-
26	PC	23/01/2009	SMITH	SBC 12	Supplements	0	T1	30.00		30.00	N	-
							Totals:		2,819.34	30.00		
							History Balance:		2,789.34			

N/C:	5001		Name:	Purchases-Health Foods				Account Balance:		4,079.96 DR	

No	Type	Date	Account	Ref	Details	Dept	T/C	Value	Debit	Credit	V	B
23	PI	02/01/2009	SMITH	SB427	Health Foods	0	T0	2,986.20	2,986.20		N	-
25	PI	12/01/2009	EDWARD	E 1098	Health Foods	0	T0	1,093.76	1,093.76		N	-
							Totals:		4,079.96			
							History Balance:		4,079.96			

End of Report

IAB Level 3 Diploma Marking Scheme

L3 DipCA-June 2009-Skornia's Health Products

Aged Debtors Analysis (Detailed)

Date From:	01/01/1980		Customer From:	
Date To:	31/01/2009		Customer To:	ZZZZZZZZ
Include future transactions:	No			
Exclude later payments:	No			

** NOTE: All report values are shown in Base Currency, unless otherwise indicated **

| A/C: | COUNTRY | Name: | Country Kitchen | | Contact: | | | Tel: | | |

No	Type	Date	Ref	Details	Balance	Future	Current	Period 1	Period 2	Period 3	Older
2	SI	15/12/2008	AS 804	Opening Balance	896.63	0.00	0.00	896.63	0.00	0.00	0.00
				Totals:	896.63	0.00	0.00	896.63	0.00	0.00	0.00

Turnover: 6,980.90
Credit Limit £ 0.00

| A/C: | COUNTY | Name: | County Stores | | Contact: | | | Tel: | | |

No	Type	Date	Ref	Details	Balance	Future	Current	Period 1	Period 2	Period 3	Older
3	SI	22/11/2008	AS 787	Opening Balance	3,505.80	0.00	0.00	0.00	3,505.80	0.00	0.00
4	SC	25/11/2008	PoA	Opening Balance	-3,000.00	0.00	0.00	0.00	-3,000.00	0.00	0.00
				Totals:	505.80	0.00	0.00	0.00	505.80	0.00	0.00

Turnover: 0.00
Credit Limit £ 0.00

| A/C: | HEALTHY | Name: | The Healthy Way | | Contact: | | | Tel: | | |

No	Type	Date	Ref	Details	Balance	Future	Current	Period 1	Period 2	Period 3	Older
21	SI	12/01/2009	AS 842	Health Foods	1,098.35	0.00	1,098.35	0.00	0.00	0.00	0.00
				Totals:	1,098.35	0.00	1,098.35	0.00	0.00	0.00	0.00

Turnover: 1,098.35
Credit Limit £ 0.00

| | | | | Grand Totals: | 2,500.78 | 0.00 | 1,098.35 | 896.63 | 505.80 | 0.00 | 0.00 |

End of Report

317

| Date: | 20/06/2009 | **L3 DipCA-June 2009-Skornia's Health Products** | Page: | 1 |
| Time: | 10:58:41 | **Aged Creditors Analysis (Detailed)** | | |

| Date From: | 01/01/1980 | | Supplier From: | |
| Date To: | 31/01/2009 | | Supplier To: | ZZZZZZZZ |

Include future transactions: No
Exclude later payments: No

** NOTE: All report values are shown in Base Currency, unless otherwise indicated **

A/C: EDWARD Name: Edward & Son Health Foods   Contact: Tel:

No:	Type	Date	Ref	Details	Balance	Future	Current	Period 1	Period 2	Period 3	Older
7	PI	26/11/2008	E1003	Opening Balance	785.40	0.00	0.00	0.00	0.00	785.40	0.00
8	PI	10/12/2008	E1036	Opening Balance	927.50	0.00	0.00	0.00	927.50	0.00	0.00
				Totals:	1,712.90	0.00	0.00	0.00	927.50	785.40	0.00

Turnover: 1,093.76
Credit Limit £ 0.00

A/C: PARR Name: Parr's Performance Supplements Ltd   Contact: Tel:

No:	Type	Date	Ref	Details	Balance	Future	Current	Period 1	Period 2	Period 3	Older
10	PI	19/11/2008	PP 1978	Opening Balance	929.17	0.00	0.00	0.00	0.00	929.17	0.00
11	PI	22/12/2008	PP 2007	Opening Balance	1,006.24	0.00	0.00	0.00	1,006.24	0.00	0.00
24	PI	09/01/2009	PP 2027	Supplements	1,274.07	0.00	0.00	1,274.07	0.00	0.00	0.00
				Totals:	3,209.48	0.00	0.00	1,274.07	1,006.24	929.17	0.00

Turnover: 1,084.32
Credit Limit £ 0.00

A/C: SMITH Name: Smith Bros   Contact: Tel:

No:	Type	Date	Ref	Details	Balance	Future	Current	Period 1	Period 2	Period 3	Older
9	PI	14/12/2008	SB 407	Opening Balance	1,835.34	0.00	0.00	0.00	1,835.34	0.00	0.00
22	PI	02/01/2009	SB427	Supplements	5,024.84	0.00	0.00	5,024.84	0.00	0.00	0.00
26	PC	23/01/2009	SBC 12	Supplements	-35.25	0.00	-35.25	0.00	0.00	0.00	0.00
				Totals:	6,824.93	0.00	-35.25	5,024.84	1,835.34	0.00	0.00

Turnover: 4,691.22
Credit Limit £ 0.00

| | | | | Grand Totals: | 11,747.31 | 0.00 | -35.25 | 6,298.91 | 3,769.08 | 1,714.57 | 0.00 |

End of Report

IAB Level 3 Diploma Marking Scheme

L3 DipCA-June 2009-Skornia's Health Products
VAT Return

Page: 1

Date From: 01/01/2009
Date To: 31/01/2009

Inc Current Reconciled: No
Inc Earlier Unreconciled: No

Transaction Number Analysis

Number of reconciled transactions included	0
Number of unreconciled transactions included (within date range)	21
Number of unreconciled transactions included (prior to date range)	0
Total number of transactions included	21

VAT due in this period on sales	1	572.86
VAT due in this period on EC acquisitions	2	0.00
Total VAT due (sum of boxes 1 and 2)	3	572.86
VAT reclaimed in this period on purchases	4	499.20
Net VAT to be paid to Customs or reclaimed by you	5	73.66
Total value of sales, excluding VAT	6	9,676.32
Total value of purchases, excluding VAT	7	7,087.62
Total value of EC sales, excluding VAT	8	0.00
Total value of EC purchases, excluding VAT	9	0.00

End of Report

IAB Level 3 Diploma Marking Scheme

L3 DipCA-June 2009-Skornia's Health Products

Profit and Loss

Page: 1

From: Month 1, January 2009
To: Month 1, January 2009

Chart of Accounts: Default Layout of Accounts

	Period		Year to Date	
Sales				
Product Sales	9,489.72		9,489.72	
		9,489.72		9,489.72
Purchases				
Purchases	6,836.49		6,836.49	
Purchase Charges	12.26		12.26	
Stock	(200.00)		(200.00)	
		6,648.75		6,648.75
Direct Expenses				
		0.00		0.00
Gross Profit/(Loss):		2,840.97		2,840.97
Overheads				
Gross Wages	1,572.47		1,572.47	
Rent and Rates	1,200.00		1,200.00	
Heat, Light and Power	300.00		300.00	
Motor Expenses	42.54		42.54	
Printing and Stationery	470.00		470.00	
Bank Charges and Interest	120.00		120.00	
Depreciation	656.67		656.67	
Bad Debts	70.02		70.02	
General Expenses	15.00		15.00	
		4,446.70		4,446.70
Net Profit/(Loss):		(1,605.73)		(1,605.73)

End of Report

IAB Level 3 Diploma Marking Scheme

L3 DipCA-June 2009-Skornia's Health Products
Balance Sheet

From: Month 1, January 2009
To: Month 1, January 2009

Chart of Account: Default Layout of Accounts

	Period		Year to Date	
Fixed Assets				
Property	(50.00)		14,950.00	
Office Equipment	(106.67)		9,493.33	
Motor Vehicles	5,500.00		16,700.00	
		5,343.33		41,143.33
Current Assets				
Stock	200.00		4,000.00	
Debtors	2,160.38		4,850.76	
Deposits and Cash	120.00		320.00	
Bank Account	2,535.98		1,479.00	
		5,016.36		10,649.76
Current Liabilities				
Creditors : Short Term	7,013.66		12,497.31	
Taxation	153.82		668.58	
VAT Liability	227.94		75.14	
		7,395.42		13,241.03
Current Assets less Current Liabilities:		(2,379.06)		(2,591.27)
Total Assets less Current Liabilities:		2,964.27		38,552.06
Long Term Liabilities				
Loan-Mrs Skornia	(5,380.00)		14,620.00	
		(5,380.00)		14,620.00
Total Assets less Total Liabilities:		8,344.27		23,932.06
Capital & Reserves				
Capital – Anton	(800.00)		31,541.90	
Capital – Alison	10,750.00		(6,004.11)	
P&L Account	(1,605.73)		(1,605.73)	
		8,344.27		23,932.06

End of Report

321

L3 DipCA – June 2009 – Skornia's Health Products

Task 2

a. A friend has suggested that the partners could control the business better if they produced an annual budget broken down on a month by month basis.
Explain how they could do this with the accounting package you have used and the benefits it will bring for the business owners. **(4 Marks)**

b. A friend has suggested to Anton that he and his wife have separate Capital and Current Accounts, rather than the present set up. Give two advantages of this suggestion. **(4 Marks)**

c. Print out the Chart of Accounts and indicate on it where you would expect to find the Current Accounts. **(2 Marks)**

It is expected candidate's answers will include:

a) The answer to this will depend on the accounting package used in the examination; however, in Sage for example:
- Budget and Prior year figures can be entered on each Nominal account record.
- Can be entered as a year's figure divided equally between the twelve months, or each of the months can be entered individually.
- In Financials, budget and prior year reports can be run for individual months, or a period of months, to compare actual to budget or this year to prior year, showing the variances.
- Keeping "finger on the pulse" - Enables the partners to be aware of current situation and spot changes/trends earlier than if they just received annual figures.
- Added information for management planning/cash flow etc.

b)
- It enables the partners to see the situation in the current financial year in terms of drawings taken etc
- This would enable to partners to clearly see if drawings were excessive.
- Keeps their original investment in the business quite separate
- Keeps capital account clear of small, minor entries.

c) Chart of Accounts – A current account should be set up for each Partner, located in the "Capital and Reserves" section, e.g. account numbers 3002 and 3003.

OCR Level 1 Question Paper

RECOGNISING ACHIEVEMENT

OXFORD CAMBRIDGE AND RSA EXAMINATIONS

LEVEL 1 CERTIFICATE IN BOOKKEEPING   01870

UNIT 4 MAINTAINING LEDGERS (COMPUTERISED)

2007 – 2008 SET A   **TIME: 1 HOUR 30 MINUTES**

INSTRUCTIONS TO CANDIDATES

1   You have TEN minutes to read through this question paper before the start of the examination.

2   You must write the following assignment code in the appropriate boxes on the front of the Unit Submission Folder: 407A.

3   You should answer **all** questions.

4   You should place your printouts in the Unit Submission Folder provided.

5   You **must** carry out the printing of all documents **yourself**.

6   Printing may be undertaken outside the 1½ hours allowed for this examination but no amendments may be made to the text after that time has expired other than the insertion of characters not available on the keyboard or printer.

7   Any printouts generated that are additional to those required **must** be clearly marked as additional with a line drawn through and enclosed in your Unit Submission Folder.

QCA Accreditation Number: M/100/9349

This document consists of 15 printed pages and 1 blank page

01870/01/04/2007-2008/A   © OCR 2007   Registered Company Number: 3484466   **[Turn over**

2

INSTRUCTIONS - SCENARIO

You are employed as a bookkeeper by **All Things Cricket**, a supplier of cricket goods. The business is a partnership and the partners are Jennifer and Mark Bevan. Recently, a new computerised accounting system was installed, and the outstanding sales and purchase invoices and credit notes/returns were transferred to the new system. The company's current financial year ends at **31 May 2008** (year beginning 1 June 2007).

All Sales Invoices and Sales Credit Notes/Returns are analysed to two separate nominal accounts: **equipment** and **clothing**. Similarly, Purchase Invoices and Purchase Credit Notes/Returns are analysed to two separate nominal accounts: **equipment** and **clothing**. The bookkeeping entries up to the end of June 2007 have been dealt with, and the month end has been updated ready for you to process transactions for **July 2007**.

BUSINESS DETAILS (BOLD ITEMS WILL ALREADY HAVE BEEN ENTERED BY THE TUTOR):	
Business Name	**All Things Cricket**
Address	**Unit 16 West Way, Richmond Road, Salisbury, Wiltshire SP6 2NW**
VAT Scheme	**Standard** (the VAT Reg No is **321 5461 211**)
Current year ends	**31 May 2008** (year beginning 1 June 2007)
VAT Rates in use	**17.5%, 5.0%, 0.0%, VAT Exempt and Transactions Not Involving (not liable to) VAT**

Terminology - to help avoid any misunderstanding

WE MAY USE THE TERM . . .	WHICH MAY ALSO BE KNOWN AS . . .
Sales Ledger	Debtors Ledger containing the accounts of Customers
Purchase Ledger	Creditors Ledger containing the accounts of Suppliers
Nominal Ledger	General Ledger containing Real, Nominal and Control Accounts
Sales/Purchase Daybooks	Sales/Purchase Journals
Returns Daybooks	Sales/Purchase Credit or Returns Journals
Trade Debtors/Creditors	Sales/Purchase Ledger Accounts and/or Balances (owing/owed)
Payment 'On Account'	A payment or receipt which is **not** to be allocated against outstanding items
Part-payment	A payment or receipt **to be allocated against** an outstanding invoice/item

IMPORTANT NOTES:

You are *strongly* advised to carry out the tasks in this examination paper in the order in which they appear.

On the next page, you will find a Nominal Ledger Account listing which shows the balances of all the Nominal Ledger Accounts as at the end of June 2007. **It is important that you <u>do not open or use</u> any additional Nominal Ledger Accounts unless instructed to do so.**

All Things Cricket

NOMINAL LEDGER LISTINGS AND TRIAL BALANCE AS AT 30 JUNE 2007

N/C	NAME	CR £	DR £
0030	Computer Equipment		987.55
1100	Debtors Control Account		6,725.52
1103	Prepayments		
1200	Bank Current Account		
1230	Petty Cash Account		
2100	Creditors Control Account	4,641.06	
2109	Accruals		
2200	VAT on Sales	1,001.67	
2201	VAT on Purchases		676.06
3200	Profit and Loss Account		
4000	Sales - Equipment	5,934.85	
4009	Discounts Allowed		
4050	Sales Returns - Equipment		211.00
4400	Credit Charges (Late Payments)		
5000	Purchases - Equipment		2,691.83
5001	Purchases - Clothing		311.32
5009	Discounts Taken		
5050	Purchase Returns - Equipment	243.75	
5051	Purchase Returns - Clothing	18.95	
7200	Electricity		142.50
7501	Telephone & Internet		
7502	Courier Services		94.50
7906	Exchange Rate Variance		
8100	Bad Debt Write Off		
9998	Suspense Account		
9999	Mispostings Account		
	TOTALS	**11,840.28**	**11,840.28**

[Turn over

4

			Assessment Objectives

1   Open the accounting software application.

1(a)

Restore the backup file to your accounting software and set an appropriate program date.

1(b), 1(c)

2   Three new customers need to be added to the Sales Ledger:

2(a)

(a)   Ref: **BWA05**
          Name: **Bulbury Woods Academy**
          Address: **15 Bulbury Lane**
                      Southampton
                      SO12 4DW

          Contact: **Matthew Reynolds**
          Tel: **02380 942382**

(b)   Ref: **MPA02**
          Name: **Meyrick Park Association**
          Address: **24 South Baddesley Road**
                      Wareham
                      DT9 4JR

          Contact: **Janice Donnelly**
          Tel: **01929 551315**

(c)   Ref: **SFA08**
          Name: **Sports For All Ltd**
          Address: **Unit 8 Walton Retail Park**
                      Milborne St Andrew
                      DT14 2HZ

          Contact: **Keith Fletcher**
          Tel: **01305 987416**

			Assessment Objectives

3 Three new supplier records need to be added to the Purchase Ledger: 2(b)

(a) Ref: **BS04**
     Name: **Buchannan Supplies Ltd**
     Address: **12 Little Plympton Road**
               Christchurch
               BH23 6LB

     Contact: **Anne Morris**
     Tel: **01425 346981**

(b) Ref: **SFB07**
     Name: **Support For Business**
     Address: **72 Millbank Avenue**
               Salisbury
               SP2 9JT

     Contact: **Teresa Morgan**
     Tel: **01722 456322**

(c) Ref: **SOW03**
     Name: **Sound Of Willow**
     Address: **17 Eastbrook Avenue**
               Blandford Forum
               DT11 8PW

     Contact: **Nigel Bosher**
     Tel: **01258 655352**

4 Four new nominal accounts need to be created: 2(c)

(a) **0040 Fixtures and Fittings**

(b) **4001 Sales - Clothing**

(c) **4051 Sales Returns - Clothing**

(d) **7505 Computer Support**

[Turn over

6

		Assessment Objectives
5	Enter the purchase invoices and purchase returns/credit notes on **pages 8 – 10**.	3(a)
	Ensure that the dates, references, amounts, VAT rates and values are accurately entered and the correct purchase ledger and nominal ledger accounts are identified and updated.	
	Analyse purchase invoices and purchase returns between **equipment** and **clothing**.	
6	Enter the sales invoices and sales returns/credit notes on **pages 11 – 13**.	3(b)
	Ensure that the dates, references, amounts, VAT rates and values are accurately entered and the correct sales ledger and nominal ledger accounts are identified and updated.	
	Analyse sales invoices and sales returns between **equipment** and **clothing**.	
7	Enter the counterfoils for supplier cheques paid, together with any discounts received, to be found on **page 14**, using the procedures appropriate to your accounting software. Ensure that the correct purchase ledger and nominal ledger accounts are updated.	3(c)
8	Enter the customer receipts, together with any discounts allowed, to be found on **page 15**, using the procedure appropriate to your accounting software. Ensure that the correct sales ledger and nominal ledger accounts are updated.	3(d)
	The PYN number is used as the reference for all cheques received. Cheques are banked on the same day as they are received.	
9	Two errors have been found relating to the June 2007 transactions. Please correct these. Details are as follows:	3(e)

    (a)   The sales invoice to **Castlemead College**, Ref **6004** and dated **8 June 2007,** has been incorrectly entered by us. The amounts should be **£60.50 Net, £10.59 VAT** and **£71.09 Gross**, and not £600.50 Net, £105.09 VAT and £705.59 Gross as processed.

    (b)   The purchase invoice, Ref **33056**, dated **21 June 2007** for the sum of **£72.42 Net, £12.67 VAT** and **£85.09 Gross** to **Allsports Supplies Ltd** was posted to the account of Barnard & Green Ltd in error.

		Assessment Objectives

10 Make a backup copy of your accounting data.   4(f)

11 Print the following reports:

<u>Please note</u>: **ALL printouts should be assembled in the requested order.**

(a) A trial balance as at **31 July 2007**. Number it P1.   4(a)

(b) A summary audit trail showing ALL transactions (a 'brief' audit trail is **not** acceptable). Number it P2.   4(b)

(c) A detailed customer activity report/transaction history showing ALL transactions as at **31 July 2007**. Number it P3.   4(c)

(d) A detailed supplier activity report/transaction history showing ALL transactions as at **31 July 2007**. Number it P4.   4(d)

(e) A customer address list. Number it P5.   4(e)

(f) A supplier address list. Number it P6.   4(e)

12 Exit from the accounting software application, ensuring that all data is secure.   4(g)

[Turn over

Material for Task 5: Purchase Invoices and Credit Notes

Sound Of Willow
17 Eastbrook Avenue
Blandford Forum DT11 8PW
01258 655352

INVOICE

All Things Cricket
Unit 16 West Way
Richmond Road
Salisbury, Wiltshire SP6 2NW

Inv No:	4682
Date:	5 July 2007
Order No:	A982
Our Ref:	NB/cw
VAT No:	982 3716 28

DESCRIPTION	Net	VAT 17.5%
2 Glory Custom Bats @ £99.00 each	198.00	34.65
4 Duellist 692 Bats @ £39.50 each	158.00	27.65
PURCHASES - EQUIPMENT	356.00	62.30
4 Technik trousers (large) @ £19.99 each	79.96	13.99
PURCHASES - CLOTHING		
TOTAL DUE	435.96	76.29
	512.25	

Terms: 30 days

Support For Business
72 Millbank Avenue Salisbury SP2 9JT
01722 456322

INVOICE

All Things Cricket
Unit 16 West Way
Richmond Road
Salisbury, Wiltshire SP6 2NW

Inv No:	9621
Date:	9 July 2007
Order No:	F96234
Our Ref:	TM/bh
VAT No:	750 1692 35

DESCRIPTION	£
Web Page Design	475.00
Training – 2 hours	80.00
COMPUTER SUPPORT	
Net	555.00
VAT at 17.5%	97.12
TOTAL DUE	**652.12**

30 days

Invoice 1

Buchannan Supplies Ltd
12 Little Plympton Road Christchurch
BH23 6LB   01425 346981

INVOICE

All Things Cricket
Unit 16 West Way
Richmond Road
Salisbury, Wiltshire
SP6 2NW

	Inv No:	1842
	Date:	19 July 2007
	Our Ref:	B/WES

	NET £	17.5% VAT £
1 Cricket Bat Display Stand @ £372.50 each	372.50	65.19
1 Ball Dispenser @ £115.75 each	115.75	20.25

FIXTURES AND FITTINGS

Sub Totals	488.25	85.44
AMOUNT DUE	**£573.69**	

VAT Reg No: 896 3257 12

Invoice 2

Solent Power plc
36 Basepoint House Basepoint Road
Broadstone   BH12 5RT

INVOICE

To: All Things Cricket
Unit 16 West Way
Richmond Road
Salisbury   SP6 2NW
Wiltshire

	Inv No:	19552
	Date:	19 July 2007
	Our Ref:	TRM02

DETAILS

	NET £	5% VAT £
Electricity supplied 980 units @ 8.1 pence per unit	79.38	3.97

ELECTRICITY

Sub total	79.38	3.97
Invoice Total	83.35	

VAT Reg No 145 9276 81

Batch Totals: £1,558.59 Net, £262.82 VAT, £1,821.41 Gross

[Turn over

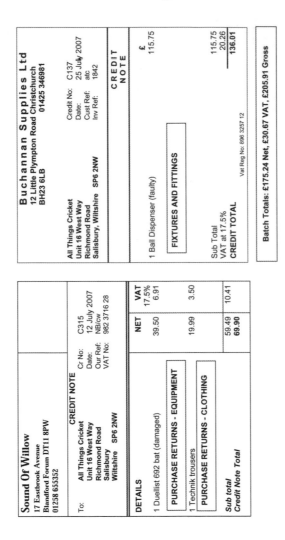

Sound Of Willow
17 Eastbrook Avenue
Blandford Forum DT11 8PW
01258 655352

CREDIT NOTE

Cr No: C315
Date: 12 July 2007
Our Ref: NB/cw
VAT No: 982 3716 28

To: **All Things Cricket**
Unit 16 West Way
Richmond Road
Salisbury
Wiltshire   SP6 2NW

DETAILS	NET	VAT 17.5%
1 Duellist 692 bat (damaged)	39.50	6.91
PURCHASE RETURNS - EQUIPMENT		
1 Technik trousers	19.99	3.50
PURCHASE RETURNS - CLOTHING		
Sub total	59.49	
Credit Note Total	**69.90**	10.41

Buchannan Supplies Ltd
12 Little Plympton Road Christchurch
BH23 6LB   01425 346981

Credit No: C137
Date: 25 July 2007
Cust Ref: atc
Inv Ref: 1842

All Things Cricket
Unit 16 West Way
Richmond Road
Salisbury, Wiltshire   SP6 2NW

CREDIT NOTE

	£
1 Ball Dispenser (faulty)	115.75
FIXTURES AND FITTINGS	
Sub Total	115.75
VAT at 17.5%	20.26
CREDIT TOTAL	**136.01**

Vat Reg No: 896 3257 12

Batch Totals: £175.24 Net, £30.67 VAT, £205.91 Gross

Material for Task 6: Sales Invoices and Credit Notes

All Things Cricket
Unit 16 West Way
Richmond Road
Salisbury
Wiltshire   SP6 2NW
Tel: 01722 372548

ATC

INVOICE

Inv No: 6013
Date: 6 July 2007
Order No: 85

To: Sports For All Ltd
     Unit 8 Walton Retail Park
     Milborne St Andrew
     DT14 2HZ

DESCRIPTION	£ NET	£ 17.5% VAT
6 Panama Sun Hats @ £6.70 each	40.20	7.04
2 Umpires Jackets @ £24.98 each	49.96	8.74
		15.78
SALES - CLOTHING		
Sub totals	90.16	
Total Due	**105.94**	

VAT Reg No: 321 5461 211

All Things Cricket
Unit 16 West Way
Richmond Road
Salisbury
Wiltshire   SP6 2NW
Tel: 01722 372548

ATC

INVOICE

Inv No: 6014
Date: 11 July 2007
Order No: 86

To: Bulbury Woods Academy
     15 Bulbury Lane
     Southampton
     SO12 4DW

DESCRIPTION	£ NET	£ 17.5% VAT
9 Reactive balls @ £9.36 each	84.24	14.74
SALES - EQUIPMENT		
		14.74
Sub totals	84.24	
Total Due	**98.98**	

VAT Reg No: 321 5461 211

[Turn over

333

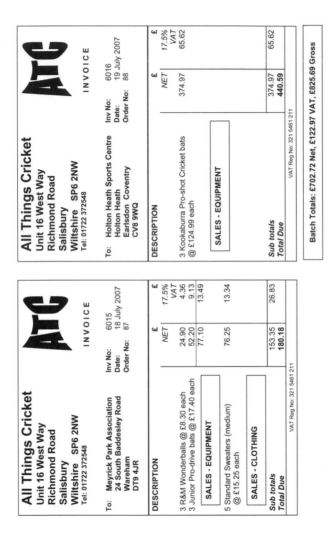

All Things Cricket
Unit 16 West Way
Richmond Road
Salisbury
Wiltshire   SP6 2NW
Tel: 01722 372548

INVOICE

Inv No: 6015
Date: 18 July 2007
Order No: 87

To: Meyrick Park Association
24 South Baddesley Road
Wareham
DT9 4JR

DESCRIPTION	£ NET	£ VAT 17.5%	£
3 R&M Wonderballs @ £8.30 each	24.90	4.36	
3 Junior Pro-drive bats @ £17.40 each	52.20	9.13	
	77.10		13.49
SALES - EQUIPMENT			
5 Standard Sweaters (medium) @ £15.25 each	76.25		13.34
SALES - CLOTHING			
Sub totals	153.35		26.83
Total Due	**180.18**		

VAT Reg No: 321 5461 211

All Things Cricket
Unit 16 West Way
Richmond Road
Salisbury
Wiltshire   SP6 2NW
Tel: 01722 372548

INVOICE

Inv No: 6016
Date: 19 July 2007
Order No: 88

To: Holton Heath Sports Centre
Holton Heath
Earlsdon Coventry
CV8 9WQ

DESCRIPTION	£ NET	£ VAT 17.5%
3 Kookaburra Pro-shot Cricket bats @ £124.99 each	374.97	65.62
SALES - EQUIPMENT		
Sub totals	374.97	65.62
Total Due	**440.59**	

VAT Reg No: 321 5461 211

Batch Totals: £702.72 Net, £122.97 VAT, £825.69 Gross

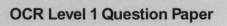

All Things Cricket
Unit 16 West Way
Richmond Road
Salisbury
Wiltshire   SP6 2NW
Tel: 01722 372548

CREDIT NOTE

To: Meyrick Park Association
       24 South Baddesley Road
       Wareham
       DT9 4JR

Credit No: C63
Date: 23 July 2007
Order No: 87

DESCRIPTION	£ NET	£ 17.5% VAT
1 Standard Sweater (wrong size)	15.25	2.67
SALES RETURNS - CLOTHING		
Sub totals	15.25	2.67
Credit Total	**£17.92**	

VAT Reg No: 321 5461 211

All Things Cricket
Unit 16 West Way
Richmond Road
Salisbury
Wiltshire   SP6 2NW
Tel: 01722 372548

CREDIT NOTE

To: Priory Cricket Association
       23 Chapel Gate
       Hurn Approach Ringwood
       BH24 9SF

Credit No: C64
Date: 25 July 2007
Order No: 82

DESCRIPTION	£ NET	£ 17.5% VAT
4 Delta Powerbow Force Bats @ £49.99 each (no longer required)	199.96	34.99
SALES RETURNS - EQUIPMENT		
Sub totals	199.96	34.99
Credit Total	**£234.95**	

VAT Reg No: 321 5461 211

Batch Totals: £215.21 Net, £37.66 VAT, £252.87 Gross

[Turn over

335

14

Material for Task 7: Cheque Counterfoils

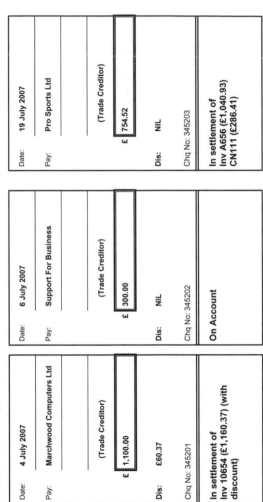

Date: 4 July 2007

Pay: Marchwood Computers Ltd

(Trade Creditor)

£ 1,100.00

Dis: £60.37

Chq No: 345201

In settlement of Inv 10654 (£1,160.37) (with discount)

Date: 6 July 2007

Pay: Support For Business

(Trade Creditor)

£ 300.00

Dis: NIL

Chq No: 345202

On Account

Date: 19 July 2007

Pay: Pro Sports Ltd

(Trade Creditor)

£ 754.52

Dis: NIL

Chq No: 345203

In settlement of Inv A656 (£1,040.93) CN111 (£286.41)

Material for Task 8: Cheque Receipts

PYN No: 701

Trade debtor

received and
banked on
6 July 2007

Dis: NIL

FIRST ROYAL BANK
123 Glendale Road, Totton, Southampton SO24 9GF

44-25-78

Date: 4 July 2007

Pay   **All Things Cricket**

Seven hundred and fifty pounds only

£ 750.00

Wayfarers Cricket Club

Geoff Norris

Cheque No	Sort Code	Account No
020556	442578	0034934

In Part Payment of Inv 6007 (£810.22)

PYN No: 702

Trade debtor

received and
banked on
23 July 2007

Dis: NIL

ALLIED NATIONAL BANK
16 The Square, Bournemouth BH2 4TR

83-28-71

Date: 20 July 2007

Pay   **All Things Cricket**

Nine hundred and eighty eight pounds and 18p

£ 988.18

West Moors Sports Club

Chris O'Rourke

Cheque No	Sort Code	Account No
001578	832871	0048934

In settlement of Inv 6009 (£429.17) and Inv 6012 (£559.01)

RECOGNISING ACHIEVEMENT

OXFORD CAMBRIDGE AND RSA EXAMINATIONS

LEVEL 1 CERTIFICATE IN BOOKKEEPING　　　　　**01870**

UNIT 4 MAINTAINING LEDGERS (COMPUTERISED)

2007 – 2008 TUTOR

TUTOR PAPER

Please do not send any disks to OCR in respect of this examination. Examiners will be able to gather all the evidence they need from the printouts produced.

It is therefore vital that all of the printouts for submission to the OCR Examiner-moderator are placed with the candidates' Unit Submission Folders.

You must also submit your tutor set-up printouts in the batch with the candidates' Unit Submission Folders.

QCA Accreditation Number: M/100/9349

This document consists of 9 printed pages and 1 blank page

01870/01/04/2007-2008/TUTOR　　　© OCR 2007　　Registered Company Number: 3484466　　　　　**[Turn over**

INSTRUCTIONS TO TUTORS

On the following pages are all the ledger accounts and opening balances for the company **All Things Cricket**. These need to be set up by you prior to the examination, **ready for candidates** to complete their task.

To do this you must either:

(a)   import the **CSV files** using the checklist shown on the next page (recommended method)

   OR

(b)   input the **Sales, Purchase** and **Nominal Account** details and transactions using the information on **pages 4 to 9.**

   Please note: remember to set the **Financial Year** to **year ending 31 May 2008** (year beginning 1 June 2007) and the program date to **30 June 2007** before you begin inputting data.

BUSINESS DETAILS (items shown **bold** are to be entered **by the tutor**):	
Business name	**All Things Cricket**
Address	**Unit 16 West Way, Richmond Road, Salisbury, Wiltshire SP6 2NW**
VAT Scheme	**Standard** (the VAT Reg No is **321 5461 211**)
Current year end	**31 May 2008** (year beginning 1 June 2007)
VAT Rates in use	**17.5%, 5.0%, 0.0%, VAT Exempt and Transactions Not Involving (not liable to) VAT**

TUTOR PRINTOUTS

Tutors must provide a printed copy of each of the following:

- a Detailed Aged Debtors Analysis
- a Detailed Aged Creditors Analysis
- a Customer Address List
- a Supplier Address List
- a Trial Balance
- a Nominal List of Accounts
- a Summary Audit Trail
- a list of VAT Codes and Rates (as noted above) used by your software

all as at **30 June 2007**.

These are to be submitted with the candidates' scripts, clearly marked **'Tutor Copy'**.

PLEASE BE SURE TO CHECK YOUR PRINTOUTS AGAINST THE INFORMATION PROVIDED IN THIS TUTOR PAPER.

Checklist for importing CSV files for:
Certificate in Bookkeeping (Computerised) Level 1, Unit 4 – 2007- 2008 (Sets A/B)

All Things Cricket

Step	Action	Done
1	Restore an unused set of ledger accounts to the computer or rebuild files	
2	Set the Financial Year to year ending **31 May 2008** (year beginning **1 June 2007**)	
3	Preview Trial Balances as at **31 May 2008**. There should be no balances in this Trial Balance	
4	Check there are no customers and no suppliers in the Sales and Purchase Ledgers	
5	Check that ALL nominal accounts, with the exception of the Control Accounts and Bank Accounts, have been deleted	
6	Add the company name **All Things Cricket** and details as shown on the previous page	
7	Set the program date to **30 June 2007**	
8	Import Sales Ledger CSV file **(cb407cus.csv)**	
9	Import Purchase Ledger CSV file **(cb407sup.csv)**	
10	Import Nominal Accounts CSV file **(cb407nom.csv)**	
11	Check Nominal Account Codes for compatibility against Nominal Trial Balance on page 8 of Tutor Paper. You must only use the accounts listed	
12	Check VAT rates of 17.5%, 5%, 0%, Exempt and Transactions Not Involving (not liable to) VAT have been entered into the system	
13	Check Bank Account (1200) and Petty Cash Account (1230) are set up as Bank Accounts	
14	Import Nominal Transaction CSV file **(cb407tra.csv)**	
15	Check whether any imported transactions use **5% VAT Rate**. If your centre uses a different tax code from OCR for those transactions, you will have to amend the tax code of the imported transactions accordingly	
16	Write out a list of the VAT Codes and Rates detailed on the previous page, as used by your Centre software. Print the following reports as at **30 June 2007**: Detailed Aged Debtors Analysis, Detailed Aged Creditors Analysis, Customer Address List, Supplier Address List, Trial Balance, Nominal List of Accounts and Summary Audit Trail. Mark all printouts **'Tutor Copy'**	
17	Check your Trial Balance for accuracy as at **30 June 2007**	
18	Run a month end	
19	Backup the assignment accounting data to a data disk or secure location	
20	After the accounting data has been backed up, please maintain data security by overwriting the accounting data on the Centre computer or server	
21	Prior to the start of the examination, a backup file, containing the accounting data and suitable for restoring to the accounting software, must be made available to candidates.	

Please note: The above steps may vary between software applications.

[Turn over

All Things Cricket

CUSTOMER ADDRESS LIST AS AT 30 JUNE 2007

CMC01
Castlemead College
19 Cannon Hill
Merley
Broadstone
BH18 9PE

Contact: Heather Tipney
Tel: 01202 845783

JP01
J Patel Ltd
Unit 2 Endeavour Park
Crow Arch Lane
Lymington
SO14 6LG

Contact: Helen Parkinson
Tel: 01590 335788

TSA01
The Sports Academy
24 Morton Park
Pynes Hill
Exeter
EX2 5HD

Contact: Dee Ciantar
Tel: 01392 564892

WMSC01
West Moors Sports Club
Flat 19 Jubilee House
23 Bond Avenue
West Moors
BH25 3DA

Contact: Chris O'Rourke
Tel: 01202 548320

HHSC01
Holton Heath Sports Centre
Holton Heath
Earlsdon
Coventry
CV8 9WQ

Contact: Katy Khan
Tel: 024 76 470186

PCA01
Priory Cricket Association
23 Chapel Gate
Hurn Approach
Ringwood
BH24 9SF

Contact: David Aitken
Tel: 01425 474921

WCC01
Wayfarers Cricket Club
15 Westwood Avenue
Totton
Southampton
SO17 4JS

Contact: Geoff Norris
Tel: 023 945 6325

5

All Things Cricket

SALES LEDGER ACCOUNTS AS AT 30 JUNE 2007

CUSTOMER	DATE	REF	N/C		VALUE		D £
Castlemead College	01-Jun-07	4000	665.93				
	08-Jun-07	6004			4000		
	06-Jun-07	C61			4050		
Holton Heath Sports Centre	07-Jun-07	6003	4000	304.44	304.44		
J Patel Ltd	6002	05-Jun-07	418.59				
	18-Jun-07	6008			4000		
	13-Jun-07	C62			4050		
Priory Cricket Association	11-Jun-07	6005	4000	304.27			
	20-Jun-07	6010			4000		
The Sports Academy	16-Jun-07	4000	429.17	429.17			
Wayfarers Cricket Club	18-Jun-07	6007	4000	810.22			
	22-Jun-07	6011	4000	1,004.33	1,814.55		
West Moors Sports Club	19-Jun-07	6009	4000	429.17			
	25-Jun-07	6012	4000	559.01	988.18		

TOTALS: 6,725.52   00.00

BALANCE: 6,725.52

If you decide not to use the CSV files provided and instead choose to input the transactions manually, you must process all Sales Invoices and Credit Notes to show Net, VAT and Gross amounts, ie as invoices and credit notes and NOT as opening balances.

[Turn over

342

All Things Cricket

SUPPLIER ADDRESS LIST AS AT 30 JUNE 2007

AS01	BG01
Allsports Supplies Ltd	Barnard & Green Ltd
19a Herringston Barn	61-63 Bargates Place
Woodstock	Richmond
Oxford	Congresbury
OX7 2FD	BS22 8KG
Contact: Nigel Carr	Contact: Mark Barnard
Tel: 01865 446395	Tel: 01934 687231
CE01	MC01
Cricket Essentials	Marchwood Computers Ltd
Unit 9 Woolsbridge Estate	18-20 Nuffield Enterprise Park
Commercial Road	Adel
Taunton	Leeds
TA4 3LD	LS14 5JR
Contact: Candice Frampton	Contact: Alex Sutherland
Tel: 01823 972536	Tel: 0113 8912457
NC01	PS01
National Couriers Ltd	Pro Sports Ltd
Unit 15 Somerville Park	17 Bailey Road
East Way	Currock
Dorchester	Carlisle
DT4 6KC	CA8 6BW
Contact: Rob Cantrell	Contact: Joanna Pearson
Tel: 01305 758945	Tel: 01228 987365
SP01	
Solent Power plc	
36 Basepoint House	
Basepoint Road	
Broadstone	
BH12 5RT	
Contact: Amir Hussein	
Tel: 01202 456325	

All Things Cricket

PURCHASE LEDGER ACCOUNTS AS AT 30 JUNE 2007

SUPPLIER	DATE	REF		N/C			VALUE	
								£
Allsports Supplies Ltd	19-Jun-07	5001	65.98					
	26-Jun-07	151			5001			
Barnard & Green Ltd	18-Jun-07	5001	142.88					
	21-Jun-07	33056			5001			
	21-Jun-07	C341			5051			
Cricket Essentials	07-Jun-07	5000	840.48					
	15-Jun-07	571			5000			
Marchwood Computers Ltd	04-Jun-07	10654	0030	1,160.37	1,160.37			
National Couriers Ltd	14-Jun-07	7502	111.04	111.04				
Pro Sports Ltd	05-Jun-07		1,040.93					
	11-Jun-07	A685	5000	675.04				
	26-Jun-07	A698	5000	304.77				
	15-Jun-07	CN111	5050	(286.41)		1,734.33		
Solent Power plc	29-Jun-07	19134	7200	149.63		149.63		

TOTALS: 0.00   **4,641.06**

BALANCE: **4,641.06**

If you decide not to use the CSV files provided and instead choose to input the transactions manually, you must process all Purchase Invoices and Credit Notes to show Net, VAT and Gross amounts, ie as invoices and credit notes and NOT as opening balances. The Solent Power plc invoice 19134 has a 5% VAT rate.

[Turn over

All Things Cricket

NOMINAL LEDGER LISTING AND TRIAL BALANCE AS AT 30 JUNE 2007

N/C	NAME	DR £	CR £
0030	Computer Equipment	987.55	
1100	Debtors Control Account	6,725.52	
1103	Prepayments		
1200	Bank Current Account		
1230	Petty Cash Account		
2100	Creditors Control Account		4,641.06
2109	Accruals		
2200	VAT on Sales		1,001.67
2201	VAT on Purchases	676.06	
3200	Profit and Loss Account		
4000	Sales - Equipment		5,934.85
4009	Discounts Allowed		
4050	Sales Returns - Equipment	211.00	
4400	Credit Charges (Late Payments)		
5000	Purchases - Equipment	2,691.83	
5001	Purchases - Clothing	311.32	
5009	Discounts Taken		
5050	Purchase Returns - Equipment		243.75
5051	Purchase Returns - Clothing		18.95
7200	Electricity	142.50	
7501	Telephone & Internet		
7502	Courier Services	94.50	
7906	Exchange Rate Variance		
8100	Bad Debt Write Off		
9998	Suspense Account		
9999	Mispostings Account		
	TOTALS	**11,840.28**	**11,840.28**

All Things Cricket

AUDIT TRAIL AS AT 30 JUNE 2007

NO	TP	DATE	A/C	N/C	REF	DETAILS	NET	VAT	GROSS	VAT %	TC
1	SI	01-Jun-07	CMC01	4000	6001	Invoice	566.75	99.18	665.93	17.5%	T1
2	SI	05-Jun-07	JP01	4000	6002	Invoice	356.25	62.34	418.59	17.5%	T1
3	SI	07-Jun-07	HHSC01	4000	6003	Invoice	259.10	45.34	304.44	17.5%	T1
4	SI	08-Jun-07	CMC01	4000	6004	Invoice	600.50	105.09	705.59	17.5%	T1
5	SI	11-Jun-07	PCA01	4000	6005	Invoice	258.95	45.32	304.27	17.5%	T1
6	SI	16-Jun-07	TSA01	4000	6006	Invoice	365.25	63.92	429.17	17.5%	T1
7	SI	18-Jun-07	WCC01	4000	6007	Invoice	689.55	120.67	810.22	17.5%	T1
8	SI	18-Jun-07	JP01	4000	6008	Invoice	510.65	89.36	600.01	17.5%	T1
9	SI	19-Jun-07	WMSC01	4000	6009	Invoice	365.25	63.92	429.17	17.5%	T1
10	SI	20-Jun-07	PCA01	4000	6010	Invoice	632.10	110.62	742.72	17.5%	T1
11	SI	22-Jun-07	WCC01	4000	6011	Invoice	854.75	149.58	1,004.33	17.5%	T1
12	SI	25-Jun-07	WMSC01	4000	6012	Invoice	475.75	83.26	559.01	17.5%	T1
13	SC	06-Jun-07	CMC01	4050	C61	Credit Note	112.50	19.69	132.19	17.5%	T1
14	SC	13-Jun-07	JP01	4050	C62	Credit Note	98.50	17.24	115.74	17.5%	T1
15	PI	04-Jun-07	MC01	0030	10654	Invoice	987.55	172.82	1,160.37	17.5%	T1
16	PI	06-Jun-07	PS01	5000	A656	Invoice	885.90	155.03	1,040.93	17.5%	T1
17	PI	07-Jun-07	CE01	5000	555	Invoice	715.30	125.18	840.48	17.5%	T1
18	PI	11-Jun-07	PS01	5000	A685	Invoice	574.50	100.54	675.04	17.5%	T1
19	PI	14-Jun-07	NC01	7502	2471	Invoice	94.50	16.54	111.04	17.5%	T1
20	PI	15-Jun-07	CE01	5000	571	Invoice	256.75	44.93	301.68	17.5%	T1
21	PI	18-Jun-07	BG01	5001	33045	Invoice	121.60	21.28	142.88	17.5%	T1
22	PI	19-Jun-07	AS01	5001	141	Invoice	56.15	9.83	65.98	17.5%	T1
23	PI	21-Jun-07	BG01	5001	33056	Invoice	72.42	12.67	85.09	17.5%	T1
24	PI	26-Jun-07	PS01	5000	A698	Invoice	259.38	45.39	304.77	17.5%	T1
25	PI	26-Jun-07	AS01	5001	151	Invoice	61.15	10.70	71.85	17.5%	T1
26	PI	29-Jun-07	SP01	7200	19134	Invoice	142.50	7.13	149.63	5.0%	T10
27	PC	15-Jun-07	PS01	5050	CN111	Credit Note	243.75	42.66	286.41	17.5%	T1
28	PC	21-Jun-07	BG01	5051	C341	Credit Note	18.95	3.32	22.27	17.5%	T1

Key to Transaction Codes

SI = Sales Invoice   SC = Sales Credit   PI = Purchase Invoice   PC = Purchase Credit

OCR Level 1 Question Paper

RECOGNISING ACHIEVEMENT

OXFORD CAMBRIDGE AND RSA EXAMINATIONS

LEVEL 1 CERTIFICATE IN BOOKKEEPING   01870

UNIT 5 PROCESSING SALES AND PURCHASES DOCUMENTS
(COMPUTERISED)

2007 – 2008 SET A   **TIME: 1 HOUR 30 MINUTES**

INSTRUCTIONS TO CANDIDATES

1   You have TEN minutes to read through this assignment before the start of the examination.

2   You must write the following assignment code in the appropriate boxes on the front of the Unit Submission Folder: 507A.

3   You should answer **all** questions.

4   You should place your printouts in the Unit Submission Folder provided.

5   You **must** carry out the printing of all documents **yourself**.

6   Printing may be undertaken outside the 1½ hours allowed for this examination but no amendments may be made to the text after that time has expired other than the insertion of characters not available on the keyboard or printer.

7   Any printouts generated that are additional to those required **must** be clearly marked as additional with a line drawn through and enclosed in your Unit Submission Folder.

QCA Accreditation Number: H/100/9350

INSTRUCTIONS - SCENARIO

You are employed as a bookkeeper, responsible for processing supplier payments, service invoices and service credit notes, by **Sammy Gee Music Co**, retailers of musical instruments who also offer a studio and editing service. The business is a partnership and the directors are Sam Groves & Gavin Williamson. Recently, a new computerised accounting system was installed, and the outstanding sales and purchase invoices and credit notes/returns were transferred to the new system. The company's current financial year ends at **30 June 2008** (year beginning 1 July 2007).

All Sales Invoices and Sales Credit Notes/Returns are analysed to three separate nominal accounts: **acoustic**, **drums** and **studio services income**. All Purchase Invoices and Purchase Credit Notes/Returns are posted to **acoustic** and **drums**. The bookkeeping entries up to the end of July 2007 have been dealt with, and the month end has been updated ready for you to process transactions for **August 2007**.

BUSINESS DETAILS (BOLD ITEMS WILL ALREADY HAVE BEEN ENTERED BY THE TUTOR):	
Business Name	**Sammy Gee Music Co**
Address	**90/92 Sycamore Street, Greenhill, Sheffield, South Yorkshire S8 5KL**
VAT Scheme	**Standard** (the VAT Reg No is **989 8059 33**)
Current year end	**30 June 2008** (year beginning 1 July 2007)
VAT Rates in use	**17.5%, 5.0%, 0.0%, VAT Exempt and Transactions Not Involving (not liable to) VAT**

Terminology - to help avoid any misunderstanding

WE MAY USE THE TERM...	WHICH MAY ALSO BE KNOWN AS ...
Sales Ledger	Debtors Ledger containing the accounts of Customers
Purchase Ledger	Creditors Ledger containing the accounts of Suppliers
Nominal Ledger	General Ledger containing Real, Nominal and Control Accounts
Sales/Purchase Daybooks	Sales/Purchase Journals
Returns Daybooks	Sales/Purchase Credit or Returns Journals
Trade Debtors/Creditors	Sales/Purchase Ledger Accounts and/or Balances (owing/owed)
Payment 'On Account'	A payment or receipt which is **not** to be allocated against outstanding items
Part-payment	A payment or receipt **to be allocated against** an outstanding invoice/item

IMPORTANT NOTES:

You are *strongly* advised to carry out the tasks in this examination paper in the order in which they appear.

On the next page, you will find a Nominal Ledger Account listing which shows the balances of all the Nominal Ledger Accounts as at the end of July 2007. **It is important that you do not open or use any additional Nominal Ledger Accounts unless instructed to do so.**

Sammy Gee Music Co

NOMINAL LEDGER LISTINGS AND TRIAL BALANCE AS AT 31 JULY 2007

N/C	NAME	DR	CR
		£	£
0020	Studio Equipment	3,008.75	
0030	Office Equipment	1,010.00	
1100	Debtors Control Account	23,896.81	
1103	Prepayments		
1200	Bank Current Account		
2100	Creditors Control Account		23,507.86
2109	Accruals		
2200	Sales Tax Control Account		3,559.10
2201	Purchase Tax Control Account	3,571.82	
2202	VAT Liability		
3000	Share Capital		
3200	Profit & Loss Account		
4000	Sales – Guitars		16,995.99
4001	Sales – Drums		1,786.72
4009	Discounts Allowed		
4400	Credit Charges (Late Payments)		
4900	Studio Services Income		1,555.00
5000	Purchases – Guitars	11,085.56	
5001	Purchases – Drums	2,410.25	
5009	Discounts Received		
7500	Printing & Stationery	1,031.50	
7502	Telephone	115.63	
7600	Advertising	708.75	
7800	Studio Equipment Repairs	565.60	
7906	Exchange Rate Variance		
8100	Bad Debt Write Off		
9998	Suspense Account		
9999	Mispostings Account		
	TOTALS	**47,404.67**	**47,404.67**

[Turn over

			Assessment Objectives
1		Open the accounting software application.	1(a)
		Restore the backup file to your accounting software and set an appropriate accounting date.	1(b), 1(c)
2		The details of three customers need to be amended:	
	(a)	Drum Beats: change the **Trade Discount** to **20%**, amend the **Default Nominal Sales Code** to **4001** and enter company details as follows:	2(a)
		Chantry Youth Centre **80 Pinder Street** **Edale** **S36 2AW**	
	(b)	Niranja Stritharan: change the first line of address to **5 Holbrook Avenue** and the post code to **S60 5FG**. Amend the **Default Nominal Sales Code** to **4000** and add **15% Trade Discount**	2(a)
	(c)	Driscoll: delete the **Trade Discount**, amend the **Default Nominal Sales Code** to **4900** and change the company name to **Dancemania**	2(b)
3		The details of three suppliers need to be amended:	2(c)
	(a)	Ashford Associates plc: Change the address to read:	
		155 Broomspring Lane **Rusthall** **Tunbridge Wells** **Kent** **TN4 5ER**	
	(b)	TM Services: Change the name to **Tune Monitoring Systems**, change the first line of the address to **87 Charnock Dale** and the post code to **S12 7WE**	
	(c)	System Computers Co: Enter the company details as follows:	
		78 Tyler Crescent **Lowfields** **Sheffield** **South Yorkshire** **S8 4DF**	

		Assessment Objectives
4	Four nominal accounts need to be amended:	2(d)

(a) Studio Equipment: change to **Sound & Recording Equipment**

(b) Sales - Guitars: change to **Sales - Acoustic**

(c) Purchases - Guitars: change to **Purchases - Acoustic**

(d) Advertising: change to **Media Publicity**

5 Create service invoices from the sales orders shown on **pages 7-9**. Ensure the following details will be shown on each document: 3(a)

Invoice Ref, Order No, Invoice Date, Customer Details, Quantity, Description, Unit Price and Trade Discounts.

Check your processing details and save each service invoice.

Do not update the ledgers at this point.

6 Print the service invoices for **August 2007**. Number these printouts P1.

7 Create the service credit notes from the goods returned notes shown on **page 10**. Ensure the following details will be shown on each document: 3(b)

Credit Note Ref, Order No, Customer Details, Quantity, Description, Unit Price and Trade Discounts.

Check your processing details and save each service credit note.

Do not update the ledgers at this point.

8 Print the service credit notes for **August 2007**. Number these printouts P2.

9 Update the ledgers and print an Update Report. Ensure that all transactions have been updated correctly. Number the printout(s) P3.   3(c)

10 Print a Service Invoice and Credit Note Report(s) to show all service invoices and service credit notes generated. Number the printout(s) P4.   3(d), 3(e)

[Turn over

		Assessment Objectives

11 Enter details from cheque counterfoils including any discounts received on **pages 11-12**. Printed **Remittance Advice Notes**, displaying supplier name, address, payment amount and reference details **MUST** be produced for each payment. Number these P5.

4(a), 4(b), 4(c)

12 Make a backup copy of your data.

6(a)

13 Print the following reports:

<u>Please note</u>: **ALL printouts should be assembled in the requested order.**

(a) Customer statements as at **31 August 2007** for the following customers (showing ALL transactions):

Acoustic Academy
Drum Beats
Dancemania
Niranja Stritharan

Number these statements P6.

5(a)

(b) A summary audit trail showing ALL transactions (a 'brief' audit trail is **not** acceptable). Number this printout P7.

5(b)

(c) Trial balance as at **31 August 2007**. Number this printout P8.

14 Exit from the accounting software application, ensuring that all data is secure.

6(b)

Sales Orders for TASK 5: Service Invoices

Sammy Gee Music Co
90/92 Sycamore Street
Greenhill
Sheffield
South Yorkshire
S8 5KL

Order Queries: 0114 2610223

SALES ORDER

To: **Drum Beats**
  Chantry Youth Centre
  80 Pinder Street
  Edale
  S36 2AW

Customer Ref: DB1
Order Date: 1 August 2007
Order No: POL56

Qty Ordered	Product Description	Per Unit Price	Amount
10	Mountain rhythm Havana bongos	39.95	399.50
3	Tribal black panther snare drums with stainless steel shell	199.99	599.97
1	Blackhawk fusion kit with sabian solar cymbals	489.75	489.75
			1,489.22
		Trade Discount	297.84
		Net	1,191.38
		VAT	208.50
		Total	1,399.88

Trade Discount: **20%**
Invoice date: **4 August 2007**
Invoice number: **960**

Sammy Gee Music Co
90/92 Sycamore Street
Greenhill
Sheffield
South Yorkshire
S8 5KL

Order Queries: 0114 2610223

SALES ORDER

To: **Obadiah Brown**
  10 High Street
  Shiregreen
  Sheffield
  South Yorkshire
  S5 9NJ

Customer Ref: OB1
Order Date: 3 August 2007
Order No: YHT991

Qty Ordered	Product Description	Per Unit	Amount
5	12 string with solid spruce top	199.00	995.00
2	6 string solid mahogany with grover super rotomatic gold tuners	249.45	498.90
1	Ali Q tomboy with grover tuners in lilac metallic finish	269.00	269.00
			1,762.90
		Trade Discount	0.00
		Net	1,762.90
		VAT	308.52
		Total	2,071.42

Trade Discount: **NONE**
Invoice date: **6 August 2007**
Invoice number: **961**

[Turn over

Sales Order 1

Sammy Gee Music Co
90/92 Sycamore Street
Greenhill
Sheffield
South Yorkshire
S8 5KL

Order Queries: 0114 2610223

SALES ORDER

To: Obadiah Brown
10 High Street
Shiregreen
Sheffield
South Yorkshire
S5 9NJ

Customer Ref: OB1
Order Date: 2 August 2007
Order No: LKU87

Qty Ordered	Product Description	Per Unit Price	Price
1	Jumbo acoustic guitar with solid mahogany top	619.00	619.00
2	Crafted 12 string in solid Queensland maple	1,029.75	2,059.50
			2,678.50
	Trade Discount		0.00
	Net		2,678.50
	VAT		468.74
	Total		3,147.24

Trade Discount: **NONE**
Invoice date: **8 August 2007**
Invoice number: **962**

Sales Order 2

Sammy Gee Music Co
90/92 Sycamore Street
Greenhill
Sheffield
South Yorkshire
S8 5KL

Order Queries: 0114 2610223

SALES ORDER

To: Niranja Stritharan
5 Holbrook Avenue
East Estate
Rotherham
South Yorkshire
S60 5FG

Customer Ref: NS8
Order Date: 4 August 2007
Order No: JND105

Qty Ordered	Product Description	Per Unit Price	Price
4	12 string with mother of pearl trimmings	299.00	1,196.00
2	Drifter travel 6 string with gig bag	149.80	299.60
1	Dual input acoustic pickup with solid spruce top	789.00	789.00
			2,284.60
	Trade Discount		342.69
	Net		1,941.91
	VAT		339.84
	Total		2,281.75

Trade Discount: **15%**
Invoice date: **11 August 2007**
Invoice number: **963**

9

SALES ORDER

Sammy Gee Music Co
90/92 Sycamore Street
Greenhill
Sheffield
South Yorkshire
S8 5KL

Order Queries: 0114 2610223

To: Dancemania
25 Rowan Tree Dell
Old Whittington
Chesterfield
Derbyshire
S41 6KW

Customer Ref: D9
Order Date: 10 August 2007
Order No: WEV851

Qty Ordered	Product Description	Per Unit	Price
10	hour studio hire with backing track facility	35.50	355.00
4	hour editing and production of demo CD	40.25	161.00
		Trade Discount	516.00
			0.00
		Net	516.00
		VAT	90.31
		Total	606.31

Trade Discount: **NONE**
Invoice date: **14 August 2007**
Invoice number: **965**

SALES ORDER

Sammy Gee Music Co
90/92 Sycamore Street
Greenhill
Sheffield
South Yorkshire
S8 5KL

Order Queries: 0114 2610223

To: Acoustic Academy
89 Brinsworth Lane
Brinsworth
Rotherham
South Yorkshire
S60 7LM

Customer Ref: AA1
Order Date: 4 August 2007
Order No: POL674

Qty Ordered	Product Description	Per Unit	Price
2	Drifter travel 6 string with gig bag	149.80	299.60
1	Dual input acoustic pickup with solid mahogany top	789.00	789.00
3	12 string with solid spruce top	199.00	597.00
		Trade Discount	1,685.60
			0.00
		Net	1,685.60
		VAT	294.99
		Total	1,980.59

Trade Discount: **NONE**
Invoice date: **12 August 2007**
Invoice number: **964**

Batch Totals: £9,776.29 Net; £1,710.90 VAT; £11,487.19 Gross

[Turn over

355

10

Goods Returned Notes for TASK 7: Service Credit Notes

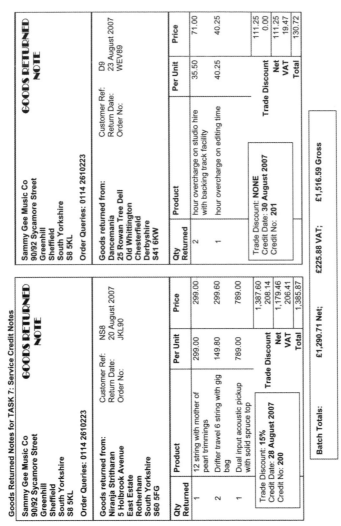

Sammy Gee Music Co
90/92 Sycamore Street
Greenhill
Sheffield
South Yorkshire
S8 5KL

GOODS RETURNED NOTE

Order Queries: 0114 2610223

Goods returned from:
Niranja Stritharan
5 Holbrook Avenue
East Estate
Rotherham
South Yorkshire
S60 5FG

Customer Ref: NS8
Return Date: 20 August 2007
Order No: JKL90

Qty Returned	Product	Per Unit	Price
1	12 string with mother of pearl trimmings	299.00	299.00
2	Drifter travel 6 string with gig bag	149.80	299.60
1	Dual input acoustic pickup with solid spruce top	789.00	789.00
		Trade Discount	1,387.60
			208.14
		Net	1,179.46
		VAT	206.41
		Total	1,385.87

Trade Discount: 15%
Credit Date: 28 August 2007
Credit No: 200

Sammy Gee Music Co
90/92 Sycamore Street
Greenhill
Sheffield
South Yorkshire
S8 5KL

GOODS RETURNED NOTE

Order Queries: 0114 2610223

Goods returned from:
Dancemania
25 Rowan Tree Dell
Old Whittington
Chesterfield
Derbyshire
S41 6KW

Customer Ref: D9
Return Date: 23 August 2007
Order No: WEV89

Qty Returned	Product	Per Unit	Price
2	hour overcharge on studio hire with backing track facility	35.50	71.00
1	hour overcharge on editing time	40.25	40.25
		Trade Discount	111.25
			0.00
		Net	111.25
		VAT	19.47
		Total	130.72

Trade Discount: NONE
Credit Date: 30 August 2007
Credit No: 201

Batch Totals: £1,290.71 Net;   £225.88 VAT;   £1,516.59 Gross

11

Cheque Counterfoils for TASK 11
Please note: Remittance Advice Notes are required for payments to ALL trade creditors

	Cheque 2024	Cheque 2025	Cheque 2026
Date:	2 August 2007	8 August 2007	14 August 2007
Pay:	Ashford Associates plc	Tune Monitoring Systems	Paper Clips
	(Trade Creditor)	(Trade Creditor)	(Trade Creditor)
	£ 832.78	£ 241.58	£ 550.00
Dis:	NONE	NONE	NONE
	Cheque No: 2024	Cheque No: 2025	Cheque No: 2026
	In settlement of Invoice AA56 £885.95 Credit note CR56 £53.17	In settlement of Invoice TM19 £241.58	In part settlement of Invoice PR/1 £1,152.09

[Turn over

357

12

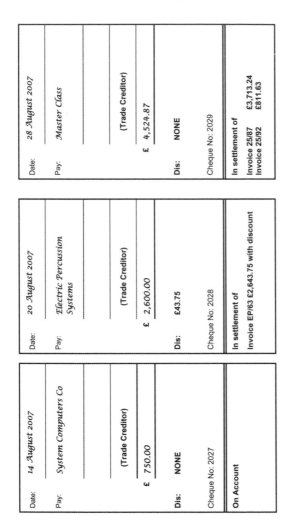

Date:	14 August 2007
Pay:	System Computers Co
	(Trade Creditor)
	£ 750.00
Dis:	NONE
Cheque No: 2027	
On Account	

Date:	20 August 2007
Pay:	Electric Percussion Systems
	(Trade Creditor)
	£ 2,600.00
Dis:	£43.75
Cheque No: 2028	
In settlement of	
Invoice EP/63 £2,643.75 with discount	

Date:	28 August 2007
Pay:	Master Class
	(Trade Creditor)
	£ 4,524.87
Dis:	NONE
Cheque No: 2029	
In settlement of	
Invoice 25/87	£3,713.24
Invoice 25/92	£811.63

OXFORD CAMBRIDGE AND RSA EXAMINATIONS

LEVEL 1 CERTIFICATE IN BOOKKEEPING   **01870**

UNIT 5 PROCESSING SALES AND PURCHASES DOCUMENTS
(COMPUTERISED)

2007 – 2008 TUTOR

TUTOR PAPER

Please do not send any disks to OCR in respect of this examination. Examiners will be able to gather all the evidence they need from the printouts produced.

It is therefore vital that all of the printouts for submission to the OCR Examiner-moderator are placed with the candidates' Unit Submission Folders.

You must also submit your tutor set-up printouts in the batch with the Candidates' Unit Submission Folders.

QCA Accreditation Number: H/100/9350

This document consists of 9 printed pages and 1 blank page

01870/01/05/2007-2008/TUTOR   © OCR 2007   Registered Company Number: 3484466   **[Turn over**

INSTRUCTIONS TO TUTORS

On the following pages are all the ledger accounts and opening balances for the company **Sammy Gee Music Co.** These need to be set up by you prior to the examination, **ready for candidates** to complete their task.

To do this you must either:

(a)   import the **CSV files** using the checklist shown on the next page (recommended method)

OR

(b)   input the **Sales**, **Purchase** and **Nominal Account** details and transactions using the information on **pages 4 to 9.**

Please note: remember to set the **Financial Year** to **year ending 30 June 2008** (year beginning 1 July 2007) and the program date to **31 July 2007** before you begin inputting data.

BUSINESS DETAILS (items shown **bold** are to be entered **by the tutor**):

Business name	**Sammy Gee Music Co**
Address	**90/92 Sycamore Street, Greenhill, Sheffield, South Yorkshire, S8 5KL**
VAT Scheme	**Standard** (the VAT Reg No is **989 8059 33**)
Current year end	**30 June 2008** (year beginning 1 July 2007)
VAT Rates in use	**17.5%, 5.0%, 0.0%, VAT Exempt and Transactions Not Involving (not liable to) VAT**

TUTOR PRINTOUTS

Tutors must provide a printed copy of each of the following:

- a Detailed Aged Debtors Analysis
- a Detailed Aged Creditors Analysis
- a Customer Address List
- a Supplier Address List
- a Trial Balance
- a Nominal List of Accounts
- a Summary Audit Trail
- a list of VAT Codes and Rates (as noted above) used by your software

all as at **31 July 2007.**

These are to be submitted with the candidates' scripts, clearly marked **'Tutor Copy'.**

PLEASE BE SURE TO CHECK YOUR PRINTOUTS AGAINST THE INFORMATION PROVIDED IN THIS TUTOR PAPER.

3

Checklist for importing CSV files for:
Certificate in Bookkeeping (Computerised) Level 1, Unit 5 – 2007- 2008 (Sets A/B)
Sammy Gee Music Co

Step	Action	Done
1	Restore an unused set of ledger accounts to the computer or rebuild files	
2	Set the Financial Year to year ending **30 June 2008** (year beginning 1 July 2007)	
3	Preview Trial Balances as at **30 June 2008**. There should be no balances in this Trial Balance	
4	Check there are no customers and no suppliers in the Sales and Purchase Ledgers	
5	Check that ALL nominal accounts, with the exception of the Control Accounts and Bank Accounts, have been deleted	
6	Add the company name **Sammy Gee Music Co** and details as shown on the previous page	
7	Set the program date to **31 July 2007**	
8	Import Sales Ledger CSV file **(cb507cus.csv)**	
9	Import Purchase Ledger CSV file **(cb507sup.csv)**	
10	Import Nominal Accounts CSV file **(cb507nom.csv)**	
11	Check Nominal Account Codes for compatibility against Nominal Trial Balance on page 8 of Tutor Paper. You should only use the accounts as listed	
12	Check VAT rates of 17.5%, 5%, 0%, Exempt and Transactions Not Involving (not liable to) VAT have been entered into system	
13	Check Bank Account (1200) is set up as a Bank Account	
14	Import Nominal Transaction CSV file **(cb507tra.csv)**	
15	Check whether any imported transactions use the **5% VAT Rate**. If your Centre uses a different tax code from OCR for those transactions, you will have to amend the tax code of the imported transactions accordingly	
16	Ensure **Customer Trade Discounts** and **Default Nominal Codes** have been added to the customer records as per the details on Page 4	
17	Write out a list of the VAT Codes and Rates detailed on the previous page, as used by your Centre software	
	Print the following reports as at **31 July 2007**: Trial Balance, Nominal List of Accounts, Summary Audit Trail, Detailed Aged Debtors Analysis, Detailed Aged Creditors Analysis, Customer Address List and Supplier Address List	
	Mark all printouts '**Tutor Copy**'	
18	Check your Trial Balance for accuracy as at **31 July 2007**	
19	Run a month end	
20	Backup the assignment accounting data to a data disk or secure location	
21	After the accounting data has been backed up, please maintain data security by overwriting the accounting data on the Centre computer or server	
22	Prior to the start of the examination, a backup file, containing the accounting data and suitable for restoring to the accounting software, must be made available to candidates	

Please note: The above steps may vary between software applications

[Turn over

4

Sammy Gee Music Co

CUSTOMER ADDRESS LIST AS AT 31 JULY 2007

AA1 Acoustic Academy 89 Brinsworth Lane Brinsworth Rotherham South Yorkshire S60 7LM Trade Discount: NONE Default Nominal Code: 4000	BBS18 Big Band Sound 35 Norton Avenue Norton Lees Sheffield South Yorkshire S8 6JN Trade Discount: NONE Default Nominal Code: 4000
BM5 Blessing Mungo Trade Discount: 20% Default Nominal Code: 4900	CYP7 Connie Yin-Peng 23 Lynbrook Road Hardwick Hall Chesterfield Derbyshire S40 8BG Trade Discount: NONE Default Nominal Code: 4000
D9 Driscoll 25 Rowan Tree Dell Old Whittington Chesterfield Derbyshire S41 6KW Trade Discount: 15% Default Nominal Code: 4001	DB1 Drum Beats Trade Discount: 10% Default Nominal Code: 4000
DB8 Down Beats 45 Newstead Road Hackenthorpe Sheffield South Yorkshire S12 3WE Trade Discount: 15% Default Nominal Code: 4000	NS8 Niranja Stritharan 115 Blake Close East Estate Rotherham South Yorkshire S66 8AR Trade Discount: NONE Default Nominal Code: 4900
OB1 Obadiah Brown 10 High Street Shiregreen Sheffield South Yorkshire S5 9NJ Trade Discount: NONE Default Nominal Code: 4000	SS5 Swingin Sisters Highmead Convent Graves Park Sheffield South Yorkshire S18 8QP Trade Discount: NONE Default Nominal Code: 4001

362

Sammy Gee Music Co

SALES LEDGER ACCOUNTS AS AT 31 JULY 2007

CUSTOMER	DATE	REF	N/C	VALUE £	BALANCE VALUE £	DR £	CR
Acoustic Academy	01/07/2007	944	4000	1,479.95			
	06/07/2007	948	4000	5,933.46			
	28/07/2007	197	4000	(100.93)	7,312.48		
Big Band Sound	15/07/2007	956	4000	4,206.50			
	19/07/2007	959	4000	528.75	4,735.25		
Blessing Mungo	02/07/2007	945	4000	2,891.00			
	11/07/2007	953	4000	1,050.92	3,941.92		
Connie Yin-Peng	07/07/2007	949	4001	243.63			
	11/07/2007	952	4001	733.02			
	30/07/2007	198	4001	(88.13)	888.52		
Driscoll	10/07/2007	950	4000	723.60			
	19/07/2007	958	4000	288.99	1,012.59		
Drum Beats	18/07/2007	957	4001	356.00			
	31/07/2007	199	4001	(142.70)	213.30		
Down Beats	10/07/2007	951	4000	2,968.05	2,968.05		
Niranja Stritharan	05/07/2007	947	4900	940.00			
	18/07/2007	196	4900	(52.88)	887.12		
Obadiah Brown	12/07/2007	954	4900	940.00	940.00		
Swingin Sisters	04/07/2007	946	4001	646.25			
	15/07/2007	955	4001	351.33	997.58		
TOTALS:					**23,896.81**	**0.00**	

If you decide not to use the CSV files provided and instead choose to input the transactions manually, you must process all Sales Invoices and Credit Notes to show Net, VAT and Gross amounts, ie as invoices and credit notes and NOT as opening balances.

Sammy Gee Music Co

SUPPLIER ADDRESS LIST AS AT 31 JULY 2007

AA5 Ashford Associates plc 15a Holly Lane Walkley Sheffield South Yorkshire S6 5BB	EPS1 Electric Percussion Systems High Meadow Industrial Estate Blackberry Hill Chesterfield Derbyshire D43 7VC
ES4 Electronic Sounds Ltd	FS1 Freya Systematic Co 131 Kilner Way Netherthorpe Sheffield South Yorkshire S6 7BZ
GG9 Great Guitars plc 7 Adel Towers Adel Leeds North Yorkshire LS15 3MN	MC16 Master Class 54/56 Chamber Close Westminster London SW1 8JH
PC1 Paper Clips Unit 41 Crystal Peaks Arcade Sheffield South Yorkshire S21 4DS	RT13 Ring Tone plc Holly Street Broomhall Sheffield South Yorkshire S11 6VF
SC1 System Computers Co	TM2 TM Services 1 Brimsfields Avenue Scowerdons Estate Sheffield South Yorkshire S12 6CG

7

Sammy Gee Music Co

PURCHASE LEDGER ACCOUNTS AS AT 31 JULY 2007

SUPPLIER	DATE	REF	N/C	VALUE	DR
Ashford Associates plc	24/07/2006	7600	885.95		
	29/07/2007		CR56		7600
Electric Percussion Systems	02/07/2007	EP/63	0020	2,643.75	2,643.75
Electronic Sounds Ltd	14/07/2007	0020	891.53	891.53	
Freya Systematic Co	10/07/2007	5001	1,750.05		
22/07/2007	5001	713.88			
	30/07/2007	7925	5001	429.87	
	18/07/2007	CR9	5001	(58.75)	2,835.05
Great Guitars plc	09/07/2007	851	5000	1,556.68	
	26/07/2007	962	5000	372.90	
	18/07/2007	Ret90	5000	(118.68)	1,810.90
Master Class	02/07/2007	25/80	5000	6,862.00	
	22/07/2007	25/87	5000	3,713.24	
	30/07/2007	25/92	5000	811.63	
	20/07/2007	R-52	5000	(92.24)	11,294.63
Paper Clips	20/07/2007	PR/1	7500	1,152.09	
	26/07/2007	ST/51	7500	59.93	1,212.02
Ring Tone plc	24/07/2007	33RT	7502	135.87	135.87
System Computers Co	24/07/2007	Com67	0030	1,186.75	1,186.75
TM Services	17/07/2007	TM19	7800	241.58	
	28/07/2007	TM26	7800	423.00	664.58
TOTALS:				**0.00**	**23,507.86**

If you decide not to use the CSV files provided and instead choose to input the transactions manually, you must process all Purchase Invoices and Credit Notes to show Net, VAT and Gross amounts, ie as invoices and credit notes and NOT as opening balances.

8

Sammy Gee Music Co

NOMINAL LEDGER LISTING AND TRIAL BALANCE AS AT 31 JULY 2007

N/C	NAME	DR	CR
		£	£
0020	Studio Equipment	3,008.75	
0030	Office Equipment	1,010.00	
1100	Debtors Control Account	23,896.81	
1103	Prepayments		
1200	Bank Current Account		
2100	Creditors Control Account		23,507.86
2109	Accruals		
2200	Sales Tax Control Account		3,559.10
2201	Purchase Tax Control Account	3,571.82	
2202	VAT Liability		
3000	Share Capital		
3200	Profit & Loss Account		
4000	Sales - Guitars		16,995.99
4001	Sales - Drums		1,786.72
4009	Discounts Allowed		
4400	Credit Charges (Late Payments)		
4900	Studio Services Income		1,555.00
5000	Purchases - Guitars	11,085.56	
5001	Purchases - Drums	2,410.25	
5009	Discounts Received		
7500	Printing & Stationery	1,031.50	
7502	Telephone	115.63	
7600	Advertising	708.75	
7800	Studio Equipment Repairs	565.60	
7906	Exchange Rate Variance		
8100	Bad Debt Write Off		
9998	Suspense Account		
9999	Mispostings Account		
	TOTALS:	**47,404.67**	**47,404.67**

9

Sammy Gee Music Co

AUDIT TRAIL AS AT 31 JULY 2007

NO	TP	DATE	A/C	N/C	REF	DETAILS	NET	VAT	GROSS	VAT%	TC
1	SI	01/07/2007	AA1	4000	944	Sales	1,259.53	220.42	1,479.95	17.5%	T1
2	SI	02/07/2007	BM5	4000	945	Sales	2,460.43	430.57	2,891.00	17.5%	T1
3	SI	04/07/2007	CC6	4001	946	Sales	550.00	96.25	646.25	17.5%	T1
4	SI	05/07/2007	NS8	4900	947	Studio	800.00	140.00	940.00	17.5%	T1
5	SI	06/07/2007	AA1	4000	948	Sales	5,049.75	883.71	5,933.46	17.5%	T1
6	SI	07/07/2007	CYP7	4001	949	Sales	207.34	36.29	243.63	17.5%	T1
7	SI	10/07/2007	D9	4000	950	Sales	615.83	107.77	723.60	17.5%	T1
8	SI	10/07/2007	DB8	4000	951	Sales	2,526.00	442.05	2,968.05	17.5%	T1
9	SI	11/07/2007	CYP7	4001	952	Sales	623.85	109.17	733.02	17.5%	T1
10	SI	11/07/2007	BM5	4000	953	Sales	894.40	156.52	1,050.92	17.5%	T1
11	SI	12/07/2007	OB1	4900	954	Studio	800.00	140.00	940.00	17.5%	T1
12	SI	15/07/2007	SS5	4001	955	Sales	299.00	52.33	351.33	17.5%	T1
13	SI	15/07/2007	BBS18	4000	956	Sales	3,580.00	626.50	4,206.50	17.5%	T1
14	SI	18/07/2007	DB1	4001	957	Sales	302.98	53.02	356.00	17.5%	T1
15	SI	19/07/2007	D9	4000	958	Sales	245.95	43.04	288.99	17.5%	T1
16	SI	19/07/2007	BBS18	4000	959	Sales	450.00	78.75	528.75	17.5%	T1
17	SC	18/07/2007	NS8	4900	196	Refund	45.00	7.88	52.88	17.5%	T1
18	SC	28/07/2007	AA1	4000	197	Sales returns	85.90	15.03	100.93	17.5%	T1
19	SC	30/07/2007	CYP7	4001	198	Sales returns	75.00	13.13	88.13	17.5%	T1
20	SC	31/07/2007	DB1	4001	199	Sales returns	121.45	21.25	142.70	17.5%	T1
21	PI	02/07/2007	EPS1	0020	EP/63	Recording deck	2,250.00	393.75	2,643.75	17.5%	T1
22	PI	02/07/2007	MC16	5000	25/80	Purchases	5,840.00	1,022.00	6,862.00	17.5%	T1
23	PI	09/07/2007	GG9	5000	851	Purchases	1,256.75	299.93	1,556.68	17.5%	T1
24	PI	10/07/2007	FS1	5001	7856	Purchases	1,489.40	260.65	1,750.05	17.5%	T1
25	PI	14/07/2007	ES4	0020	1010	Synthesizer	758.75	132.78	891.53	17.5%	T1
26	PI	17/07/2007	TM2	7800	TM19	Tape deck repair	205.60	35.98	241.58	17.5%	T1
27	PI	20/07/2007	PC1	7500	PR/1	Leaflet printing	980.50	171.59	1,152.09	17.5%	T1
28	PI	22/07/2007	FS1	5001	7921	Purchases	605.00	108.88	713.88	17.5%	T1
29	PI	22/07/2007	MC16	5000	25/87	Purchases	3,160.20	553.04	3,713.24	17.5%	T1
30	PI	24/07/2007	RT13	7502	33RT	Phone charges	115.63	20.24	135.87	17.5%	T1
31	PI	24/07/2007	AA5	7600	AA56	Advertising	754.00	131.95	885.95	17.5%	T1
32	PI	24/07/2007	SC1	0030	Com67	IT Equipment	1,010.00	176.75	1,186.75	17.5%	T1
33	PI	26/07/2007	PC1	7500	ST/51	Copier paper	51.00	8.93	59.93	17.5%	T1
34	PI	26/07/2007	GG9	5000	962	Purchases	317.36	55.54	372.90	17.5%	T1
35	PI	28/07/2007	TM2	7800	TM26	Test sound system	360.00	63.00	423.00	17.5%	T1
36	PI	30/07/2007	FS1	5001	7925	Purchases	365.85	64.02	429.87	17.5%	T1
37	PI	30/07/2007	MC16	5000	25/92	Purchases	690.75	120.88	811.63	17.5%	T1
38	PC	18/07/2007	FS1	5001	CR9	Purchase returns	50.00	8.75	58.75	17.5%	T1
39	PC	18/07/2007	GG9	5000	Ret90	Purchase returns	101.00	17.68	118.68	17.5%	T1
40	PC	20/07/2007	MC16	5000	R-52	Purchase returns	78.50	13.74	92.24	17.5%	T1
41	PC	29/07/2007	AA5	7600	CR56	Overcharge	45.25	7.92	53.17	17.5%	T1

Key to Transaction Codes

SI = Sales Invoice   SC = Sales Credit   PI = Purchase Invoice   PC = Purchase Credit

Accruals. Expenses incurred, but not yet billed to the firm.

Activity view. A window which is accessed from within a customer record in which you can explore different aspects and different levels of a customer's various transactions with the firm. The details can be viewed in tabular or graph format. It is accessed by clicking on the Activity tab at the top of the window.

Assets. The term comes from the French word *assez*, meaning 'enough'. It is used because the property of a proprietor is judged in terms of whether it is sufficient to discharge his/her liabilities, i.e. to settle his/her debts.

Assets: fixed and current. Assets are classified into fixed assets and current assets. The former are those which will be retained in the business, e.g. machines, motor vehicles, etc. The latter, it is assumed, will be consumed in the business within the fiscal year and includes stock, debtors, cash in hand and cash at bank.

Authorised share capital. The amount of capital a company is permitted to raise by means of issuing shares.

Bad debts. Debts which a firm regards as uncollectable.

Balance sheet. A listing of the ledger balances remaining after compilation of the revenue account. (It is not, as some think, called a balance sheet merely because it balances.)

Balance. This term is used in three different ways in double-entry book-keeping:

- for the balancing item transferred as the opening figure for the subsequent accounting period (balance b/d);
- for the balancing item required to equalise the two column totals (balance c/d);
- for the debit and credit column totals.

Bank reconciliation. The process of explaining a discrepancy between the bank statement balance and the cashbook balance.

Bill of materials. The list of products used to make up another, more complex, product. For example, a car care gift set may comprise a bucket, a sponge, a bottle of shampoo, a brush, a cloth and a bottle of wax.

Bought ledger. The division of the ledger that contains personal accounts of suppliers. It is also sometimes referred to as the purchase ledger or creditors account.

Capital. This term derives from the Latin words *capitalis*, meaning 'chief', and *capitali*, meaning 'property', giving us the combined meaning of 'property of the chief'. The chief of a business is, of course, the proprietor.

Cashbook. The book in which records of cash and banking transactions are made.

Chart of accounts. A list of accounts that make up the general ledger, presented in a way deemed to facilitate best understanding. The list is normally subdivided into assets, liabilities, income and expenses, and these are subcategorised according to whether they appear in the revenue accounts or the balance sheet. Income may be further subdivided into, for example, sales revenue and income from other sources. Expenses are normally subdivided into direct expenses and administrative expenses. Assets are normally subdivided into fixed and current assets, and liabilities are normally subdivided into current liabilities, long-term liabilities and capital (for which the business is liable to its owners). Further subdivisions will be made according to company preferences, but administrative expenses will almost certainly contain accounts such as heat and light, advertising and promotion, wages, motor expenses, etc. Fixed assets will include things like land and buildings, plant and machinery, motor vehicles and fixtures and fittings. Current assets will include things such as debtors, cash at bank and cash in hand, and current liabilities will include things like creditors and bank overdraft.

Credit note. A document which reverses the effect of an invoice.

Creditors. People or firms to whom the business owes money.

Debtors. People or firms who owe money to the business.

Depreciation. The writing down of an asset's value in the books of a business to allow for wear and tear.

Dividends. Shares of profit paid to shareholders.

Drawings. The retrieval of capital by a proprietor or partners for private use.

Early settlement discount. A discount allowed to customers as an enticement to pay their bills on time.

Expenses. Purchases of goods or services for consumption by the business within the financial year. They do not enhance the value of any fixed assets, though they may include repairs to them. Examples are: goods for resale, wages, repairs, heat and lighting costs, petrol and professional fees.

Final accounts. The revenue accounts and balance sheet of a firm at a particular moment in time and covering a particular financial period, e.g. a financial year.

Goodwill. The intangible fixed asset of a business's reputation.

Gross profit margin. Gross profit as a percentage of sales.

Gross profit. Sales revenue minus cost of sales.

Imprest system. A system of managing petty cash in which a fund is regularly replenished to a set amount by the cashier.

Input tax. VAT charged by a supplier on goods or services it has supplied and which will be subsequently reclaimed by the business from HMRC.

Invoice. A bill for goods or services rendered.

Issued share capital. The nominal value of shares actually issued by a company.

Journal. A book of prime entry used for initial entries of a miscellany of transactions for which no other book exists, e.g. the initial recording of opening figures, bad debt, depreciation and the correction of errors.

Ledger. The essential double-entry accounting system consisting of a number of divisions, e.g. the general ledger, personal ledger, cashbook and petty cash book.

Liabilities. Financial obligations to others – debts owed out. Capital too is listed under liabilities in the balance sheet since it is owed to the proprietor by the business.

LIFO. Last In First Out. A method of stock valuation based on the assumption that the latest prices prevail.

Liquidity. The ability of a firm to pay its debts.

Net profit. Gross profit minus overhead expenses.

Nominal ledger. That division of the ledger in which impersonal accounts are kept.

Ordinary shares. Shares in a company which earn the holders a percentage of profits. In the event of a liquidation, this category of investors will be the last in the queue for recovery of their investment.

Output tax. VAT charged to customers by a business and which it will have to subsequently remit to HM Revenue and Customs.

Overhead expenses. Expenses which cannot be directly related to turnover.

Petty cash book. The book of prime entry in which records of small cash transactions are kept.

Preference shares. Shares in a company which entitle the holders to a fixed rate of dividend on profits. Their claim on profits comes before ordinary shareholders, as would their claim on residual assets in the event of a liquidation.

Product assembly. A product made up of a number of other products from the firm's stores.

Profit. The reward to the proprietor, partners or shareholders for the business risk they have taken.

Profit and loss account. The section of the revenue accounts which shows the calculation of net profit, by deduction of overhead expenses from gross profit.

Provision for bad debts. A suitable provision set against the value of debtors to allow for some which will become uncollectable.

Provision for depreciation. An allowance set against an asset for wear and tear.

Purchase day book. A book of prime entry in which the initial record of purchases is made prior to posting to the ledger.

Purchase returns day book. A book of prime entry in which the initial record of goods returned to suppliers is made prior to posting to the ledger.

Radio buttons. A line of button-shaped images which appear on the computer screen inviting you to choose between alternatives by moving the cursor over and clicking on the centre of the button that matches your choice.

Redeemable shares. Shares which the company is empowered to buy back.

Revenue accounts. The set of accounts which shows the net profit earned by a business, how it is calculated and how it is to be distributed.

Revenues. Inflows of money or money's worth to the firm, e.g. sales figures, rents, discounts received, etc. They must be distinguished from proceeds of sale of fixed assets, which is capital income rather than revenue income and is ultimately shown in the balance sheet rather than the trading, profit and loss account.

Sales day book. A book of prime entry in which the initial record of all sales is made prior to posting to the ledger.

Sales ledger. The division of the ledger which contains personal accounts of customers. It is also sometimes referred to as the debtors ledger.

Sales return day book. A book of prime entry in which the initial record of goods returned by customers is made prior to posting to the ledger.

Stock. Goods for resale or for use in a manufacturing process for the production of goods for resale.

Suspense account. An account into which a value equal to an error can be posted temporarily in order to make the books balance while the source of the error is being sought.

Trading account. The section of the revenue accounts which explains the calculation of gross profit.

Trial balance. A listing and summing of all the ledger balances at a particular moment in time to confirm that the total debits equal the total credits and, thus, provide some measure of confidence in the accuracy of the ledger posting.

Value Added Tax (VAT). A tax on goods and services. Businesses act as subcollectors by charging VAT on goods they sell and remitting it to HM Revenue and Customs.

Wizard. A software routine designed to guide you through a process, such as setting up a new record or recording the disposal of an asset.

Working capital. The difference between current assets and current liabilities.

Index

Index